The World
I Dream Of

The World
I Dream Of

Curt Butz

BOOKS

Winchester, UK
Washington, USA

First published by O-Books, 2010
O Books is an imprint of John Hunt Publishing Ltd., The Bothy, Deershot Lodge, Park Lane, Ropley,
Hants, SO24 0BE, UK
office1@o-books.net
www.o-books.com

Distribution in:	South Africa
	Stephan Phillips (pty) Ltd
UK and Europe	Email: orders@stephanphillips.com
Orca Book Services Ltd	Tel: 27 21 4489839 Telefax: 27 21 4479879
Home trade orders	Text copyright Curt Butz 2010
tradeorders@orcabookservices.co.uk	
Tel: 01235 465521 Fax: 01235 465555	ISBN: 978 1 84694 315 7
Export orders	Design: Stuart Davies
exportorders@orcabookservices.co.uk	
Tel: 01235 465516 or 01235 465517	All rights reserved. Except for brief quotations
Fax: 01235 465555	in critical articles or reviews, no part of this
	book may be reproduced in any manner
USA and Canada	without prior written permission from the
NBN	publishers.
custserv@nbnbooks.com	
Tel: 1 800 462 6420 Fax: 1 800 338 4550	The rights of Curt Butz as author have been
	asserted in accordance with the Copyright,
Australia and New Zealand	Designs and Patents Act 1988.
Brumby Books	
sales@brumbybooks.com.au	A CIP catalogue record for this book is
Tel: 61 3 9761 5535 Fax: 61 3 9761 7095	available from the British Library.
Far East (offices in Singapore, Thailand,	
Hong Kong, Taiwan)	
Pansing Distribution Pte Ltd	
kemal@pansing.com	
Tel: 65 6319 9939 Fax: 65 6462 5761	Printed in the UK by CPI Antony Rowe

We operate a distinctive and ethical publishing philosophy in all
areas of its business, from its global network of authors to
production and worldwide distribution.

CONTENTS

To my parents

Acknowledgements

I would like to thank John Silliphant, Llyn Roberts, John Hunt and all the contributors for their inspiration, kindness, openness, and vision. And Nancy Guillemette for her love.

Introduction

This book is a dream.

As a writer I dreamed of writing a positive book. I had written four previous books that were not so positive. I decided to change my ways. Instead of promulgating life's negatives, I'd promote its positives. I dreamed of a book of inspiration. I dreamed of a book of unification. I would introduce myself and my readers to people doing good in the world, people breaking new ground and forging new paths, enlightening myself and my readers to the limitless potential of what can be accomplished in the world and what infinite futures lie ahead. This book would be my own inner journey for peace, hope and faith and the meditation of my discoveries. This book would add to the harmonic of love consciousness. This book I wouldn't feel awkward about if it fell into the hands of my little nieces... This was my dream.

The dream becomes an idea.

I read a book by John Perkins, *The World Is As You Dream It: Teachings from The Amazon and the Andes*, detailing Mr. Perkins's life with, among others, the Shuar people of the Amazon in Equador. At the time he was concerned with the state of the western world and its consumptive and destructive ways. He shared this with his shaman friends. "The world is as you dream it," they told him (to paraphrase). In order for the western world to change its destructive pattern it must "change the dream."

The idea: I would help "change the dream" of my western world. The world I grew up in. The world I felt, after studying permaculture for many years and understanding how far we were from living sustainably and in harmony with our planet, needed a serious change of its dream.

Idea to vision.

I would title the book *The World I See: A Foundation For The Co-Creation Of Our Future*. Why this title? At the time I was intrigued with Field Theory in combination with indigenous philosophies of universal connection. I was inspired by the Law of Attraction and our human ability to affect reality through thoughts. Along with these interests were books about the Mayan calendar, a calendar measuring time based not on physical reality but on the evolution of consciousness. According to this calendar humanity will advance in consciousness again, entering the Ninth Underworld, that of "Conscious Co-Creation."

Field Theory: western science's acknowledgement of what our indigenous ancestors already knew—that everything is connected; the mind as an electro-magnet with thoughts vibrating and attracting like frequencies; dreaming our reality into existence; the end of duality creationism; consciousness evolving…all of this sounded "positive" to me, so I pushed ahead with these thoughts and title in mind (obviously the title has since transformed).

Idea to vision, vision to action.

I emailed all the people from my past who had, in whatever way, garnered my respect and from there *followed the links*. I researched speaking circuits and environmental conferences. I emailed people who founded their own charities or social organizations. I emailed people creating solutions and dedicating their lives to positive transformation in whatever field, discipline or lifestyle they had chosen for their accomplishments. These artists, activists, authors, educators, speakers, environmentalists, scientists, young entrepreneurs, Elders and visionaries were sent the following request:

> *I'm compiling a book entitled, The World I See—A Foundation For The Co-Creation Of Our Future, for which I'm requesting your*

participation. I would like to ask you for a written description of your "dream" world...

...this can be one sentence or many pages; a poem or researched essay—there is no structure you need to follow. All that is requested is your image of a perfect world: What is it that you really want in the world? How would you live? What is your Utopia; your "Heaven on Earth"? What would your perfect world look like? These are some of the ways to approach the question. Your dream world can be as fantastic and marvelous as you want it to be. There are no rules, no right or wrong descriptions, only the world of your imagination and the world of your dreams....

From the action, a reality.

114 people resonated with the project enough to send "dream world" quotes to a complete stranger (3 were prior acquaintances). 117 in total. After reading about an author *reverse tithing* his book earnings the "positive" book would become more positive. I would do the same, giving each contributor the option of choosing a charity. To these charities 90% of my earnings will be donated. The community grew with an added 60 charity organizations (listed in the back of the book).

I dreamed of creating a "positive" book and here it is. I dreamed this book into existence and all those who are now a part of it and all their visions of the future. (This might sound boastful, but isn't it so? If only in my own world?) More importantly, though, I realized that this book, this dream, is only a tiny example of what a dream can do.

The world you dream of.

What is it you desire in the world? Perhaps meditating on the dreams in this book will provide clarity for your own dream world. Dreaming is important. Dreaming is necessary:

"Dream lofty dreams, and as you dream, so you shall become. Your

vision is the promise of what you shall one day be; your ideal is the prophecy of what you shall at last unveil." - *James Allen*

This book is a dream. And within this dream are 117 more dreams. Loftier dreams...important dreams. Dreams of our future.

I look forward to the ideas, the visions, the actions, and the new reality that will surely follow.

As our shaman say, "The world is as you dream it." - *Curt Butz*

Contributors

Adisa, Opal - *writer, performer, photographer, storyteller*

Aggrey, Isaac - *founder Women Business Center, South Africa*

Agnivesh, Swami - *religious teacher, author, activist, India ·*

Allan, Sterling D. - *founder and chief executive officer PES Network, Inc. and New Energy Congress*

Allen, Laura - *educator, greywater activist*

Alvarez, Ana Maria - *activist, founder CONTRA-TIEMPO dance company*

Anderson, Ray - *founder and chairman Interface, Inc.*

Ang, Bernise - *founder Syinc, Singapore*

Ardagh, Arjuna - *awakening coach, author Leap Before You Look*

Baba, Sunny - *author The Realization of Divine Oneness*

Baraniuk, Dr Richard - *professor, internet pioneer, founder cnx.org*

Barsody, Sister Carmen - *Franciscan Sister of Little Falls, MN, co-founder Faithful Fools Street Ministry*

Beautiful Painted Arrow, Joseph - *author, artist, visionary, story-teller, founder the Peace Chamber project*

Benally, Jones - *Navajo medicine man*

Bhatt, Ela - *founder, general secretary SEWA (Self Employed Women's Association), founder chair SEWA Cooperative Bank, India*

Blackmore, Dr Susan - *lecturer, broadcaster, author Ten Zen Questions, UK*

Blincoe, Karen - *educator, designer, environmentalist, director Schumacher College, UK*

Blum, Dr Arlene - *biophysical chemist, speaker, mountaineer, author Breaking Trail: A Climbing Life*

Borges, Phil - *photographer, founder and president Bridges to Understanding*

Bosch, Jason - *founder Argusfest.*

Bostrom, Nick - *philosopher, director Oxford Future of Humanity Institute, UK*

Brown, Adrienne Maree - *executive director The Ruckus Society*

Brown, Lester - *author Eco-Economy: Building An Economy For The Earth*

Caldicott, Dr Helen - *physician, speaker, author War In Heaven*

Caldwell, Gillian - *filmmaker, attorney, campaign director 1Sky*

Carter, Dr Majora - *activist, city designer, founder and executive director Sustainable South Bronx*

Casey, Marisa Catalina - *founder Starting Artists, Inc.*

Clow, Barbara Hand - *author The Mayan Code: Time Acceleration and Awakening the World Mind*

Cremo, Michael A. - *historian of archeology, researcher in human origins*

Daoudi, Yannick - *world traveler, cycled Uganda to raise money for Invisible Children NGO, Canada*

Davis, Ron - *founder Reading Research Council, Davis Dyslexia Association International, and Davis Autism International, author The Gift of Dyslexia and The Gift of Learning*

deAngelis, Dr Angela - *author, systems theorist, social scientist, spiritual guide, psychotherapist*

de Grey, Dr Aubrey - *biomedical gerontologist, chairman and chief science officer Methuselah Foundation*

de Quincey, Ph.D., Christian - *professor, founder The Wisdom Academy, author Deep Spirit: Cracking the Noetic Code*

Dickinson, Paul - *chief executive Carbon Disclosure Project, UK*

Dixon, Frank - *founder Global System Change*

dos Santos, Feliciano - *musician, founder and director Estamos, Mozambique*

Dunbar-Ortiz, Roxanne - *activist, author Roots of Resistance: A History of Land Tenure in New Mexico*

Charles Eisenstein - *healer, author The Ascent of Humanity*

El Ebrashi, Raghda - *founder and chairperson Alashanek ya Balady Association for Sustainable Development (AYB-SD), Egypt*

Elkington, John - *co-founder SustainAbility, founding partner and director Volans, UK*

Ely, Scott - *founder and director Sunsense Solar Electric*

Feng, Master Li Jun - *qigong master, founder of Sheng Zhen Qigong*

Fletcher, Jr., Bill - *executive editor BlackCommentator.com*

Fresco, Jacque - *industrial designer, author, lecturer, artist, architectural designer, futurist, founder The Venus Project*

Gellman H.D., Dr Alex - *motivational speaker, executive coach, doctor of homeopathy, team facilitator, author Passage Ways to Your Soul, Canada*

Gellman, C.A., C.P. A., Reverend David - *director and founder Universal Oneness United Faith Canada, Canada*

Glennie, Dame Evelyn - *solo percussionist, motivational speaker, writer, UK*

Glithero, Lisa - *environmental educator, lecturer, founder EYES project, Canada*

Group, Dr Edward - *healer, teacher, chief executive officer Global Healing Center*

Guevara-Stone, Laurie - *international program manager Solar Energy International*

Hailes, Julia - *sustainability consultant, author The New Green Consumer Guide, UK*

Hairfield, Ph.D., Steven - *intuitive life coach, author A Metaphysical Interpretation of the Bible and The Twelve Sacred Principles of Karma*

Halter, Dr Reese - *founder Global Forest Science*

Haramein, Nassim - *director of research The Resonance Project Foundation*

Honoré, Carl - *speaker, author Under Pressure: Rescuing Childhood From the Culture Of Hyper-Parenting*

Jamail, Dahr - *independent journalist, author Beyond The Green Zone: Dispatches From An Unembedded Journalist In Occupied Iraq*

Jensen, Derrick - *activist, speaker, author Endgame*

Jolivette, Dr Andrew - *professor, author Louisiana Creoles: Cultural Recovery and Mixed-Race Native American Identity*

Kataria, Dr Madan - *founder Laughter Yoga, India*

Kelly, Alex - *media/arts practitioner and producer, Australia*

Kennedy, Dr Margrit - *founder Money Network Alliance for Research and Development of Complementary Currencies (MonNetA), Germany*

Kivel, Paul - *educator, mentor, social justice activist, author You Call This a Democracy? Who Benefits, Who Pays and Who Really Decides*

KMO - *founder C-Realm Podcast*

Koch, Sarah - *dreamer, believer, co-founder Development In Gardening (DIG)*

Kramer, Neil - *writer, speaker and researcher. Navigating the ancient pathways of gnosis, esoteric knowledge, consciousness and the divine, UK*

Kunstler, James Howard - *lecturer, author The Long Emergency*

Laskow, Dr Leonard - *physician, holoenergetic healer*

Leanna, Anthony - *founder Heavenly Hats Foundation, Inc.*

Lee, Katie - *author, singer, filmmaker, lecturer, activist*

Lipkis, Andy - *founder TreePeople*

Luckey, Wendy - *traditional healer (curandera)*

MacKaye, Ian - *musician, aberrationist, founder Dischord Records*

Madu, Dr Ernest Chijioke - *founder, chairman, chief executive officer Heart Institute of the Caribbean, West Indies*

Mali, Jeddah - *spiritual mentor, author Godkind: The Residents of Heaven on Earth, UK*

Manitonquat - *Assonet Wampanoag elder, philosopher, author Changing the World*

Marris, Sheree - *environmental communications consultant, documentary filmmaker, author KarmaSEAtra - Secrets of Sex in the Sea, Australia*

Martinez, James - *radio talk show host Cash Flow*

Maser, Chris - *lecturer, international facilitator, environmental consultant, author Earth In Our Care: Ecology, Economy, and Sustainability*

McKibben, Bill - *co-founder 350.org, author Fight Global Warming Now*

Miller, Dr Emmett - *physician, poet, musician, storyteller*

Mountrose, Drs Phillip & Jane - *co-directors Awakenings Institute, holistic coaches, ministers of holistic healing*

Murray, Jessica - *astrologer, author, teacher*

Nutt, Dr Samantha - *founder and executive director War Child Canada, Canada*

O'Leary, Dr Brian - *scientist, former astronaut, international speaker, author The Energy Solution Revolution*

Ortiz, Ernesto - *facilitator, teacher, therapist, founder and director Journey to the Heart*

Pascoe, Ted - *executive director Senior Support Services*

Perkins, Kelly - *author The Climb of My Life, Scaling Mountains with a Borrowed Heart*

Petersen, Carol - *traditional Elder, creation singer*

Plotkin, Ph.D., Mark J. - *ethnobotanist, author, president Amazon Conservation Team*

Powell, M.D., Diane Hennacy - *activist, psychotherapist, psychopharmacologist, author The ESP Enigma: The Scientific Case for Psychic Phenomena*

Ramirez, Magdala - *medicine woman, speaker, author I Am You*

Roberts, M.A., Llyn - *teacher, spiritual ecologist, director of Dream Change, Inc., author Shapeshifting into Higher Consciousness*

Rosling, Hans - *professor, director Gapminder.org, Sweden*

Ross, Steven A. - *researcher, lecturer, philosopher, chief executive officer World Research Foundation*

Russell, Peter - *author, speaker, personal development consultant, philosopher, futurist, UK*

Salingaros, Dr Nikos - *mathematician and polymath, urban, architectural and complexity theorist, design philosopher*

Schwartz, Robert - *author Your Soul's Plan: Discovering the Real Meaning of the Life You Planned Before You Were Born*

Schwartz, Stephan - *remote viewer, founder Schwartz Report, author*

Opening To The Infinite

Secours, Molly - *writer, filmmaker, speaker, activist*

Silliphant, John - *artist, servant, lover of life, founder Seva Café, India*

Stamets, Paul - *mycologist, speaker, author Mycelium Running: How Mushrooms Can Help Save The World*

Steffen, Alex - *co-founder and executive editor Worldchanging*

Tamminen, Terry - *author Lives Per Gallon: The True Cost Of Our Oil Addiction*

Tennenbaum, Carla - *artist, artisan, designer, history graduate, Brazil*

Tilsen, Nick - *community organizer, executive director Thunder Valley Community Development Corporation*

Frank Tugwell - *president and chief executive officer Winrock International (nonprofit global development organization)*

Vaughan-Lee, Emmanuel - *founder and director Global Oneness Project*

Von Ward, Paul - *interdisciplinary cosmologist, author The Soul Genome: Science and Reincarnation*

Wagalla, Zablon - *founder Trees For Clean Energy Network, Kenya*

Wann, David - *father, gardener, filmmaker, futurist, author Simple Prosperity: Finding Real Wealth in a Sustainable Lifestyle*

Wise, Tim - *writer, speaker, anti-racist activist*

Wolf, Ph.D., Fred Alan - *physicist, lecturer, author The Yoga of Time Travel: How the Mind Can Defeat Time*

Wright, Machaelle Small - *author, researcher Perelandra Center for Nature Research*

Ye, Quanzhi - *undergraduate student, discoverer of Comet Lulin, China*

Z., Mickey - *author No Innocent Bystanders: Riding Shotgun in the Land of Denial*

Zoriah - *photojournalist, war photographer*

In the very near future,
There will come a Wave
Sweeping across our spinning Earth,
Bringing Divine,
Wholly unexpected change.
-anonymous prophecy

Quotes

The sun, the sea, singing saturating the day with blissful melodies.

The pale blue, white cloudy sky, sweet mangoes and stories sweating the air with pungent aromas.

Sitting on the veranda with friends, drinking cool sorrel, eating fish and festival, laughing so hard that tears roll down your cheeks and you fall off the chair in stitches, the joke so sweet, and knowing that you and everyone else in the world is safe, have food and shelter, and life would not and could not be without you.

- Opal Palmer Adisa - writer, performer, photographer, storyteller

Promoting gender equality and empowering women is the only powerful weapon to address unemployment, poverty alleviation, reduction of crime, restoring the moral fabric and rebuilding of family lives.

I dream of a world free of economic hardships, wars and HIV/AIDS pandemic.

I dream of a world where people will work collaboratively to inspire one another to fight against discrimination, abuse, sexual violence, and oppression against one another.

A world where we inspire respect, acknowledge opinions to understand how we recognize and respond to issues such as gender, race, religion, culture and politics.

A world where everyone has access to good education, health, nutrition and water.

A world where we all speak the same language and accept all as one regardless of where you come from.

- Isaac Aggrey - founder Women Business Center, South Africa

A world of my dreams is a world without organised, institutionalised, hierarchical religions and a world where political boundaries will not stand in the way of people who want to cross the borders either for tourism or for making a living just to survive with human dignity. Also a world where no discrimination is allowed on the basis of gender, caste, race, religion and every child is guaranteed equal opportunities up to the age of 18 irrespective of socio-economic status of the parents. Also a world where simple living and high thinking is promoted instead of a crass materialistic and consumeristic culture—A world without alcoholism, tobacco smoking/chewing, drugs, etc. A world where every child is encouraged to be her/his own Prophet/Guru/Master and to write an A4 size scripture of ten commandments for his/her guidance in day to day life-where animals and birds and bees and all forms of lifeare respected and not killed for food and medicine or cosmetics.

- Swami Agnivesh - religious teacher, author, activist, India

The not-too distant future will see a shift to clean, affordable energy that is reliable, portable, not grid-dependent but distributed, without vulnerabilities. Each home will have its own power generator that obtains its energy in such a way that no fuel has to be added. Every vehicle will be able to run without ever stopping for fuel. Each appliance will have its own power source that never has to be recharged. Wireless devices will have wireless power that doesn't have to be recharged. We'll be able to pump water to irrigate deserts; desalinate water inexpensively; grow food cheaply in climate-controlled, local buildings. With this shift to an abundance mentality, there will be no wars over scarce resources. Society will no longer be subservient to a central authority but will thrive as individuals are able to nurture their natural talents.

- Sterling D. Allan - founder and chief executive officer PES Network, Inc. and New Energy Congress

I imagine a world full of healthy people, clean rivers, bountiful lands. As we live our lives we replenish the earth, collecting rainwater, using water from our showers to grow fruit trees, recycling nutrients through composting toilets. Our children learn about the past, when the world was filled with "isms", racism, sexism, classism. Our future world is rooted in respect for all people and all peoples, all experiences, all life.

  - Laura Allen - educator, greywater activist

I dream of living in a world where resistance isn't seen as adversarial, but instead as a fundamental key for communication and empowerment between partners and for a people. I dream of a world where my children respect, celebrate and desire difference - and where borders are recognized for what they are - arbitrary, man-made lines.

  - Ana Maria Alvarez - activist, founder CONTRA-TIEMPO dance company

As the founder and chairman of an industrial enterprise, Interface, Inc., my 'perfect world' is one that I've described as the top of Mount Sustainability—a mountain that my company is metaphorically climbing to its summit, representing zero footprint. When I talk about Mount Sustainability, I envision the summit symbolizing "The *Prototypical* Company of the 21st Century." What will it look like?

If I can put a picture into words, it will be: Strongly service - oriented by means of products that deliver service. It will be driven by renewable energy, waste-free, cyclical; it will be strongly connected to all constituencies; communities engaged, customers engaged, suppliers buying into the vision; and connected to each other within the organization; altogether, forming *an eco-system, with trust and cooperation replacing confrontation*, that includes Earth in win-win-win relationships. This company will be way ahead of the regulatory process, rendering it irrelevant; taking nothing from Earth's lithosphere that's not naturally and rapidly renewable, and doing no harm to her biosphere. All the undesirable linkages to the earth, gone! New, vital linkages, in place. Sustainable and just, an example for all, and *doing well by doing good*. Winning in the marketplace, but not at Earth's expense, nor at the expense of our descendants, but at the expense of inefficient adapters, competitors who just don't "get it". Growing, yes, even in a no-growth world, should we come to that, by increasing value and market share, but not footprint, and with declining throughput of virgin materials, eventually to *zero*. Only zero throughput of extracted natural capital is sustainable over evolutionary time (the true long run), in consideration of the thousands of generations *of Homo sapiens*, and all the other species, yet to be.

At Interface we call this entire initiative to climb this enormous mountain on all its faces, "Mission Zero™", as we aim for zero footprint by 2020.

- Ray Anderson - founder and chairman Interface, Inc.

I wish to see a world of love. Where people treat one another with dignity. Where no child, woman, man, or community is prejudiced against. Yes, even gays and HIV-positive people. I dream of a world where love and liberty of humankind are more powerful than national interests, oil, and terrorism. Where the downtrodden are not left behind, in any society. Where people of different faiths are free to immerse in these multiple truths, where those of different backgrounds can *celebrate* their difference. I think such a world is something worth fighting for.

- Bernise Ang - founder Syinc, Singapore

The World I Dream Of - interview with Arjuna Ardagh

"If you could describe your dream world what would it look like?"

Arjuna: What I would say in answer to your question is humanity has been dreaming for too long. Dreaming is not the solution, dreaming is the problem. What I mean by dreaming is people living in fantasies of what could be and what should be and what they think used to be, and not fully experiencing what is. In fact you could say humanity is sleepwalking. That we're a bunch of sleepwalkers living in a dream world, not paying full attention to how we treat other people, not paying full attention to the planet, not paying full attention to the consequences of our actions, not paying full attention to anything. And because we're caught up in dreaming, the results of our life are like the way a drunkard lives. A drunkard is intoxicated and therefore unable to fully meet any moment with presence and consciousness and you can see the results. If you go into the house of someone who is a drunkard you can see that their house is not well cared for. And if you look at the planet, it looks like a planet that's populated by drunkards – it is not well cared for. So the solution that humanity is crying out for is not more dreaming but waking up, and waking up starts with now. It starts with paying attention to what is actually here in this moment, which may be unpleasant. It's much easier to weave dreams of a fantasy future than to actually pay close attention to what is here before our very noses.

Albert Einstein said, many years ago, "You cannot solve any problem in the same state of consciousness in which it was created." So actually, everything you see on this planet that feels out of balance, whether it's child abuse, domestic abuse; whether it's families not getting along together or neighbors not getting along together; whether it's the quality of education in our schools, expanding to the inadequacy of our healthcare system— and you can expand that globally to huge environmental abuse.

Really we've become on this planet not inhabitants, but termites. We behave on this planet like an infestation. If you fly an airplane over any big city and look out the window at the urban sprawl of a city like Denver, or Phoenix, or Detroit, it looks like the earth has some kind of skin infection. It looks like you want to apply some sort of cream to remove the infection—so all of these problems that we face and everything that seems to be out of balance, in one way, is a separate, disconnected problem state. And in another way they are all expressions of a collective state of consciousness.

I've made my work lately about asking people how they would describe the collective state of consciousness dominating this planet. Most people will say that our collective state of consciousness is one of separation. You can see the manifestation of separation as fear, as greed, as taking more than you give back. If you feel very close to someone, or if you feel intimately connected to a place, you take care of it. If you feel very close to someone, you treat them like you would like to be treated yourself. All of the things we see that are abhorrent about how we live on this planet are all functions of separation.

So I would say that my vision for the potential for humanity is not so much with external things but with a shift in consciousness. Which I would say is happening now. In the same way that when someone who's been an alcoholic bottoms out. When they've come to the most dysfunctional aspect of alcoholism, that's when they're most ripe for a breakthrough, they're most ripe to shift into something else. And in the same way, we're collectively bottoming out to the extent that many structures that we've gotten used to—economic structures, political structures, environmental structures—no longer function. They are now breaking down. You can see this particularly economically. Although there are stimulus packages happening in many different economies, I think most people realize these are Band-Aids. Right now in America, going further and further into debt is really not a long term solution. What seems to be happening is the entire basis of the economic system is crumbling because it was based upon separation. It was based upon usury. It was based upon people with money using people without money to get more money. That is a very separate way of doing things. The hope for humanity, my vision of a world we would love to live in, has more to do with a state of consciousness than anything external. Because trying to change anything external, whether it's environmental, or political, or economic is like putting a Band-Aid over a place where we have cancer in the body. It's not going to do anything except cover it up. What is needed is to address the underlying cause of the cancer which may be some sort of imbalance in the body. You can treat a bad skin problem internally by using the right herbs or medicine, by changing the inner environment of the body with your diet. But covering up a skin condition with a Band-Aid isn't going to heal it. In the same way that trying to change external circumstances isn't any kind of viable solution. What is needed is to shift consciousness.

And that is happening all over the world now in very secular ways. In ways that don't require any change of belief or lifestyle. All over the world today people are recognizing that there is another way of seeing themselves and seeing reality. We call that *awakening*. Awakening means to recognize that, although you do have a personal story, of your wife, your children, your triumphs and defeats, although there is a person, that person is actually a fleeting story. And that there is something else deeper and more abiding and actually very obvious when you notice it, which is something like an awareness, or presence, or consciousness which can get involved with the story, but in itself has no story.

As we awaken to that deeper dimension of ourselves, we awaken to something that is not separate. And as we start to live from that non-separateness, everything that we do automatically becomes an expression of a world that we would all love to live in. An expression of a world that is generated out of non-separation, out of intimacy, and out of love.

- *Arjuna Ardagh - awakening coach, author Leap Before You Look*

My Perfect World

This world, which I am about to describe, is not an imaginary world, because I have actually lived it during my life here on this beautiful Earth.

In order to manifest Heaven on Earth, or to enter the Kingdom of God upon Earth, we all must first recognize that there is only One Conscious Being, manifesting and experiencing itself as all living beings. This recognition is the realization of our inherent divinity: the acknowledgement that life on Earth *is* the Great Divine Being (God) manifesting itself as matter (all forms).

With this recognition, we see ourselves and all living beings as cells in the universal Body of God. This awareness allows us to live and act from a feeling of being One with All That Is (all that exists). This feeling of interconnected relationship is LOVE. We cannot harm "others" when we see them as manifestations of our Self, or the One Self. Thus, there is no more war, murder, rape or theft in this new world, and we all are nurturing the interconnected Web of Life.

We enrich the soil (Earth) and feed it and take good care of it because we see that it is our greater body: it is alive and we are the cells that make up that great body. We intuit that the health of the whole Earth is equal to the health of all of its parts. Thus, we acknowledge that the health and well being of the greater body is dependent on the health and well being of living beings/cells within that body. We are no longer cancerous cells in the universal body of God. Rather we are healthy, happy cells, nurturing the very body that supports us individually and collectively. We are always enhancing the Web of Life. Therefore our everyday life is our daily worship of the Living God.

Our dance of life has become an ongoing active worship of the Inherent Divinity that surrounds and engulfs us in every moment. We have ended our feeling of separation – from each other, all living beings, and God. We are living in Unity Consciousness, at One with God and each other...thus manifesting Heaven of Earth.

- Sunny Baba - spiritual counselor, author The Realization of Divine Oneness

I see a world where a high-quality education is available to everyone, everywhere, at any time for free. I see a world where learners become teachers and teachers become learners.

- Dr Richard Baraniuk - professor, internet pioneer, founder cnx.org

I believe in the potential of every being to care about someone or something, and the ability to embody that care, no matter what the cost. Thus I dream of a world where every living being knows the joy of fearlessly caring about someone or something, AND being fearlessly cared about.

- Carmen Barsody, OSF - Franciscan Sister of Little Falls, MN, co-founder Faithful Fools Street Ministry

Beauty that crystallizes wisdom into awareness and connects us to a oneness not seen before.

- Joseph Beautiful Painted Arrow - author, artist, visionary, story-teller, founder the Peace Chamber project

Heaven on Earth

On this world now there is no time. We as Native American

people don't follow the clocks. The creator made us only for this world that we are living in since the beginning of time.

We belong to this world. The earth owns us, even if you buy it you can not own it.

In the beginning of time, all over the world the human people all have the same roots. That's how the creator made us. Just like you, the trees, the animals, all is made by nature which is responsible for the earth.

So, we belong to traditional ways. We follow nature's rules. We have our laws that are not written on paper. We follow Nature.

So, there is no other world. This is the perfect world. From the bottom of our hearts we belong to the earth.

But, don't kill your brothers and sisters.

P.S. Respect this Planet.

- Jones Benally - Navajo medicine man

India's greatest unleashed enterprise lies in its millions of poor and women who against all odds each day survive crushing poverty with success and smile.

- Ela Bhatt - founder, general secretary SEWA (Self Employed Women's Association), founder chair SEWA Cooperative Bank, India

In my ideal world there is no prohibition of drugs; all recreational drugs from the relatively harmless, like cannabis, to the addictive and destructive, like heroin, are sold in shops, properly regulated and controlled. So anyone who wants to use them properly can.

In this world there are no gangs fighting turf wars over drugs, no dealers stalking the streets trying to sell, no desperate users buying rubbish because it's all they can find, no heroin addicts dying of overdoses for lack of quality control, no party-goers taking one drug thinking it's another, no children brought up on estates where the only income comes from drugs, no burglars breaking into homes to steal TVs and selling them for a fiver for drugs, no prisons full to bursting point.

This world would be a better place just for removing the horrors of prohibition, but to really gain the benefits we'd need to know how to use drugs wisely. So in my ideal world we would all have learned how to use drugs, not abuse them. Yes, I know there will always be people who abuse drugs, who take too much, too often, in the wrong place and at the wrong times, but even so, in my ideal world most people would use drugs well. There would be social norms on how and when to use what, we would have plentiful and truthful advice, we would know lots of people who knew more than we did about each drug and how to use it, we could learn from books, from the media, and from friends how to make the most of each kind of drug. Doses would be accurate, packaging helpful, and regulations sensible. There would be no more "Just say No!" and children would be given honest drugs education. We could bring up our children to understand how to use different drugs for the best results. Rules about use when driving or at work, and age limits would help reduce abuse.

In this world I could buy cannabis in its many varieties and concoctions—hash and grass, oils and solutions, the old-fashioned get-you-high type or the modern dope-you-down type, and probably much else besides. In this world I could buy pure MDMA, rather than what passes as ecstasy now, and use it for the fun of dancing, the intimacy of friendship, or the fun of sex. But I would also know that MDMA is addictive and that after 5 or 6 doses it would never have the same effect as the first time. So I would judge my use well and make the most of it. I would be able to buy magic mushrooms in countless variations, containing psilocybin in natural forms and complex mixtures, for fun and exploration. I could choose mescaline for amazing visual effects and wondrous emotions. And I would be able to buy the ultimate hallucinogen, LSD, for those rare occasions when I feel ready for the full thing—8 hours (that seem like a hundred) of serious insight and inner exploration.

I would not be alone. In my ideal world others who, like me, want to explore their own minds would be there to help and guide, to introduce me to new just-synthesised drugs, to help me cope with terrifying drugs like DMT, to teach me how to make the most of ancient plants like salvia divinorum, or shamanic mixtures like ayahuasca. This way I would learn so much.

I hope that one day this will all come true.

- Dr Susan Blackmore - lecturer, broadcaster, author Ten Zen Questions, UK

My Utopia

Nature is in balance,
People are in balance,
The inner, the outer.
A constant ebb and flow,
A constant cycle, give and take.
Only take what you can give back,
All in accordance with the breath,
Breathing in and breathing out,
Life is diverse, multi-faceted, multi-layered, colourful.
Life and nature are abundant for all,
but still the give and take,
and always restore.

- Karen Blincoe - educator, designer, environmentalist, director Schumacher College, UK

I dream of a world of peace and joy where every creature has the basic necessities of food, shelter, community, clean air, water, a healthy and safe environment as well as the opportunity to achieve their own potential. It is a beautiful natural world of healthy forests, prairies, grasslands, mountains and oceans.

My own contribution is reducing the unnecessary use of toxic chemicals and promoting the development of safer, greener substitutes. Untested chemicals are one of the greatest threats to our health and environment. With health and toxicity information as well as political will, we can move to less hazardous substances, preventing an enormous amount of disease and suffering and protecting the global environment.

- Dr Arlene Blum - biophysical chemist, speaker, mountaineer, author Breaking Trail: A Climbing Life

My vision is a harmonious, interconnected world in which youth are actively engaged as responsible global citizens.

- Phil Borges - photographer, founder and president Bridges to Understanding

I could never create the perfect world because individual free will is integral to my perfect world and therefore only *we* could create a more perfect world.

In this more perfect world people would make independent decisions about how to live based upon honest, intellectual, and empathetic deliberation, always maintaining ownership of, and responsibility for, their own will. These decisions would be free of the economic, psychological and physical coercions so present in modern life.

In my perfect world, power would be decentralized. No one would have the leverage to use basic living necessities to coerce others. Food, water, and energy production would be done at the local level with local democratic control. Land ownership would be limited to those individuals working or living on the land and only with respect for their neighbors and the environment. Absentee landlords would not exist. We would have a decentralized monetary system that favored circulation over amassing. Individual incomes would have a floor and a ceiling where everyone has enough but no one has so much that it threatens democracy. Corporations would not be considered persons. People would ally themselves with one another based upon their values rather than race, religion, or nationality. And this world would come about after a majority of people using their free will decided it was best.

- Jason Bosch - founder Argusfest

The blush of health on a convalescent's cheek. The sparkle of the eye in a moment of wit. The smile of a loving thought... Utopia is the hope that the scattered fragments of good that we come across from time to time in our lives can be put together, one day, to reveal the shape of a new kind of life. The kind of life that yours should have been.

I fear that the pursuit of Utopia will bring out the worst in you. Many a moth has been incinerated in pursuit of a brighter future.

Seek the light! But approach with care, and swerve if you smell your wingtips singeing. Light is for seeing, not dying.

When you embark on this quest, you will encounter rough seas and hard problems. To prevail will take your best science, your best technology, and your best politics. Yet each problem has a solution. My existence breaks no law of nature. The materials are all there. Your people must become master builders, and then you must use these skills to build yourselves up, without crushing your cores.

***

To reach Utopia, you must first discover the means to three fundamental transformations.

The First Transformation: Secure life!

Your body is a deathtrap. This vital machine and mortal vehicle, unless it jams first or crashes, is sure to rust anon. You are lucky to get seven decades of mobility; eight if you be fortune's darling. That is not sufficient to get started in a serious way, much less to complete the journey. Maturity of the soul takes longer. Why, even a tree-life takes longer.

Death is not one but a multitude of assassins. Do you not see them? They are coming at you from every angle. Take aim at the causes of early death – infection, violence, malnutrition, heart attack, cancer. Turn your biggest gun on aging, and fire. You must seize the biochemical processes in your body in order to vanquish, by and by, illness and senescence. In time, you will discover ways to move your mind to more durable media. Then continue to improve the system, so that the risk of death and disease continues to decline. Any death prior to the heat death of the universe is premature if your life is good.

Oh, it is not well to live in a self-combusting paper hut! Keep the flames at bay and be prepared with liquid nitrogen, while you construct yourself a better habitation. One day you or your children should have a secure home.

Research, build, redouble your effort!

The Second Transformation: Upgrade cognition!

Your brain's special faculties: music, humor, spirituality, mathematics, eroticism, art, nurturing, narration, gossip! These are fine spirits to pour into the cup of life. Blessed you are if you have a vintage bottle of any of these. Better yet, a cask! Better yet, a vineyard! Be not afraid to grow. The mind's cellars have no ceilings!

What other capacities are possible? Imagine a world with all the music dried up: what poverty, what loss. Give your thanks, not to the lyre, but to your ears for the music. And ask yourself, what other harmonies are there in the air, that you lack the ears to hear? What vaults of value are you witlessly debarred from, lacking the key sensibility?

Had you but an inkling, your nails would be clawing at the padlock.

Your brain must grow beyond any genius of humankind, in its special faculties as well as its general intelligence, so that you may better learn, remember, and understand, and so that you may apprehend your own beatitude.

Mind is a means: for without insight you will get bogged down or lose your way, and your journey will fail.

Mind is also an end: for it is in the spacetime of awareness that Utopia will exist. May the measure of your mind be vast and expanding.

Oh, stupidity is a loathsome corral! Gnaw and tug at the posts, and you will slowly loosen them up. One day you'll break the fence that held your forebears captive. Gnaw and tug, redouble your effort!

The Third Transformation: Elevate well-being!
What is the difference between indifference and interest, boredom and thrill, despair and bliss?

Pleasure! A few grains of this magic ingredient are worth more than a king's treasure, and we have it aplenty here in Utopia. It pervades into everything we do and everything we experience. We sprinkle it in our tea.

The universe is cold. Fun is the fire that melts the blocks of hardship and creates a bubbling celebration of life.

It is the birth right of every creature, a right no less sacred for having been trampled on since the beginning of time.

There is a beauty and joy here that you cannot fathom. It feels so good that if the sensation were translated into tears of gratitude, rivers would overflow.

I reach in vain for words to convey to you what it all amounts to... It's like a rain of the most wonderful feeling, where every raindrop has its own unique and indescribable meaning—or rather it has a scent or essence that evokes a whole world... And each such evoked world is subtler, richer, deeper, more multidimensional than the sum total of what you have experienced in your entire life.

I will not speak of the worst pain and misery that is to be got rid of; it is too horrible to dwell upon, and you are already cognizant of the urgency of palliation. My point is that in addition to the removal of the negative, there is also an upside imperative: to enable the full flourishing of enjoyments that are currently out of reach.

The roots of suffering are planted deep in your brain. Weeding them out and replacing them with nutritious crops of well-being will require advanced skills and instruments for the cultivation of your neuronal soil. But take heed, the problem is multiplex! All emotions have a natural function. Prune carefully lest you accidentally reduce the fertility of your plot.

Sustainable yields are possible. Yet fools will build fools' paradises. I recommend you go easy on your paradise-engineering until you have the wisdom to do it right.

Oh, what a gruesome knot suffering is! Pull and tug on those loops, and you will gradually loosen them up. One day the coils will fall, and you will stretch out in delight. Pull and tug, and be patient in your effort!

May there come a time when rising suns are greeted with joy by all the living creatures they shine upon.

- Nick Bostrom - philosopher, director Oxford Future of Humanity Institute, UK

The world of my dreams is not a utopia. It is a world where

resources are distributed in a way that makes us all feel abundant, able to exist and communicate from a place of pleasure, appreciation and love instead of insecurity and fear. I don't long for a world free of struggle, reason or desire...but rather a space in which we embrace our full humanity, embrace learning and evolving and transforming, embrace using truth, action and reconciliation to deepen our experience of each other, and our knowledge of the world.

- Adrienne Maree Brown - executive director The Ruckus Society

We can now see what an eco-economy looks like. Instead of being run on fossil fuels, it will be powered by sources of energy that derive from the Sun, such as wind and sunlight, and by geothermal energy from within the earth. It will be hydrogen-based instead of carbon-based. Cars and buses will run on fuel-cell engines powered by electricity produced with an electrochemical process using hydrogen as the fuel instead of internal combustion engines. With fuel cells powered by hydrogen, there is no climate-disrupting CO_2 or noxious health-damaging pollutants; only water is emitted.

In the new economy, atmospheric CO_2 levels will be stable. In contrast to today's energy economy, where the world's reserves of oil and coal are concentrated in a handful of countries, energy sources in the eco-economy will be widely dispersed—as widely distributed as sunlight and wind. The heavy dependence of the entire world on one geographic region—the Middle East—for much of its energy will likely decline as the new climate-benign energy sources and fuel-cell engines take over.

The energy economy will be essentially a solar/hydrogen economy with various energy sources deriving from the Sun used either directly for heating and cooling or indirectly to produce electricity. Wind-generated electricity, which is likely to be the lowest-cost source of energy, will be used to electrolyze water, producing hydrogen. This provides a means of both storing and transporting wind energy. Initially, existing natural gas pipelines will be used to distribute hydrogen. But over the longer term, both natural gas and oil pipeline networks can be adapted to carry hydrogen as the world shifts from a carbon-based to a hydrogen-based economy.

The transport systems of cities will change—indeed, they already are. Instead of the noisy, congested, polluting, auto-centered transport systems of today, cities will have rail-centered transport systems and they will be bicycle- and pedestrian-friendly, offering more mobility, more exercise, cleaner air, and less frustration. Historians looking back on the current system will likely see it as a dark age in urban evolution.

Urban transport systems will have the same components as they do today: automobile, rail, bus, and bicycle. The difference will be in the mix. As more and more city planners recognize the inherent conflict between the automobile and the city, new, cleaner, more efficient transport systems will develop. Urban personal mobility will increase as automobile use and traffic congestion decline.

The materials sector of the eco-economy will look far different too. Mature industrial economies with stable populations can operate largely by recycling the materials already in use. The materials loop will be closed, yielding no waste and nothing for the landfills.

One of the keys to reversing the deforestation of the earth is paper recycling; the potential here has been only partly realized. A second key is developing alternative energy sources that will reduce the amount of wood used as fuel. In addition, boosting the efficiency of wood burning can measurably lighten the load on forests.

Another promising option is the use of carefully- designed, ecologically- managed, and highly- productive tree plantations. A small area devoted to plantations may be essential to protecting forests at the global level. Plantations can yield several times as much wood per hectare as can a natural forest.

In the economy of the future, the use of water will be in balance with supply. Water tables will be stable, not falling. The economic restructuring will be designed to raise water productivity in every facet of economic activity.

In this environmentally sustainable economy, harvests from oceanic fisheries, a major source of animal protein in the human diet, will be reduced to the sustainable yield. Additional demand will be satisfied by fish farming. This is, in effect, an aquatic version of the same shift that occurred during the transition from hunting and gathering to farming. The freshwater, herbivorous carp polyculture on which the Chinese rely heavily for their vast production of farmed fish offers an ecological model for the rest of the world.

A somewhat similar situation exists for rangelands. One of the keys to alleviating the excessive pressure on rangelands is to feed livestock the crop residues that are otherwise being burned for fuel or for disposal. This trend, already well under way in India and China, may hold the key to stabilizing the world's rangelands.

And finally, the new economy will have a stable population. Over the longer term, the only sustainable society is one in which couples have an average of two children.

- Lester Brown - from his book, Eco-Economy: Building An Economy For The Earth

My perfect world would be one where man stops fighting and killing, where human growth is stabilized, where science is used only in the service of life and not death, where homo sapiens live in harmony and balance with nature and where 30 million other species are as revered and treasured as our own.

- Dr Helen Caldicott - physician, speaker, author War In Heaven

I dream of a world that is guided by love and justice. And I dream of a world that my kids can survive and thrive in—a world where we have tackled the defining challenge of our generation which is climate change, and embraced the opportunity of a smart, renewable energy future.

- Gillian Caldwell - filmmaker, attorney, campaign director 1Sky

A world where you don't have to move out of your neighborhood to live in a better one.

- Dr Majora Carter - activist, city designer, founder and executive director Sustainable South Bronx

My dream world would be one in which access to the arts is a right, not a privilege. In my dream world creativity and passion would be rewarded over greed and celebrity. Citizens of my dream world would be nurtured to find their natural talents and to contribute back to the rest of the world by utilizing those talents.

- Marisa Catalina Casey - founder Starting Artists, Inc.

In a Perfect World

When the world is perfect, which is arriving now, the clock will not dominate our sense of time. No longer will we divide our days and nights into smaller increments, while clocks will be used only to arrive on time for appointments. Instead, we will live by responding to the four seasons, the new and full moons, as well as to various astrological and cosmic cycles. For example, we will create what we want in our lives by using seasonal rhythms. During the spring equinox, the time of ultimate balance, each one of us will carefully choose three things we want to create during the year. We will initiate these intentions during the spring, deepen them in the summer, and balance them with everything else in our lives during the fall. Then during the winter, we will contemplate the spiritual meaning of our personal creations and gift them to the cosmos. This will be the end of competition and excessive striving, since creating life with the seasons is the way to live in total attunement with Nature. By working with Nature instead of being outside of her flow, we will have everything we need and plenty left over to share.

In the middle of this timeless heaven, we still will have to deal with our emotions. When we became conscious beings a hundred thousand years ago, the Moon created a method for us to utilize the power of our feelings. In the perfect world as our primary socialization, we will return to communing with the moon in groups. During the new moon, gathering together in groups in dark and secretive places, each month we will receive the new seed of creation to be implanted in the planetary field. In deep attunement with this subtle new frequency, we will feel and know each new creative essence when it arrives in Earth. We will align our emotions with creation by implanting these feelings right in our souls. Aligned with our spirits, from the new moon through the full moon, this subtle seed will germinate, grow, and flower within all the people. We will all bless Nature for creating the moon to modulate our emotions, the tides in the oceans, and the growth cycles in our gardens. Violence and loneliness will be gone when lunar light interweaves our activities causing us all to flow in these feelings. We will be delighted by the creations that Nature expresses through the moon.

Once violence, fear, neediness, and loneliness end, seven generations will create new communities based on peace and joy. Then we will be invited back into the cosmic society, we will re-enter our galaxy and the universe. Blessed with full cosmic knowledge, scientists and healers from all over the galaxy will joyfully instruct us in the heavenly powers and cycles. As responsible keepers of our planet, our home, we will be free and have the means to travel to any place in the cosmos that we desire. We will emote our consciousness from our hearts, sharing life and knowledge with the whole universe. Beings from the far reaches of time and space will commune with us and seek our wisdom.

- Barbara Hand Clow - author The Mayan Code: Time Acceleration and Awakening the World Mind

In my work as a researcher in human origins and in my personal life, I have been greatly inspired by my studies in the Vedic philosophy. There are two great schools of Vedic thought, the impersonalist and personalist. I follow the personalist school. According to this school, we originally exist as beings of pure consciousness, existing in loving harmony with the source of all conscious beings and with all other conscious beings. The ruling principle of this domain of pure consciousness is love, love for the source of all conscious beings and by extension all other individual conscious beings. Love cannot be forced. It has to be freely given at every moment. So the chance to not love is also there. The opposite of love is selfish exploitation. If a conscious self chooses to become selfish, then it can no longer exist on that level of pure consciousness. And that is why this material world exists. It gives a place where conscious selves can act on their selfish desires, using the vehicles of material bodies. This process, by which a pure conscious self descends into the world of matter is what I call devolution, and I have explained it in great detail in my book *Human Devolution*. But the process can be reversed, and consciousness can be restored to its original pure state. This is what I call spiritual re-evolution. So in an ideal world, the governments and other institutions would be encouraging people to live as simply and naturally as possible. They could thus put most of their human energy into returning to their original state. People would learn to see all other people, indeed all other living things, as beings of pure consciousness. They would realize that true happiness and satisfaction can be found by cultivating our lost loving relationship with the source of all consciousness beings. This would reduce the level of conflict in the world, reduce the level of environmental destruction. The lives of people would be full of peace, natural prosperity, and friendship. And at the end of their present lives, people would return to the level of pure consciousness. But even before that the earth would be transformed. Most people would be vegetarians, living in self-sustaining eco- villages and small towns. They would give up sectarian religion and nationalism. They would understand we are all from the same source. They would search for happiness within.

- Michael A. Cremo - historian of archaeology, researcher in human origins

I wish I could travel through a world of freedom and peace, in the largest sense of the words. A world where we are all free to live our lives the way we choose to, regardless of geographical location, ethnicity or social class; as long as that way does not encroach on another's right to freedom. A world where people are at peace with nature, at peace with each other, and at peace with themselves.

- Yannick Daoudi - world traveler, cycled Uganda to raise money for Invisible Children NGO, Canada

I am afraid that I cannot just write a few lines about my vision of the future. In fact – it will be a real challenge to get it done in only a few pages.

My vision of the future is not a simple fantasy. It is based on a sense of my own purpose for being alive. My vision of the future is not based on the way things have been for thousands of years. It is based on a change that is actually already upon us.

There is a transition occurring within the human race. About seventy years ago a very rare condition, that we now call autism, began to increase. At first the percentage of increase was very slow but it was gaining momentum with each passing year. Now, the percentage of increase has passed the 50% per year mark. The offspring of "normal" parents are coming more and more as a new form of human being. I consider myself an example of that change. I am a new one, a representative of the future.

My biography begins with my being labeled a *Kanner's baby* in 1942. (Dr Leo Kanner was the first of the two doctors to use the word *autism* to identify infants and children that fail to develop social skills.) In 1954 I was given the label of *uneducatable mental retardation* by the school system. In 1960, after extensive IQ testing, I was given the label *genius*. Later that same year I was given speech therapy where I learned to speak in sentences. At the same time I underwent a number of different therapy techniques intended to teach me how to read—none of which produced any detectable result.

Between 1960 and 1980 I was in hiding. I wasn't just hiding my illiteracy; I was really hiding that I wasn't a real human being. For as long as I could remember all I really wanted from life was to be the same as everyone else. All the while knowing that I wasn't and never would be.

The way I was hiding was to pretend to be someone that was normal. For the most part it wasn't too hard. However, it was very difficult to pretend emotional responses within social situations and relationships. Until I figured out how the human emotion system actually worked, I don't think I ever got it right.

Then in December 1980, I discovered the states of orientation and disorientation, and as a result of causing myself to be in an oriented state I could read. This led to the creation of the Reading Research Council in 1981 and the development of the Davis Dyslexia Correction program in the following years.

What this discovery and the subsequent developments did for me was to bring me out of hiding. It was slow; it took about fifteen years for me to be able to stand in front of a group of people and admit that I was different. It wasn't just admitting that I wasn't a real human being, it was also admitting that my entire life, up until then had been a lie.

In 1999, I had the opportunity to spend an afternoon with Dr Georg Kuhlewind. He was introduced to me as a retired professor of physical chemistry from a university in Hungary. One of the twenty-four books he had written is titled *Star Children*, a book about autism. He told me the reason he had sought me out was that he considered me to be one of his star children. In that afternoon's conversations he made a number of very profound statements. He said that every forty to sixty thousand years the human race goes through an evolutionary change. He said it is probably designed into the double helix structure of our DNA that after so many times of an egg and sperm joining, the placement of certain genes change. That change in the DNA structure brings about an evolutionary change in the species. He also said that the last time this happened was about sixty thousand years ago when Cro-Magnon man appeared. We are due for the next change.

Kuhlewind said that what is happening now is actually the third appearance of this transition. He went on to say, just look at history and you will see points in time where extreme genius is accompanied by autistic characteristics. They "shine like beacons of enlightenment." The first, around 1450 to 1550 when individuals who are just now being recognized as autistics, were making history. He cited Leonardo da Vinci, Michelangelo, Isaac Newton, Galileo Galilei, and many others whom I cannot now recall. He continued by saying most of these individuals did not procreate. In fact, for many there are no records of them ever having had any successful social contact or relationship with women at all.

The last appearance was around 1850 to 1900, with individuals like Edison, Bell, Einstein, Watt, Whitney, and many others. But as it happened earlier, if and when these individuals did procreate, their genius did not follow.

Then Kuhlewind made the most profound statement of all. He told me that autism is the next evolutionary change and it is the future of mankind. He said that "this time there will be no going back, this time we either successfully evolve or we are doomed to extinction. Within three generations the incidence of autistic births will reach 100%."

My thinking at the time was, this couldn't possibly be true, this old man is not looking at the mechanics of probability. If a generation is twenty years, his prediction is there won't be any normal children being born by the year 2070. Even though he liked me and was curious about the way I perceived things and seemed delighted by my answers I couldn't help but feel that Georg Kuhlewind had lost touch with reality.

But then in 2005, I received a copy of the January 2005 United States Government Accountability Office report GAO-05-220. This report begins by stating that there are about 1.5 million Americans currently living with some form of autism. Then on page two it states, "The number of children diagnosed with autism ... has increased by more than 500 percent in the last decade."

I had to do some quick arithmetic: If things keep going at the same rate 1.5 million X 500% = 6.5 million by 2015. Using the same formula of a five times increase every decade I get 32.5 million by 2025, 162.5 million by 2035, 812.5 million by 2045, 4.0625 billion by 2055, 20.3125 billion by 2065. The current population of the entire planet is only about 6.5 billion, which is about one third of this fifty year projected number. Also, I started with only the U.S. figure of 1.5 million not a planet wide number. At this rate, we should pass the 100% mark around the year 2050.

According to the simple math, not only is Kuhlewind's

prediction a possibility, it is a probability. It appears almost a certainty that autism is the future of mankind.

But wait a minute—there may be other factors involved in the increased recognition of autism than simply an increase in the birth rate. The way autism is defined has changed and now includes many more individuals than the old definitions would. Also an increased awareness of the condition would cause people to be looking for and finding the condition that wouldn't have otherwise been found. These two things may account for possibly half of the recognized increase. Then again—it doesn't really matter—does it? The fact that the incidence of the condition is increasing is all that really counts. The other considerations only affect how long it will actually take.

The media has given us a list of possible causes for autism. The list includes *inoculations, heavy metal exposure, food preservatives, pesticides,* and *air pollution* just to name the more common ones. However, the World Health Organization states that the incidence of autism is increasing world wide at the same rate. That means that autism is increasing among the indigenous population of the Amazon basin at the same rate as in the United States. It is obvious that what we have been told about the cause(s) of autism is, at best, only erroneous speculations. Of all of the possible causes for autism, I consider Georg Kuhlewind's genetic evolution to be the most plausible.

The simplest perspective or statement about what autism is would be that the sufferers fail to develop acceptable social skills (behaviors). If this, according to Kuhlewind, is the future of mankind, then in the worst-case scenario, we would have a population that lacks the social skills necessary to develop relationships resulting in procreation.

If I leave my vision of the future here it would be quite bleak.

However, I cannot leave my vision of the future with only this perspective. I have spent about thirty years looking for and developing a method of addressing autism. The result is a counseling program that can allow an autistic individual to realize the skills necessary to live life to its fullest. This includes the development of the full spectrum of social skills and behaviors. And it can be done without losing the autistic gifts of innocence, empathy, and intellect.

The most rewarding results of the Davis Autism Approach for Nurturing The Seed of Genius programs are autistic individuals who have flawless reasoning and logic skills—individuals who have unwavering discipline—individuals who will not violate responsibility—individuals who have intellects that go beyond anything that mankind has ever seen. All of this while at the same time we also have individuals who retain their innocence and empathy of being everything and nothing at the same time.

From this view, my vision of the future is utopian. I see the future composed of a population of the "new ones" who are an evolutionary step above what exists today. The new ones will bring about a different world. Simply based upon the inherent nature of autism we can predict some of the changes that will occur.

A "new one" would not take a weapon from a government representative or a religious official with the idea of hurting or killing someone. It simply wouldn't or couldn't happen. Therefore, in my vision of the future there will not be war.

An individual that can feel the pain and sense of violation of another's being a victim of a criminal act would not be able to commit such an act. Therefore, in my vision of the future there will be no need for jails or prisons.

An individual that knows the mechanics of emotions and appropriately accepts responsibility will not experience guilt or inappropriate emotions, will not experience mental illness. Therefore, in my vision of the future there will be no need for mental institutions.

And last, but not least, a government composed of responsible individuals that govern out of respect for the population would find itself above corruption. Therefore, in my vision of the future, the primary concern of humanity will be the welfare of humanity. Utopia!

- *Ronald D. Davis - founder Reading Research Council, Davis Dyslexia Association International, and Davis Autism International, author The Gift of Dyslexia and The Gift of Learning*

I see the full transformation of our human species, as a collective consciousness, now underway. The vibration, the resonance, the chorus of change is here. We stand at the threshold of a new perception of reality, a new understanding of where we live in the cosmos of Creation—and of where we as a species can go now. All we need to rise above our presently knotted web of ecologic, biologic, economic, sociologic, spiritual-logic conditions is to see what is beyond these knots, and to realize that we can be there. Our evolution is a long journey, and we are merely in the early phases. We will face the challenges of this remarkable era, and we will rise above these, unfolding the power of our consciousnesses as individuals and as a species, and as members of the cosmic biosphere.

- *Dr Angela deAngelis (also known as Dr Angela Browne-Miller) - author, systems theorist, social scientist, spiritual guide, psychotherapist*

You don't have to be a futurophile, these days, to have heard of "the Singularity". What was once viewed as an oversimplistic extrapolation has now become mainstream: it is almost heterodox in technologically sophisticated circles **not** to take the view that technological progress will accelerate within the next few decades to a rate that, if not actually infinite, will so far exceed our imagination that it is fruitless to attempt to predict what life will be like thereafter.

Which technologies will dominate this march? Surveying the torrent of literature on this topic, we can with reasonable confidence identify three major areas: software, hardware and wetware. Artificial intelligence researchers will, numerous experts attest, probably build systems that are "recursively self-improving"—that understand their own workings well enough to design improvements to themselves, thereby bootstrapping to a state of ever more unimaginable intellectual performance. On the hardware side, it is now widely accepted as technically feasible to build structures in which every atom is exactly where we wish it to be. The positioning of each atom will be painstaking, so one might view this as of purely academic interest—if not for the prospect of machines that can build copies of themselves. Such "assemblers" have yet to be completely designed, let alone built, but cellular automata research indicates that the smallest possible assembler is probably quite simple and small. The advent of such devices would rather thoroughly remove the barrier to practicability that arises from the time it takes to place each atom: exponentially accelerating parallelism is not to be sneezed at. And finally, when it comes to biology, the development of regenerative medicine to a level of comprehensiveness that can give a few extra decades of healthy life to those who are already in middle age will herald a similarly accelerating sequence of refinements—not necessarily accelerating in terms of the rate at which such therapies are improved, but in the rate at which they diminish our risk of succumbing to aging at any age, as I've described using the concept of "longevity escape velocity".

The transformative technologies I have mentioned will, in my view, probably all arrive within the next few decades—a timeframe that I personally expect to see. And we will use them, directly or indirectly, to address all the other slings and arrows that humanity is heir to: biotechnology to combat aging will also combat infections, molecular manufacturing to build unprecedentedly powerful machines will also be able to perform geo-engineering and prevent hurricanes and earthquakes and global warming, and superintelligent computers will orchestrate these and other technologies to protect us even from cosmic threats such as asteroids—even, in relatively short order, nearby super-novae. (Seriously) Moreover, we will use these technologies to address any irritations of which we are not yet even aware, but which grow on us as today's burdens are lifted from our shoulders. Where will it all end?

You may ask why it should end at all—but I think it will. I think it is reasonable to conclude, based on the above, that there will come a time when **all** avenues of technology will, roughly simultaneously, reach the point seen today with aviation, as epitomised by the non-existence of flying cars: where we are simply not motivated to explore further sophistication in our technology, but prefer to focus on enriching our and each other's lives using the technology that already exists. Progress will still occur, but fitfully and at a **decelerating** rather than accelerating rate. Humanity will at that point be in a state of complete satisfaction with its condition: complete identity with its deepest goals. Human nature will at last be revealed.

- Dr Aubrey de Grey - biomedical gerontologist, chairman and chief science officer Methuselah Foundation

This is my vision for "Future Earth"—a world where humans live in balance with all other species, and give up the dangerous myth that "humans are special." All species are special (it's what makes them different species). And there is nothing especially special about human specialness. Only when we let go of that self-serving myth will our planet stand a chance of sustaining the bountiful variety of living systems that Earth has so beautifully created and nourished for the billions of years we have circled around the life-giving light of our Sun. May it long continue. And may we continue to walk the journey of evolution.

Earth Song

A time when Earth sings
joyously of soul's long-forgotten dream

when the spirit of humanity calls out
across the centuries,
reclaiming and reclaimed by,
our long lost lineage of natural wisdom

a time when ancient stories sound
their mythical truth
in the hidden chambers of every heart
and silence echoes like drops of lunar rain
in the vast vast space of each eternal moment
replenishing and reconnecting
blood and breath with sacred mineral and precious air

and skin meets scales in a watery embrace
and oceans pulse again with new vitality
and mountains roar in celebration
as wild things fly free once more

ozone sky screens and greens the land
and immemorial glaciers stand firm,
monuments to hidden ages
preserving the fingerprints of time

listen, you can hear the whisper of intelligence
from deep inside the atoms
guiding the ever-spiraling adventure of matter
orchestrating the symphony and dance of all species

humanity finds its home, at last
ceasing the hopeless search for ever more
ever more ever more
and releases Earth to dream its song

- Christian de Quincey, for Earth Day 2009 - professor, founder The
Wisdom Academy, author Deep Spirit: Cracking the Noetic Code

The opportunity to create a forum for companies to voice their collective views promoting dematerialized growth

Invitation to participate in the creation of a Confederation of Dematerialized Industries

1. The great majority of commerce in the world today is heavily dependent on fossil fuels.

2. The looming catastrophe of climate change compels nations to reduce these emissions by a very significant percentage.

3. New energy generation processes may be developed in 30 or 60 years that could permit a return to current levels of energy consumption.

4. The critical challenge for the 21st Century is therefore to massively reduce greenhouse gas (ghg) emissions and hold them down until a new technology emerges (nuclear fusion or some other).

5. In every country citizen perception of greater wealth through a growing economy has become the minimum requirement demanded of governments. Attempts to

change this expectation may prove dangerous.

As Financial Times columnist Martin Wolff wrote on 18 December 2007:

> "The biggest point about debates on climate change and energy supply is that they bring back the question of limits. If, for example, the entire planet emitted CO2 at the rate the US does today, global emissions would be almost five times greater. The same, roughly speaking, is true of energy use per head. This is why climate change and energy security are such geopolitically significant issues. For if there are limits to emissions, there may also be limits to growth. But if there are indeed limits to growth, the political underpinnings of our world fall apart. Intense distributional conflicts must then re-emerge—indeed, they are already emerging—within and among countries."

6. Economic growth can proceed without increased energy consumption when consumer expenditure migrates from physical goods to increased consumption of 'dematerialized' products. These are carried by electronic media and include:

- Films
- TV
- Games
- Music
- News
- Education
- Culture
- Literature
- People, live

7. To give a picture of the home in 2012 imagine first that a significant percentage of expenditure on cars and fuel has been transferred to the 'dematerialized' economy.

8. A billion people's homes in the industrialized world should have more than 20MB of high quality internet bandwidth both down and up.

9. A combination of high definition broadband (HDB) and video telephony would then permit people in their homes to:

- Avoid commuting (videophones left on during working hours to allow managers to 'be with' and therefore supervise home workers). Workers can also virtually 'sit together'.

- HDB videophones with true eye contact will permit friends and families to spend time together remotely and offer extraordinary potential for social and business networking.

- HDB will permit any film, TV or other piece of recorded media to be enjoyed in cinema quality.

- HDB allows for every school class and university lecture in the world to be recorded and watched by any number of people who wish to study any thing at any time.

- HDB allows the infinite mass of content available to be edited and repackaged in any form by any person and made available on demand for a price.

- HDB video telephony allows for one billion broadcasters to emerge and educate, entertain and inform us all.

In this near future a young person might naturally want to be rich and famous, but would not necessarily assume that leaving their local area was the most effective first step to achieve their goal. We can also imagine that in this world all energy consumption will be monitored and managed by billions of embedded sensors ensuring high efficiency.

10. To me this future seems very exciting and alive with delightful possibilities. But under all circumstances, dematerialization is the necessary prerequisite for economic growth that is consistent with human survival.

11. If the reader accepts the points made above consider what a bright this future lays ahead for Information and Communications Technology (ICT) companies and their content providers.

12. It is inevitable that companies pioneering dematerialization will grow turnover and profit whilst those associated with significant ghg production will lose revenues. The impact on profitability could be dramatic, see table below.

13. This paper suggests that the migration to a much more dematerialized economy is an unavoidable necessity over the next 20 years. However, if this change happens over 20 years or 5 years is a function of how quickly taxation and regulation of ghgs can be implemented at a sufficient scale to migrate expenditure to the dematerialized alternatives.

14. This paper recommends a single issue lobbying company is established to stimulate, unite and direct lobbying efforts by the Information and Communications Technology (ICT) companies, as well as content providers, who all stand to benefit dramatically financially from migration to a dematerialized economy.

15. The first target for such a company might be to promote investment in expanded procurement of travel substitution technology by government agencies. A secondary target would be to financially support campaigns for increased taxation and regulation of ghgs in all areas.

Below is a rudimentary analysis of ghgs to revenues and profit based on Carbon Disclosure Project data. The table shows 12 companies from high emitting sectors contrasted with 12 companies from the Information and Communications Technology (ICT) sector.

High emitters include 4 Airlines, 3 Cement, 3 Steel and 2 Auto manufacturers.
ICT include 4 Hardware, 1 Software, 1 Broadcaster and 6 Network operators.

High emitters

	Sales $bn	Profit $bn	M/cap $bn	CO2 MMT
Air France	28.5	1.59	11.49	15.5
British Airways	16.5	1.2	11.14	16.1
Japan Airlines	19.9	0.52	5.93	16.97
Singapore Airlines	13.34	1.66	13.37	13.1
Lafarge	22.5	1.82	26.28	89.2
Holcim	19.82	1.73	24.81	74.51
Cemex	17.59	2.23	25.54	50.47
Arcelor	54.08	3.99	41.28	74.7

Nippon Steel	33.45	2.93	45.9	61
Posco	26.76	4.24	32.45	62.8
General Motors	206.71	4.09	16.5	12.3
Ford	160.12	4.79	14.29	8.4
Total	**619.27**	**30.79**	**268.98**	**495.05**

ICT

	Sales $bn	Profit $bn	M/cap $bn	CO2 MMT
Cisco	31.9	10.34	157	0.5
Intel	35.38	12.49	110	4
HP	94.08	10.16	106.82	1.54
IBM	91.42	18.95	140.39	2.67
Microsoft	46	17.94	267.62	0.46
Sky	8.03	1.06	19.1	0.03
Vodafone	56.99	22.83	142.77	1.3
BT	37.86	2.9	48.15	0.74
Bell Canada	15.06	1.7	20.66	0.28
NTT	91.99	4.26	70.41	3.19
NTT (mobile)	40.81	5.22	77.8	0.86
Swisscom	7.98	1.31	18.63	0.02
Total	**557.5**	**109.16**	**1179.35**	**15.59**

Key observations from the above table include:

1. The high emitters generate larger revenue.
2. But high emitters generate only 28% of the earnings of ICT
3. The high emitters have only 23% of the ICT market capitalization
4. But high emitters produce 32 times more CO2
5. Per tonne of CO2 high emitters earn $62, ICT earns $6,992
6. ICT produces 112 times more profit per tonne of CO2 than high emitters.

It follows that the ICT economy can grow far more safely than for example air, autos or construction. Most importantly, ICT companies can dramatically increase profits by accelerating the development of a low carbon economy through increased taxation and regulation of ghg emissions.

The new organization, working title 'Confederation of Dematerialized Industries' could be either a not for profit trade association or private company.

The Confederation of Dematerialized Industries would offer members:
The principal forum to voice their collective views on the significant opportunities presented to the dematerialized industries in providing low energy economic development.

Technical and policy expertise to work to influence the shape of forthcoming national and international standards and legislation promoting a realistic response to climate change.

A platform to ensure policy makers at national and supranational level are aware of the issues and opinions of the dematerialized industries in support of the recommendations from the scientific community.

A media voice for the dematerialized industries, able to say things individual companies might fear to say (for fear of offending their customers).

Opportunities to share best practice to help eliminate waste and achieve sustainable improvements in quality, cost and delivery.

Help maximizing funding opportunities by accessing the wealth of national and supra -national government funding available.
Marketing opportunities through participation in technology demonstrations.

Access to an economics resource that will ensure the members are kept abreast of the key economic, market and business opportunities stemming from responses to climate change.

Regular updates on progress with sector liaison with an enormous number of organizations, legislative bodies and government departments.

- Paul Dickinson - chief executive Carbon Disclosure Project, UK

Imagine the world as if humans never existed. Instantly, you have beauty, vitality, diversity, purity, resilience, and crystal clear land, air and water. Now imagine that we add human society and keep this same level of brilliance, beauty and health. Humans would be living in perfect harmony with nature and each other. Nature without humans is perfect. Humans are part of nature. We have the capacity to be as smart as nature. We can live with the same high level of intelligence, coordination, sophistication and sustainability seen in nature. This high level of intelligence comes mostly through the heart or intuition, not the intellect. When we make the mind the servant of the heart, we access the wisdom and brilliance of nature. We become as smart as nature. We understand that we are part of one interconnected, healthy and vibrant system.

The idea that we are above nature, or separate from nature, or that nature is here to serve us is a self-serving, myopic human creation. It causes humans to act like a cancer on this planet. Obviously, we are not above nature. We are one equal part of it. When we truly understand and act on this, we will create Heaven on Earth.

- Frank Dixon - founder Global System Change

The perfect world would be one in which freedom of mind would be translated into real and physical freedom of movement which has to be equal.

- Feliciano dos Santos - musician, founder and director Estamos, Mozambique

I see a world in which everyone would have abundant and quality food, shelter, clothing, heath care, and education. There would be no rich people. Everything else would follow from the freedom from want. People would create all kinds of different societies based on that principle.

- *Roxanne Dunbar-Ortiz - activist, author Roots of Resistance: A History of Land Tenure in New Mexico*

In my dream world, when young people consider careers, they no longer ask, "How can I make a living and enjoy financial security?" but rather, "How might I best give of my gifts, to create a more beautiful world?"

That means that there will be no antagonism between work and art, or between money and art.

It also means we will have an economic system in which the best business decision is identical to the best ecological decision.

All the beautiful things that visionaries describe will come to pass, but they will arise naturally from a basic shift in the way we experience ourselves and look at life. We can start creating that world, and living in it, right now. If you ask, whenever you remember to, "How best can I give in this situation?" you will soon find yourself living in a different world.

- *Charles Eisenstein - healer, author The Ascent of Humanity*

I have always dreamed of "a world of empathy and realization." Why don't I see people standing up to leave the chair for an old woman? Why don't I see children learning from their parents to give more than to take? Why don't I see a fortunate man or woman learning persistence and humility from those unfortunate?

I am trying to see, but what I see is still few from what it should be!

I have taken two things from life: knowledge and love, and I am quite indebted to those who passed those two things to me. I am not happy I have knowledge... I am not happy I have love... I am happy because I have both of them in my brain and heart.

I have always struggled to learn knowledge to enlighten my brain, and to find love to keep my heart alive, but after all I was wrong. To be a human being, I discovered that I need love for my brain and knowledge for my heart! This is what I call "a world of empathy and realization."

- Raghda El Ebrashi - founder and chairperson Alashanek ya Balady Association for Sustainable Development (AYB-SD), Egypt

The Power of Unreasonable People

It's easy to have nightmares about the future, with another 1.5 billion people projected by 2025—and the world headed, so we are told by the demographers, for a peak population of 9-10 billion souls. I'm not at all sure that I believe that, because the system we are part of tends to convulse and our civilization is precariously fine-tuned to a narrow set of climatic conditions, while much of what we do—including our catastrophic over-harvesting of oceanic fisheries—puts us on a collision course with the capacity of our planet to support us. That, for me, is the emerging nightmare reality.

In terms of my dreams for the future, it's too easy to say a better world for pretty much all species. So my vision of a future I'd like to be part of is one where every child can look forward to a future where life expectancy, living conditions and environmental quality are all on a dramatically improving trend. That's what we're working towards at SustainAbility (http://www.sustainability.com) and at Volans (http://www.volans.com). For that to happen we don't just need one Barack Obama but hundreds of visionary pragamatists who drive positive change at every level of our societies and economies. That may seem an unreasonable expectation in the circumstances, but—as we put it in our 2008 book for Harvard Business Press of the same name—this is 'The Power of Unreasonable People'.

The excruciating economic and social pressures we will endure as the downturn impacts countries around the world is to be regretted, but the collapse of the old economic order is potentially clearing the way for a new order. I think we are confronted by the biggest set of challenges—and the biggest window of opportunity—of my lifetime. That is the message of our 2009 report, *The Phoenix Economy*, which spotlights 50 enterprises, companies, financial institutions and government agencies that are working towards this end. In the report we use that old quote, which I think derives from the U.S. Marines in the Pacific campaign of WWII, to the effect that: 'The impossible takes a little longer'.

- John Elkington - co-founder SustainAbility, founding partner and director Volans, UK

In my dream world I would explore many more worlds in hopes of finding peace and perspective.

- Scott Ely - founder and director Sunsense Solar Electric

The World I See

My concerns and my hopes for the future of the World are as follows:

1) Resources
My vision is that people will understand more and more the importance of taking care of the Earth.

Our planet has limited resources. For years people have used much more than they need and continue to do so. The new generation is even more wasteful. As the population continues to grow, people will need more and more. There is no room for excessive desires and excessive waste. If we do not awaken and become more careful, our resources could be depleted, and the Earth could become sick and weak. It could even lose balance, spin out of orbit, and collide with another planet. All life would be destroyed.

Excessive desires are the cause, the root, of this problem.

My vision is that this problem will become more obvious, so that most people will change their attitudes, become less greedy, and stop harming the Earth.

My wish is that technology will improve so much that we can get all of our energy from the Sun and will no longer have to drill into Earth to take her resources, creating a dangerous imbalance.

My vision is that people will actually begin to use wisely only what they need.

They will begin to protect this precious, living World.

2) Pollution

Another issue of concern is the continuing pollution of our air, water and food.

This, like using too many resources, is caused by greed and selfishness.

In the future I see that, through further education, our attitudes toward life will change.

We will become increasingly more gentle and sensitive toward each other and our Earth.

More and more scientists, businessmen, and factory owners will realize the mistake of polluting our Earth, act upon their knowledge, and stop ignoring the problem.

Good business skills and advanced technology will combine with good hearts to create a healthy, sustainable environment.

3) Religions

The essence of all religions is the same. They are all based on Love.

Although Love is one word, it has been fragmented by competition and conflict.

My vision for the future is that there will be more understanding between the many different religions. There will be less friction, and eventually all religions will work side by side toward the common good.

I see all religions coming together to make Love one again.

4) The end of war & the beginning of the new era

War is the most destructive of all human activities.

Fighting, anger, and hatred between individuals, religions, and countries have caused immeasurable pain and suffering.

Soon people will realize that weapons and angry words are walls.

These walls must be dissolved.

It is imperative that, collectively, we change our ways and turn toward kindness, patience, compassion and understanding. Otherwise the results could be disastrous.

The World can be peaceful only if the majority of people understand Unconditional Love and live in that Spirit.

A new World will emerge when most people begin to love everyone and love everything.

This will make possible the beginning of a new era, an era of clear and positive communication. A time when Science, technology and the economy will continue to grow, but hearts will be open and pure.

My vision for the near future is that this World will be Paradise.

I can see a future World filled with very calm, peaceful people, living in a state of ease, always smiling. A World filled with people who respect each other, enjoy life, and are always kind and friendly.

My vision is that soon there will be "Heaven on Earth."
All we have to do is open our Hearts and work together.

- Master Li Jun Feng - qigong master, founder of Sheng Zhen Qigong

When I think about a few words that summarize a critical and key vision for the future, they are actually drawn from the film *"Star Trek: First Contact."* There is a scene where Captain Picard is explaining the economics of the 24th century to a woman of the 21st century. He says: "The acquisition of wealth is no longer the driving force in our lives. We work to better ourselves and the rest of humanity." I could not put it better or more concisely.

- Bill Fletcher, Jr. - executive editor BlackCommentator.com

Proposal for a Sustainable Future

There are no "Utopias." The very notion of "Utopia" is static. However, the survival of any social system ultimately depends upon its ability to allow for appropriate change to improve society as a whole. The paths that we choose will ultimately determine whether or not there is intelligent life on earth.

The social direction being proposed has no parallel in history with any other previous political ideology or economic strategy. Establishing the parameters of this new civilization will require transcending many of the traditions, values, and methods of our past.

The Venus Project presents an alternative vision for a sustainable world civilization unlike any political, economic or social system that has gone before. It envisions a time in the near future when money, politics, self and national interest have been phased out. *The Venus Project* calls for the redesign of our social structure. Within this new structure the age-old failures of war, poverty, hunger, debt, nationalism and unnecessary human suffering are viewed not only as fully avoidable, but also totally unacceptable. Although this vision may seem idealistic, it is based upon years of study and experimental research.

As global challenges and scientific information proliferate, nations and people face common threats that transcend national boundaries. Overpopulation, energy shortages, environmental pollution, water scarcity, economic catastrophe, the spread of uncontrollable disease, and the technological displacement of people by machines threaten each of us. Although many people are dedicated to alleviating those conditions, our social and environmental problems will remain insurmountable as long as a few powerful nations and financial interests maintain control of and consume most of the world's resources.

To transcend these limitations, *The Venus Project* proposes we work toward a **worldwide, resource-based economy, in which the planetary resources are held as the common heritage of all the earth's inhabitants.** The current practice of rationing resources through monetary methods is irrelevant, counter-productive, and falls far short of meeting humanity's needs.

Today we have access to technologies that can measure and manage our resources globally to easily provide a very high standard of living for all. With the intelligent and humane application of science and technology, the people of the earth can guide and shape the future together while protecting the environment.

Simply stated, a resource-based economy utilizes existing resources—rather than money—to provide an equitable method of distribution in the most humane and efficient manner. It is a system in which all natural, man-made, machine-made, and synthetic resources are available without the use of money, credits, barter, or any other form of debt.

To better understand a resource-based economy, consider

this. If all the money in the world disappeared overnight, as long as topsoil, factories, personnel and other resources were left intact, we could build anything we needed to fulfill most human needs. It is not money that people require, but rather free access to most of their needs without worrying about financial security or having to appeal to a government bureaucracy. In a resource-based economy of abundance, money will become irrelevant.

We have arrived at a time when new innovations in science and technology can easily provide abundance to all of the world's people. It is no longer necessary to perpetuate the conscious withdrawal of efficiency by planned obsolescence, perpetuated by our old and outworn profit system. If we are genuinely concerned about the environment and our fellow human beings, if we really want to end territorial disputes, war, crime, poverty and hunger, we must consciously reconsider the social processes that led us to a world where these factors are common. Like it or not, it is our social processes—political practices, belief systems, profit-based economy, our culture-driven behavioral norms—that lead to and support hunger, war, disease and environmental damage.

We must ask why and how and when for every social construct we blindly follow. The intelligent and humane use of science and technology offers us the tools to accomplish this.

A resource-based economy uses technology to overcome scarce resources by applying renewable sources of energy, computerizing and automating manufacturing and inventories, designing safe, energy-efficient cities, providing universal health care, making relevant education available, and generating a new incentive system based on human and environmental concern.

Some question what would happen to incentive if our needs were provided without our having to work to attain them. The question assumes humans have no desires beyond basic needs. If that were true, there would be no inventors, no writers, no teachers. People work with passion on the things that interest and challenge them. Motivation and incentive exist when people take on meaningful tasks. Motivation and incentive die in the daily grind of the boring and repetitive tasks required to earn a paycheck.

True growth and development occur when people are involved in creative, challenging and constructive endeavors.

WHERE DO WE START?

The first step is a survey of all available planetary resources and personnel. This information would be compiled as a database to ascertain the possible parameters for *humanizing* social and technological development. This can be accomplished through today's fast, high capacity computer systems that will assist us in defining what we have, what the earth can supply, and how we can humanely and appropriately manage environmental and human affairs.

We are rapidly approaching the time when human intelligence will be incapable of assimilating the technological complexities necessary to manage a highly advanced society. Existing technologies are rapidly exceeding the human capacity to absorb and process essential information. The human mind is far too slow and simplistic a structure to handle the forthcoming voluminous information. We have neither the training nor the capability to handle the trillions of bits of information per second necessary to efficiently manage the new advances in technology. Only our most capable computers can carry the memory and enormous bits of data necessary to arrive at equitable and sustainable decisions involving the development and distribution of resources on a global scale.

As artificial intelligence rapidly develops, machines will be assigned the tasks of complex decision-making in industrial, military and governmental affairs. **This would not imply a takeover by machines.** Instead it will be a gradual transfer of decision-making processes to machine intelligence as the next phase of social evolution.

Today's computers are not yet linked to the necessary social and environmental information nor do they have operating indices for those issues to arrive at appropriate options and decisions. When cybernation is ultimately integrated into all aspects of this new and dynamic culture, only then can computers appropriately serve the needs of all people. One can think of this as an electronic, autonomic nervous system extending into all areas of the social complex. Their function would be to coordinate a balance between production and distribution and to maintain and operate a balanced-load economy. In this way decisions would be arrived at on the basis of human needs, feedback from the environment, the carrying capacity of each geographical area and the like.

Many nations grapple with the daunting task of piecemeal retrofitting of new, more efficient technologies into their existing infrastructures. These efforts will fall far short of the required, integrated technology because current infrastructures cannot fully accommodate the vast changes required. We graft new technology onto old ideas and old processes. Each new graft creates more stress on the process affected, and new problems and imbalances ripple across the globe.

We are already, in fact, a global community. The fiction we hold to is that nations can still be independent of others and the impact of the technological changes sprouting around us. Our city designs, industrial plants, waterways, energy systems, production and distribution centers, and transportation systems must be re-designed and operated as a coherent, integrated, global energy system. In this way we can use our technology to overcome resource shortages, provide universal abundance and protect the environment.

In this cybernated global economy, mega machines directed by sophisticated artificial intelligence will excavate canals, dig tunnels, and erect bridges, viaducts and dams without the necessity of human involvement: all of these will be based on designs that accommodate human and animal migrations and ecological dependencies. Human participation will be in the form of selecting the desired ends, yet human labor would no longer be required.

In this society, construction techniques would be vastly different from those employed today. Self-erecting structures would prove most expedient and efficient in the construction of industrial plants, bridges, buildings and eventually the entire global infrastructure. This would not create cookie-cutter cities. The notion that intelligent overall planning implies mass uniformity is absurd. Cities would be uniform only to the degree that they would require far less materials, save time and energy and yet be flexible enough to allow for innovative changes, while maintaining the highest quality possible to support the local ecology—both human and environmental. Utilizing technology in this way would make it possible for a global society to achieve social advancement and worldwide reconstruction in the shortest time possible.

Eventually factories would be designed by robots for robots, capable of doing almost any type of work once believed to be uniquely attributable to humans. The cybernated systems could also be self-programming by means of environmental feedback. Machines will be capable of self-replication and improvement of their operational range, while at the same time repairing themselves, updating their circuitry and recommending the most appropriate direction to be taken in an emergent civilization.

Since the computers and systems involved would be continuously self-monitoring, parts would be supplied and installed well in advance of any wear. The machines could operate continuously except when conducting their own maintenance and repair.

In a resource-based economy, all the work of robotics would

be directed toward the well being of all people. In such a society the monitoring of people by machines would serve no useful purpose, except where deliberate human feedback was needed.

Some people fear the possibility of machines "taking over". This is pure fantasy. Machines have no emotions nor do they seek power or control. The notion that machines will eventually take over and enslave the human race is science fiction. Machines do not possess emotions. They neither love nor hate. They do not trust or feel compassion. However, they heat and cool our homes, preserve our food, transport us around the world, maintain life support systems in hospitals, warn us of fires, enable us to communicate with one another throughout the world and much more. Machines are merely tools and extensions of the physical and mental attributes of human beings.

It is not advances in machine technology we should fear, but rather the abuse and misuse of this technology in a monetary-based society of private profit and self-interest. We can build machines to explore outer space and to enhance the quality of life on Earth. Or we can use machines to destroy ourselves. Ultimately, humans will determine the uses to which inanimate machines are directed.

The Venus Project's vision of applied machine technology to the social system would serve the common good, a goal that has eluded human civilization to this day. Although this vision is still in its infancy, the possibilities for a better life for all the inhabitants of our planet ultimately depend on the decisions we make today. *The Venus Project* offers a global concept and an invitation to explore, discuss, and develop the future together.

- Jacque Fresco - industrial designer, author, lecturer, artist, architectural designer, futurist, founder The Venus Project

The World as it should Have Been

To create an ideal world as I feel it should have been...

Once upon a time in a far away place called the Land of Elves, there is a society that humans could emulate. It is a place where children are raised by parents who are fully functioning on every level. They would not resort to relying on addictions or other destructive behaviours to deal with their stress, and therefore would not need stimulants like sugar, alcohol, drugs or junk food to feel good. The quality of their health would be far superior to that of our present world.

There would be no obesity due to the healthy eating regimes, and all of the food would be pesticide and hormone free. It would be derived directly from nature, and thus the individuals would receive the full benefits of this nutritional spectrum for their body.

Individuals would find love and fulfillment with a partner early in life. Their health would prosper, since it would be second nature to eating well, meditating, exercising and being at one with nature and a higher power. This environment would also foster the ability for an individual to find sexual and romantic bliss with a partner, without the long journey of being attracted to negative partners who ARE ONLY in our lives because they mirror the unfulfilled aspects of one or both parents.

When children are born, the stars would line up and bless the child, and yes, there would still be challenges to overcome as the child grew and matured. Lessons like perseverance and patience would still be an important part of the learning process, but life would prove to be very rewarding on every level, and from an early age.

The children would be deeply loved by both parents, and they would be raised in a home that supports who they are—not who their parents want them to be. This environment would foster positive self-esteem and confidence for the child to go off on their own path to fulfill his or her life, in their chosen area of personal passion. Most of our passions are extinguished out of us by an early age when we are told not to behave or act in certain fashions. This environment would also foster a positive self image, which would lead to healthy sexual relationships in the future.

The children would grow up with complete support in every level of emotional, intellectual and physical development. This would lead to a world where there would be less illness or need for doctors. The inner life of an individual is the core foundation for the health of our emotional life, our immune system and digestive systems for the rest of our lives; or until we begin to work deeply at healing the multiple wounds of the past.

In an ideal world, these children would be brought up with, and would grow to honour and embrace all faiths. They would honour all of the key gods and goddesses of our times, including the ancient ones. As the children matured, they would focus on their own choices, but would grow up with the understanding that all gods and goddess come from one source of the universe.

Career choices would come early to the children, since their strengths have been encouraged rather than suppressed. They would prosper financially and have a great life; for the desire to overspend would not be there. The desire to overspend and accumulate is only a result of the emotional hole from childhood.

This is a place where intuition would be encouraged rather than ridiculed; therefore individuals would grow up with a keen sense of a connection to their angels, animal totems, a higher power and their own spirit guides. Perhaps the gutsier ones would cross the invisible veil and come over to the human realm known as Earth; and start to introduce a new way of life to the humans who are motivated completely by their lifelong desire to fill the emotional hole of never feeling fulfilled or loved.

- Dr Alex Gellman H.D. - motivational speaker, executive coach, doctor of homeopathy, team facilitator, author Passage Ways to Your Soul, Canada

Have you ever wondered what life would be like if—
You were always healthy in mind, emotions, spirit and body?
You were happy?
You were fulfilled?
You were supported?
You were loved?
Well, the people of Newtopia don't wonder about any of these because they live life like that every day of their lives. How did that happen and why hasn't it happened to us?

Many years ago, the people of Newtopia were just like us. They rushed through life eating what they could, hoping one day they'd relax and do all the things they dreamed of. Funnily enough, there never was enough time. They sacrificed their health, unwittingly of course, not realizing that health emanated from inward out. Because of their busy schedules, they didn't really have the proper time to devote to their children or loved ones. There was always electronic babysitting or others to take on these more menial tasks. Mental relief from the stresses of daily life could easily be obtained from any number of pharmacologic sources. Physical activity often got in the way of work, so it too was denigrated to a lesser status. Satisfaction came from things, not ideas or feelings and unconditional love had more conditions than the most complex nuclear proliferation treaty.

Suddenly their world changed. The abuse of the environment and its gifts resulted in a people left teetering on the brink of extinction. This highly civilized, sophisticated and intelligent (using almost 5% of their brain capacity) society was faced with a crisis. Thankfully none of these things can happen to us.

Faced with the task of a lack of energy, a lack of outside stimulus but more importantly a lack of satisfactory existence, it suddenly dawned on a quiet, simple soul that everything anyone could ever want or hope for was actually already there waiting to be found and that that secret had actually been handed down from generation to generation but somehow, everyone forgot.

He realized and taught the people that the changing months with their four seasons which represented the four elements of fire, earth, air and water were the four keys to life and how to live it.

He realized and taught that there was an elemental diamond about the people which protected each and every one of them. Fire represented the desire and will and energy of life; it was the vital health force which connected everything on the planet together and by fostering it, health could be eternal. No longer would people need to eat and drink for the wrong reason and that by integrating all the elements, the people would only ingest that which would foster them. Air represented the mind and the ability to conceptualize and envision and that these were necessary to the manifestation of anything we wanted. Water was the flowing emotions which for so long had been misunderstood or denied. He taught that there was only one love and that it was based on existence and acceptance alone. Suddenly the conditions of emotion gave way to the love for existence's sake alone. Suddenly people realized that they could foster self esteem and that their children were learning they were loved because they existed and not because of their behavior. This in turn led more and more to accepting and loving and suddenly judgment fell away and jealousy disappeared and there was a spirit of connectivity which took on its own life force. But it was really a life force which was always there but splintered. Finally he taught that the earth represented the action needed to manifest what had begun as inspiration, was transformed by the creative principal of design, was fostered by the feeling of satisfaction and then made manifest. The four elements of life being the stages of the creation of everything in life which had meaning for the people.

Their world changed. The people supported one another. They created out of love. They realized that the divine spark of creation existed in everyone and that when acted upon the mind would devise what was necessary but without the heart feeling it, they would never bring to fruition that which was their desire.

And so a new world was created out of inspiration and desire, sparked by mental creation and the heartfelt feeling of satisfaction and accomplishment which were necessary to be happy, followed by the action needed to manifest that which would contribute to the benefit of the life force of the planet because all was connected.

- Reverend David Gellman, C.A., C.P. A. - director and founder Universal Oneness United Faith Canada, Canada

A perfect world is a state of mind. My mind revolves around perfect sound creation. I create the sounds for others to understand how to enjoy living in their perfect world. When their world is perfect then so is mine.

- Dame Evelyn Glennie - solo percussionist, writer, motivational speaker, UK

My ideal world is where the interconnectedness and interdependence of the human and natural worlds are understood and practiced; a world that measures well-being by the collective health, spirit and diversity of our communities and ecosystems; a world where the human footprint is minimized through widespread commitment to local living and sustainable design principles.

My ideal world is where old values of generosity, honesty, and service are bridged with new ideas around social innovation, green entrepreneurship and transformative learning; a world where elders and children learn through the exchange of their inherent qualities of wisdom and optimism respectively, for the betterment of all who fall in between; a world where words are walked and walked well.

- Lisa (Diz) Glithero - environmental educator, lecturer, founder EYES Project, Canada

The World I Dream Of - interview with Dr Edward Group

"If you could create the world you wanted, the perfect world, what would it look like?"

Dr Group: That's what my whole life has been about, is helping create the perfect dream world of what the past was and what the future can be. I guess the first thing, if I was to think about the perfect dream world, would be to wake people up and expose them to the truths about their health, about who they really are spiritually, about what power they really have, and how we're all interconnected as one. I think that people need a major shift in consciousness to be able to understand the divine power within and their connection with nature, and how we have the power to create a perfect world.

In order to create a perfect dream world, I think the first step is to have a mass consciousness change. I think everything starts from teaching, and people need to be taught why they're here and who they really are. Once mass consciousness reaches a certain point, like the hundredth monkey phenomenon—which is actually in process right now where consciousness is rising and there are a lot of high powered energy fields coming into the planet—we will start to see and feel positive transformational change. We still unfortunately have the majority of the world's population under control and believing what they hear from government and the lies spread through the world media channels. But finally, especially over the last 5 years people are finally waking up to reality and not walking around like sheep in a herd as much.

The same can be said for the brainwashing of the public about disease. We are not addressing the root cause of disease and only addressing the symptoms. The true definition of a doctor is a teacher NOT a prescriber. If people do not understand what causes disease how can they ever expect to learn how to eliminate disease? When I had my clinic I would ask people "Why do you have the disease you suffer from?" and they would say "Well, I don't know." Or I would say, "Could you explain to me about your cancer? What it is? How it got there?" and they would look at me and say, "No, I can't. I don't know about it." So in order to address a problem you need to understand why the problem exists to begin with. After I explained to them the root cause of why they have the disease due to the toxins and everything else, they understand and they're able to heal—spiritually, physically, or mentally.

So the next step to the perfect dream world would be to eliminate what is killing the world and what is killing the population and all the animals and plants. Meaning all the toxins that are in the air we breathe every day. The air's been poisoned! I would make laws to prevent the production of any substance released into the air that's not completely sustainable, provided or produced by nature. And that would also mean to stop cutting down all the trees, to clean up the oceans, to do everything possible to increase the oxygen levels to bring the planet back to an environmentally healing, co-created, space of love.

People are going to have to realize and understand what the problems are that are having such a detrimental effect on the planet which ultimately has a detrimental effect on us. All of the water systems have also been poisoned. So I would start on air and water pollution. We could still have cars, boats and airplanes, they just don't need to run on toxic gas and emit toxic fumes, they could run on magnetic, electromagnetic, or they could run on water or hydrogen. The exhaust would be nothing but pure oxygen.

The next step I would take would be to pass a law that would restrict any type of production of any types of chemicals by any country—this would include volatile organic compounds, pesticides, insecticides, POP's, paints, heavy metal processing, arsenic, etc. Or, anything that would cause harm to the environment or the human body.

Then, I would restrict the production and sale of any type of toxic beverages. And that would mean all the soft drinks and other toxic beverages out there. Anything, that would cause a major effect, as far as production is concerned, on the environment and human body. Also to teach people that the only beverage the body wants and needs is water (after breastfeeding of course).

The next step for a perfect world would be to clean up the food supply and eat healthy foods or better yet learn to live on fruit or air. I'm not a believer that the human body, after years and years of research, should eat meat or that we should slaughter animals. I've researched everything from fruitarians, to raw vegans, to vegetarianism, to half-meat half-vegetarian…and breatharianism. In a perfect scenario the body should not even need any food or liquid to survive. And in a perfect world what we'll be seeing if everything goes as planned in the future is you'll be seeing a race which lives off of air and pranic energy alone.

The air would provide the necessary life-force and energy to sustain the human body which is the way the body was originally made. Actually, there are over 10,000 humans as of todaywho are living on air alone with no food or water. And have been living like this for 10, 20, 40, even over 60 years. You can do the research yourself if this sounds strange. Just read the book *Living on Light* by Jasmuheen or type in breatharian in Google. Also what we've done is we've contaminated the fluids in our body to become acidic. Not to mention the fact that one of the major, major problems with the world today is our food supply. The fact that they're genetically modifying our foods is a scary, scary thought considering the fact they want to depopulate the world and they're going to do it by cutting off good foods. It's just unbelievable to even think about.

People need to understand and cleanse themselves and start cleansing the world. When the environment and the human body become contaminated, then microbes can create diseases of plants and diseases of the human body. Like Louis Pasteur said on his death bed, the germ is nothing, the terrain is everything. He's the one that basically, in the beginning of his research, said that the germ is everything, the germ causes disease. We now know that the germ doesn't cause disease, it's the terrain not being in the proper state that causes disease. And everything that happens with the human body also translates to the earth and the universe.

Next I would address the harmful electromagnetic frequencies which are being created with the addition of all the cell phones and all the cell phone towers around the world. We have literally created a negative harmonic frequency surrounding the globe. As well as with the HAARP systems and any of the other high-pulsed radio waves, microwaves, negative electromagnetic rays which have altered the way fish swim in the oceans, the way plants grow, the way birds fly, and it's altered the way the human body functions. Brain cancers have gone up 60% since the introduction of cell phones. So I would also restrict the use of any damaging electromagnetic rays for the perfect dream world.

Next I would change all negative media to positive by elimi-nating all negative emotional patterns sent through the media. All TV, newspapers and all other media, would only report positive life-giving, happy news. So you'd never have to taint the minds of the newborns or the new children, or the population on a daily basis with negative, negative, negative. I would change that to completely positive—about doing stories on people's gardens, or how this person was helped by this other person. Changing everything to a positive state from a negative state and ultimately creating a world in which everybody is interconnected in a space of love, and peace, and joy.

Next, I would bring people back to nature. Starting with our young children, because the children are the future of the planet.

The indigo children, the star children, and the crystal children that are coming into our planet to help raise the frequency and the vibrations of the planet are being taught the wrong things in school and having their minds corrupted with false knowledge. Also they are being mentally suppressed with pharmaceutical drugs.

And that's another thing I would immediately stop in the perfect dream world—the administration of any vaccinations to children and the administration of any prescription medications. Because all it does is decrease our own spiritual frequency levels. The most damaging part of it is that this is planned by certain groups of people involved in world government affairs that are trying to suppress the coming of a new Golden Age by inoculating children—these powerful indigo children, and crystal children that are coming in—with these harmful vaccinations. The child's immune system is not fully developed until they are eleven years old. And if you put DNA and RNA fragments from chicken embryos and monkey embryos and everything else that's contained in vaccinations it alters the genetic code and the frequencies that normally come in through the pineal gland to the child's body. The spiritual frequencies can be altered in these children. So I would immediately stop any vaccinations and pharmaceutical medications that are numbing our children from becoming attuned with each other through telepathy and through the same mission that they're here for, especially with the ADD and ADHD drugs.

With the elimination of all those things people will start to wake up again and they'll start to use their own powers and they'll start to feel their true selves once again. Ultimately, as the mass consciousness of the planet becomes cleansed, so does the planet become cleansed. And once the planet becomes cleansed everybody will be drawn into nature, and will have the faith to allow nature and their own spiritual ability to progress to a world of love, happiness, peace, and joy.

To create a heaven on earth I think you have to address the main problem on why we don't have a heaven on Earth right now. And the main problem is because the earth is being polluted and our bodies are being polluted. It's inevitable, the earth naturally cleanses itself. Everything cleanses itself on a regular basis. We have a whole society now that's tried to play God and tried to break down God's natural structure. And what they don't understand is that there's a life-force component which they can't see with their microscopes that sustains all life. And what they can take and isolate out of plants, and create chemicals, is just the opposite of the living force and beauty of what the world needs. By using man-made science we've literally, in the last hundred years, practically destroyed the human population as well as the natural environment. We have 2500 medicinal plants going extinct every three months. Every medicinal plant has been harvested by the pharmaceutical companies. Even in the wild, it's very hard to find Ginseng or a lot of other medicinal herbs anymore. If so, there's a cell phone tower nearby, or something else polluting the environment disturbing the potency and growth patterns.

Now the good news with all that being said is there are many, many people waking up and we're on the verge of reaching a mass consciousness level. And the powers that are trying to control the populations and eliminate the populations are running scared right now. Things are happening at an extremely high rate. There's a lot of different theories about what's going to happen in 2012 with the Mayan Calendar. Nobody really knows what's going to be happening, though we are on the path — regardless of what happens in the near future, the next five years, ten years — to be coming into another Golden Age. Whether the earth ascends into another dimension, or whether once we reach mass consciousness everybody wakes up and understands and is then able to communicate through telepathy and communicate through spirituality and create their own space of love. Regardless, I think we're getting extremely close. I know that's why I was put on this planet—to do good. Many are gathering together. It's the gathering of Eagles and the last times to put forth the new heaven on Earth, and so that's ultimately where we're heading. I'm not saying that we might not have to go through some bad times. But we've all known about this. These things have all been put in front of our faces to prepare us for these times that we're going to be going through.

- Dr Edward Group - healer, teacher, chief executive officer Global Healing Center

My ideal world would be a world where the majority of our energy is produced by clean renewable sources such as solar and wind power, and everyone has access to the energy that they need, but nobody uses more than their fair share. All agriculture is grown organically, and the rivers are so clean people can drink right out of them. There is no hunger because there is no poverty. Exports take a back seat to creating and developing local industry and economy, and exporting food is a lower priority than growing food for the local community's consumption. Cycling and riding public transportation is the norm, and every road has bike lanes which are more utilized than the car lanes. Women have equal opportunities to education and employment, and are paid as much as men are for a comparable job. War is obsolete because there is no shortage of food or energy, and because we respect and celebrate people's differences. Higher education, health care, birth control, and chocolate are first-rate, abundant and free.

- Laurie Guevara-Stone - international program manager Solar Energy International

It's easy to come up with reasons why we can't save the world and use that as an excuse to do nothing. I believe that we should stop worrying about whether we're going to succeed or not and just do as much as we can. As Edmund Burke said, *"Nobody made a greater mistake than he who did nothing because he could only do a little" ....*

- *Julia Hailes - sustainability consultant, author The New Green Consumer Guide, UK*

Atlantis Rising
Utopia Revealed

For a moment in time, please simply sit back, relax, and allow your mind to be free from all thoughts concerning the present external world and the environment in which you may find yourself. As you do this, open your mind to a new and seemingly unbelievable reality, an entirely new way of life, a completely new way of living and sharing. Allow your mind to drift into a new paradigm, and as you begin to release your thoughts, focus on the concepts of consciousness and our inseparable connectedness to each other and all life. Envision a world where no conflict exists—personal or global—a world where there is no need for weapons of any kind, including those of mass destruction. In this place, the idea or concept of struggle is now unheard of in any form. Imagine a world without crime, without police, without any human-made law, hence no need for jails or prisons. See a world in which both greed and ego do not exist in any form; in fact, you cannot find any act of selfishness anywhere anytime in anyone, for you can only see a place where all people are as friends, even when they encounter each other for the very first time. And only one language is spoken. Can you picture an environment which is free of any pollution and filled only with self-less-ness, a place where even illness and disease do not exist? Can you imagine a place of great joy and laughter where the idea of stress is incomprehensible, a place simply filled with loving people, each loving the other and all life? Can you visualize a world where life is celebrated to the fullest extent, a place where people consciously lift others in all they do while being filled with creative genius?

This is, indeed, a new and coming reality for us to behold, especially since only unison prevails between all things—even animals and humans live in complete harmony! This is a place where deception cannot fit because it has no need; in fact, it would be totally useless. Why? The use of the intuitive sense would be commonplace for all inhabitants; therefore, deception is instantly revealed. Can you see a world where there is no limitation, one in which you are free to have any experience you so choose? Imagine a world where the need to work would also be virtually non-existent, a world with very little government, if any. This is a place where being homeless is unheard of and where hunger or starvation cannot occur. Imagine an environment in which instant manifestation would be second nature, thereby eliminating any need to harm or kill any thing for food. In such a world, all things are implicitly perfect in all respects, a world in which every human lives in perfect harmony with the animal kingdom and nature. This is a place where death is completely unknown to all things. Can this truly take place? Is this even possible?

Do you realize this new reality may actually come to pass, whether or not we like it or even want it? How can this be? The ancients left messages through their prophecies so we may understand this so-called shift of the ages. Please continue to read on as I outline this journey so you may more easily under-stand and envision the new world just presented to you, a journey of us all awakening to this transcendent, ideal reality. This future time has been termed as the Golden Age which occurs approximately every twenty-five thousand years, and appears as a grand cycle according to the ancient Mayan texts of Meso-America. Allow me to unfold the journey we are on as a world, and the subsequent paths we are going to travel on in order to arrive in our utopian reality. Consider, what if all of the perceived struggles and so-called crises in our world are nothing more than the pangs of birth, a natural process through which the Golden Age must travel before entering our reality? Before it arrives, however, we must let go and leave the old ways of doing things far behind, allowing them to come upon their very own death. Put another way, we must pass off the old in order for the new to arrive in our world. Let us begin our journey in the fields of science and geology, and then look into the impacts—individually and collectively—along our present road of life. This journey will end in a new way of living, the rising of Atlantis based on our new level of understanding and true appreciation of life—the birth of Divine Human. But make no mistake. Because this path leads us to full enlightenment, we do have an arduous journey ahead.

Let us first look into the concept of magnetic fields as presented by geophysics. These scientists generally refer to and view these fields only as they relate to our world, explaining in detail how they can and will change the earth and their significance on weather patterns. Curiously, very few sciences—if even any—truly take an interest into the potential impact these fields may have on the human itself, and to my knowledge, still fewer have even considered studying this effect. Who today really knows the full ramifications these fields have on both the earth and human as they shift and change? The truth is we are one of the most significant—living and moving—electro-magnetic fields in the world. Why? This in and of itself implies that we will experience the greatest of impacts as these fields shift in polarity because we are capable of thinking and to self-realize. Weather and geology cannot. You see, even though everything down to the cellular level, the human mind, by far, is the largest magnetic field we have. My point is these shifting fields will have a greater effect on us than possibly anything else. Will it affect our minds? Will it impact our ability to think and to comprehend? Will such a shift even impact our cellular structure? Will these shifting fields generally affect all life? Every answer is a resounding yes! Allow me to offer some food for thought. As a global society, we shall face the full impact from these changing fields of magnetism; in fact, all of life shall shift and forever alter the journey we undertake on our wonderful planet. Do you realize this is not the first time these fields have shifted? Science has determined this will be the 171st time for such an occurrence, and it will not be the last one as we travel from one grand cycle into the next—endlessly. In this present cycle, interestingly enough, we are the most physically oriented creatures than we have ever been in the last twenty-five thousand years. We are also the most logically and analytically developed than in any other time period, which implies we have a low level of sensitivity. It is actually not far-fetched to state that we currently exist at the lowest point of the pendulum swing; however, the truth is, the pendulum has already begun its rise toward the new cycle as the electro-magnetic fields shift. Yes, it will indeed become more dramatic and obvious as we approach the New Age or Golden Age, progressing ever forward in our cycle—in perfect concordance to prophecy.

Yet another prophecy written millennia ago simply states that our world will shift from patriarchal to matriarchal in its full nature. What exactly does that imply? This one single concept contains many ramifications which shall affect each human directly by reaching into so many arenas; yet, it simply implies a complete transition of our world. Allow me to offer a few examples, keeping in mind that "patriarchal" is male dominant whereas "matriarchal" is female dominant. Water is matriarchal or feminine while land is patriarchal or masculine. The sun is masculine; the moon is feminine. The same relationship holds true for the earth and air, respectively. Even between soul and physical form. Ancient schools of thought would clearly reveal these very same ideas to us; however, observing the manner in which we presently live and work in the world, perhaps now we can clearly see how so many humans rely heavily and exclusively on their logical mind and the outer environment, both patriarchal or masculine natures. Our modern world also clearly reveals the manner and degree to which we have become entirely too reliant on our material reality, not to mention how caught up we are with our bodies in how they appear to others—masculine natures again. These areas are simply going to shift from their patriarchal positions into their opposite ones—matriarchal—as the magnetic fields move into their new paradigms which will affect us to the point that these views will become potentially and completely reversed. In truth, all arenas will shift from dominant patriarchal to dominant matriarchal, and we have absolutely no choice or place to hide since, in reality, there is no way to get around this. As a visual, see this shift as nothing more than switching the cables to a car battery by simply connecting the positive cable to the negative post and vice versa. Although this does not appear at all logical—even dangerous at this point in time—it is this precise mindset from which we shall be moving away, entering instead into a more right brain metaphorical school of thought in much the same manner as the ancients. We will also shift into a higher level of sensitivity, hence moving us more into the intuitive realms of mind, thought and feel. This shift will also create a deeper—more meaningful—way of operating with our emotions, and the material reality will diminish in its importance to us along with the physical body. The body will simply become what it always has been, our vehicle of experience to which there shall be little attachment to it other than this, a tool. When this occurs we shall be creating a much more divine and spiritually-oriented individual and world. We simply shall become matriarchal by our very inherent and true nature. Soul and form literally merge into one and the same idea, not as the duality by which we all live today.

When this matriarchal shift of the magnetic fields takes place our utopian reality will be upon us because we now enter into more of a spiritual state of being or paradigm, a fully unified state with our self and life. We will be operating in a new reality of life as we return to more of an expressive metaphorical manner—matriarchal—as opposed to following the literal concepts of logic as we do today—patriarchal. As the unification of form and spirit takes place we become much lighter as a physical form with less density which, in its present state, could also be referred to as patriarchal. Due to the new human image, we would no longer be able to see duality in any form since all things are now unified in the concept of oneness. The ideas being presented will have their impacts, for certain. And the truth is they already are beginning to appear on the horizon. Please allow me to share with you the reasons for and the mechanics of these events.

Before I do, however, take just a few moments to consider the following questions so you may also see what is on the horizon. To think these are now going on right before our very eyes is amazing! So I ask you, what out there is actually working today? Are world governments and economies working smoothly? How about the health and education systems—are they working well? Looking at the corporate world on a global scale, you can easily see that it, too, is faltering. Do you see people—maybe even yourself!—speak, think, or act in a strange or different manner? Believe or not, these questions bring to light how the above subjects are already shifting in this new direction, just as we each are; yet, in our case it continues unnoticed. It seems material things are easier to see than our innermost self because the diffi-culty is going to be in the actual shift. If we look around, it is starting to show in the human itself. "How so?" one might ask. Two more ancient prophecies assist us: 1) "what is hidden will be shown," and 2) "the truth will come forth." These prophecies merely reveal that whatever lies dominant or as a strong temptation within the human must come out and will be seen by all for it can no longer remain hidden. For example, if you are an angry person then your anger must show at some point. As another example, if you have the desire to create fire then the arsonist within you will compel you to start one—anywhere, anytime. Or, if you have the tendency to steal then it will come upon you as though a thief in the night, no pun intended. Whatever our deepest desire, we and every other human in our world will no longer be able to contain it, for it must rise to the surface. Certainly not as a punishment, mind you! The purpose of this is to remove those urges from the human. At least this is the intention which remains to be seen. We could even go so far to say that it is a cleansing of sorts because these things will not be able to remain in the coming utopian world. They will not fit.

What is my point? To be sure, this shift is going to create the potential of upheaval in our world. Because these things must be worked through by the individual them self, they must choose to either carry out these things in the external and literal sense, or to simply acknowledge and release them. In order for the New Age to come, remember what was shared with you in the beginning. None of these things can exist in this upcoming Golden Age; therefore, they must be removed. Sadly, many humans are removing themselves rather than their inner impulses. If this all seems somewhat far-fetched in reality, the truth is, it is not. We merely need to look into recent world events, with still more coming to light every day. People must play them out to fulfill ancient prophecy. Consider the recent fires throughout our world, stretching from Australia to Greece, and all up and down California. Most were intentionally started by humans. Unfortunately, innocent people lost their lives while others lost their homes and all personal belongings. In Brussels, a knife-wielding man walks into a day-care center and attacks people, including children. Another young man goes on a shooting spree throughout his rural town in South Alabama, killing ten before taking his own life. We now look into the economy and clearly see greed showing itself with the likes of Bernard Madoff and Robert Stanford, to name only two, who took billions of dollars from innocent people. We are seeing the fall of people in power, governors either resigning or being impeached. This seems to be happening anywhere at anytime from all walks of life. One may respond, "Is this all really necessary?" If we are going to cleanse our world of these kinds of actions then yes, it is! To understand and realize just how magnificently powerful we truly are, we must first sense or feel the point of being utterly powerless.

If catastrophes and collapses are going to be shown, then so also are their opposites going to show, such as calm and kindness. I ask, what is the truth of you? Are you a person of peace? Are you one of unconditional love? Are you filled with compassion and empathy? These, too, are going to come forth; in fact, all truth is going to come out, from the individual level through the organizational level, all the way up to the level of world governments. All is going to be made known. After all, didn't the ancient teachers tell us the meek shall inherit the earth? Please understand, meek does not suggest weakness; on the contrary, it symbolizes the power of true strength simply because the meek are the peacemakers. They are the ones filled with unconditional love, compassion and empathy. They are the people of great flexibility and possess incredible knowledge. They are the individuals willing to follow the idea of acceptance, to accept all others and life. For them, no turmoil exists, only peace and sharing. These are what shall remain in the Golden Age. Perhaps the descriptions offered through the opening paragraphs are truly nothing more than the meek living life to the fullest extent.

Let us now look into another part of the equation to our

present paradigm shift. Have you noticed the weather changes and the seemingly odd patterns now taking shape? Consider the following. Even though our weather appears out of control, what if this is nothing more than Mother Nature purely reflecting to us what we have become to each other? What is meant here? Please answer this: overall, our world is filled with which—peace or anger? Most likely the consensual answer is anger, unfortunately. But the answer actually makes total sense because, if only oneness exists, then it stands to reason that our weather must follow our anger, the dominant inner turmoil of the human. Yes, we are much more powerful than we yet realize. Was it not stated centuries ago that we have dominion over all things? In truth, we are actually witnessing pent-up anger and frustration now releasing, all from human emotions which have built up and compounded over the millennia. Sadly, it seems every human is walking into the crossfire, remember that this is to remove these energies from our world and this process is not going to be stopped.

Such a release from so many humans undeniably contains a massive amount of energy, and as the human releases this energy, it is being cast into our very atmosphere. Most people realize, energy is not seen by the naked eye—at least at this time—but it can surely be sensed. Therefore, as this violent energy unleashes, it stands to reason that it would have an overall impact on all things, especially the weather as sensitive as it is and conceivably on geology as well. Let us for a moment look at another recent event—Hurricane Ike. Why this one? The sheer magnitude of it! Do you realize the eye wall of a hurricane is sixty to seventy miles wide, on average? The eye wall for Hurricane Ike measured a staggering two-hundred and fifty miles wide! This is unheard of and extremely rare, meteorologists admit. Another key point to keep in mind is that Hurricane Ike nearly covered the entire Gulf of Mexico, from the west coast of Florida to the east coast of Mexico, an event never witnessed before. What with all the weather anomalies and geologic changes, not to mention the current global economic turmoil, this process shall continue. The truth is it must continue to grow and expand, and it will utterly defy our comprehension by their degree of frequency and magnitude; however, looking at this from the positive side of the coin, an exquisite order seems apparent. The beauty of all this is that every time our ability to comprehend is defied, our comprehension then expands through the very same vehicle. In other words, we are slowly traveling from a limited mindset to an infinite mindset; hence, we will comprehend greater things. This expanded awareness will ultimately lead us to the very truth of our own higher nature and the real ability we all have imbedded within us.

There is one more area we must travel through before our utopian world rises from the darkness of mind. That remaining arena is the global geologic activity, and there will be a lot as we progress. The changes in this area alone will grow to the likes never before recorded or ever witnessed in our modern world. The shifting magnetic fields will not only impact the human and weather, but will also physically stress most lands and seas. These areas may very well become stretched to the point where the earth will have to release her pressure just as the human is currently doing; subsequently, we will observe an increase in geologic activity, both in frequency and magnitude. It is stated as an ancient prophecy, "in that time the lands and islands will be moved from their places." Do you remember the massive Indian Ocean earthquake which occurred off the west coast of Indonesia a few short years ago? Do you realize the island of Sumatra was physically moved by this event? Utilizing a high-resolution, multi-beam sonar system, the Royal Navy vessel HMS Scott surveyed and confirmed the resulting transformation to the undersea landscape. Imagine continents being moved from their places! This simply staggers the mind! Is such a change even possible? Archaeology says yes, for this is not the first time these kinds of things have occurred. All present continents, indeed, used to be one very large land mass known as Pangaea, and on many occasions during earth's history, they have separated and come together. If they come together again would this not be the return of Atlantis? Yes, it is compassionately understood that many lives will be given up as these events unfold throughout the world, all the while challenging our current level of comprehension. Is any human truly able to imagine an earthquake of, say, a magnitude 12 on the Richter scale—even greater? Can you comprehend land masses colliding? Can you imagine the sun rising in the west and setting in the east? This, too, has occurred before, so it would stand to reason that if the magnetic fields change then so could the tilt of our world's axis and its direction of rotation. According to the fields of geology and archaeology, all of these have occurred in the distant past, yet remain inconceivable today simply because we do not know what occurs as the world's and our own magnetic fields shift and change. All of these have the ability to defy our comprehension which—once more—expands our ability to understand and to know even greater things than we realize today.

The full shift has not yet come to pass for humankind, or should I say for the remaining humans in our world. Let us now look into its final phase. Believe it or not, another prophecy is revealed right within the pages of the Bible in the Book of Revelation, and states in these words, "...there shall be three days of darkness..." Hollywood portrays this as war and destruction. Perhaps so, but this is entertainment's point of view. Consider switching our perspective to the field of psychology. Instead of destruction in the literal sense, we ought to perceive the prophecy from the mind's point of view—three days of possible insanity. Keep in mind, the full impact of these shifting magnetic fields on the human mind and its realms of thought are not at all known; therefore, so-called insanity may become a very real possibility. Well, just look around you! If the events going on in our world today are any indication, then it would stand to reason that there shall surely come a tipping point in the mind of every human, and this indeed could easily produce the effects of insanity. The sciences do tell us the shift will have consequences, both on the way we do things at present and all life. Also, a period of time may be necessary in order to adjust to the new paradigm in which we shall suddenly find ourselves, to adjust to the new realms of thinking and interaction with each other — equal to three days perhaps? No doubt, it shall truly be a new reality no matter how it unfolds. As we awaken, we will each find our self working with each other shoulder to shoulder. We will find our self assisting others, and as we do, we will pull together to form one world, one people, all with the same ability of comprehension, a realization which has been greatly expanded into the new paradigm. We will travel from a limited mindset to more of an infinite one in our newly expanded world of consciousness where only oneness is known, a world where duality can never exist.

As each shock wave encompasses the human, wave after wave, it opens up new arenas for the individual and the collective to work with — and through. These will ultimately enhance us to the point where we can accomplish nearly anything in our new environment. For instance, imagine living in a well-lit home with no power necessary from the utility company. Yes, that is correct. We will be able to power it all simply through our thoughts! Envision the ability to put warm, satisfying, healthy food on the table for each meal without the need for refrigeration, killing, or cooking. Yes, that is correct. We will be able to instantly manifest any fine feast and to share it with all who decide to eat with us! Can you picture in your mind any type and style of living space you desire, all without harming any living thing or the environment? Yes, this is also correct. We will be able to do nothing less than to harmoniously create through our very own divine power! After all, the ancients told us that every thing is all already here, infinitely waiting so patiently for us to bring it all into our own reality. As of yet, however, we have not realized how and we cannot as long as we rely on the external world, patriarchal! The new world will be an internal world where all of our true power resides, matriarchal. Whether an individual chooses to walk on the path so outlined within these few pages matters not, for every human shall have this ability. In truth, it will actually become magnified by the coming events and require us to work together without any concern for race or belief system. This is how we learn about each other and how we ultimately become unified throughout our world, a place where we now live only as one in our reality, totally free of conflict, and a lush garden where the human has the greatest value of all and takes advantage of nothing. This is all created simply because of the magnetic fields of our world shifting into a new paradigm, a reality which has been written about for millennia, yet no one has paid attention to the ever-present as it unfolds right before our very eyes.

Ultimately, our world shall only be filled with humans living and expressing through unconditional nature, a divine being who individually and collectively stands in complete acceptance of all life, innocent in all they say and do. These are people backed by the creative power of the universe. They operate in union with it rather than against it as they realize their true alignment. The new human realizes their true perfection and the reality of their divine nature; hence, they use it to the fullest extent in support of life. These two ideas—perfection and divine nature—have been with us since the dawn of creation; however, their presence has been cleverly hidden by the cloak of external conditioning, completely unnoticed by all, for we have simply been led astray from the very idea of pure divine being, an attribute lying dormant within each human. It has been stated, the best place to hide something is right in plain sight. Perhaps it will take all of the events which have been outlined in the previous pages, including a short period of potential insanity, before this inner aspect finally finds its way to the surface of our life. Once this is completed, we then learn to live from within and extend it to the outer world—the true power of manifestation. The days of living only for external reasons are long gone and the bodies are pure in their nature. Peace is all what is known in this Golden Age, an Atlantean lifestyle where it is now one people and one language as all things are now unified into one ideal, one world. The "Garden" returns to its rightful throne and proper place, our world as it was originally intended!

- Steven L. Hairfield, Ph.D. - author A Metaphysical Interpretation of the Bible and The Twelve Sacred Principles of Karma

Earth is a glorious and abundant home; each of us is its custodian.
A walk in the woods soothes the souls and welcomes us home.
Salubrious spring flowers remind us that life is a continual kalei-doscope of color and abundance.
The sweet smell of wafting pine on a summer's afternoon is heavenly.

- Dr Reese Halter - founder Global Forest Science

The world we live in is about to ascend. It is about to discover and experience the true dynamics of the fundamental forces of nature. These dynamics have been hidden from the human eyes for millennia, veiled by a developing global consciousness in a state of infancy.

Now, through all of our experiences, traumas and struggles we are about to mature into a new world where the primary force of creation—gravity—is understood and utilized so that humanity may ascend and transform its limitations and scarcities into true freedom and abundance. All societies in the universe must at one point or another reach this level of understanding and liberate their world from living directly on the unstable and unsustainable surface of their planet, to living in an infinitely abundant universe. This comes as a result of their capacity to travel across vast distances, reaching infinite supplies of resources and allowing the surface of their planet to regain an Edenic state, having developed technologies based on the appropriate understanding and use of the fundamental creative powers of the universe. All that's required for this to occur on earth is for humanity to reach a deep understanding of the clues that were left by ancient masters in many of our cultures and to apply them appropriately to science and technology so that we reach profound levels of understanding of the structure of spacetime, its fluid and spin dynamics and literally ascend our world. This is the world of Utopia, of an advanced civilization truly freed from its limitations and living in a world of infinite energy and resources. This is the world that awaits us if we collectively transcend our perceived limitations and walk into a future of infinite possibilities.

- *Nassim Haramein - director of research The Resonance Project Foundation*

I see a world where we are no longer slaves to the clock and the inbox. Where we have enough time—for others, for ourselves, for Nature, for life itself.

- *Carl Honoré - speaker, author Under Pressure: Rescuing Childhood From the Culture Of Hyper-Parenting*

I envision a world where telling the truth is not a revolutionary concept.

- *Dahr Jamail - independent journalist, author Beyond The Green Zone: Dispatches From An Unembedded Journalist In Occupied Iraq*

I want to live in a world with more wild salmon in it every year than the year before, and more migratory songbirds. I want to live in a world with more wild amphibians every year than the year before. I want to live in a world with more native forest every year than the year before, and more native grasslands, and more coral reefs and more tundra. I want to live in a world with fewer dams every year than the year before. I want to live in a world with less plastic in the ocean every year than the year before, and more large fish. I want to live in a world with less dioxin in every (human and nonhuman) mother's breastmilk every year than the year before. I want to live in a world with fewer machines and less plastic every year than the year before. I want to live in a world without industrial civilization. I want to live in a world that is not being murdered. And I will do whatever it takes to get there.

- Derrick Jensen - activist, speaker, author Endgame

A WORLD without time.
A WORLD without fear.
A WORLD of multiples rather than either/or.
A WORLD with enough space to wrap all of us—Yes ALL of us...
Up into the arms of a peaceful universe.
A WORLD of constant and unending seas.
A WORLD where all creatures, all colors, all genders, all creeds, all eyes, are made whole because we simply EMBRACE AND ACCEPT our RIGHT to EXIST.
OUR right to exist I say...to exist in the Unique Beauty that is Each and Everyone of US.
We seek Peace. We Seek Justice. We Seek Liberation.
This is the World if unmasked that we will all someday SEE.

- Dr Andrew Jolivette - professor, author Louisiana Creoles: Cultural Recovery and Mixed-Race Native American Identity

My Dream

Normally people dream while sleeping, but I dream in all states of awareness; whether asleep or awake. The most important fact about my dreams is that they are not mine alone – they are for the whole universe.

I BELIEVE IN THEM AND THEY'RE ALREADY COMING TRUE.

At 4 am on 13th March, 1995, an idea flashed in my mind to start a laughter club. This dream came true within three hours when I set up the first Laughter Club in Mumbai, India with just five people. As the concept spread, today there are more than 6000 laughter clubs in 60 countries. Laughter Yoga clubs are non-religious and non- political organization. It aims at connecting people from different cultures and countries to spread Good Health, Joy and World Peace through laughter.

In addition to social laughter clubs, Laughter Yoga is being practiced in companies and corporations, fitness centers, yoga studios, old age homes, prisons, schools and colleges, universities and also with the underprivileged people and those with special needs like blind schools, physically and mentally challenged, deaf and mute children, street children, orphanages, and cancer self-help groups and for multiple sclerosis and other chronic diseases groups.

One Million Social Laughter Clubs!

To accomplish this mission we set up Laughter Yoga International (LYI) which avidly works towards generating an awareness of the unique concept of Laughter Yoga and its manifold health benefits.

My dream is to set up ONE MILLION laughter clubs in the next ten years which will connect all laughter club members from around the world into an extended family.

No Control on Laughter Clubs, No Posts, No Hierarchy

All Laughter Clubs are individual entities and are free functioning units and are available to one and all free of cost. They are not under control of any other organization, group or institution anywhere in the world. Though there are no rules and regulations that oversee the conduct of Laughter Clubs, we do offer guidelines for functioning. The Laughter Yoga Movement recognizes no hierarchy, positions or titles.

World Peace through Laughter

The ultimate objective is to bring World Peace through laughter. Laughter in Laughter Yoga is unconditional thought-free laughter and does not involve any language mechanism. People anywhere, belonging to any culture can laugh easily without any reason. Laughter is a common language and is a powerful connector of people.

How can we bring world peace through laughter?—Very simple.

When you laugh, you change and when you change the whole world changes around you.

Unconditional laughter brings positive attributes like unconditional love, generosity and willingness to help each other. Normally, when we are laughing, we are not killing each other! The day when even a percent of the whole world's population starts laughing it is going to change the consciousness of the world. This will lead to world peace.

My Vision
International Laughter Yoga University

The proposed International Laughter Yoga University will be one of its kinds to explore all aspects of human body, mind, emotions and relationships, art, culture, music, dance through the basis of unconditional laughter. We will organize laughter festivals and world conferences. To fulfill this endeavor, we will be setting up

5 centers in each continent that will provide all necessary knowledge and comprehension of the rapidly spreading concept of Laughter Yoga. The first center is already underway in Bangalore, India.

Laughter Ship—A Mobile University

We are already envisioning an unusual project of a mobile University - a huge ship called SS Shanti (Peace Boat). This will go around the world connecting different people from different cultures through laughter. There will be a museum and laughter festivals and training programs on board.

Laughter Townships (Hasya Nagari)

We plan to create community living townships of the happiest people in this world. Our vision is to have a 'Laughter City' on the outskirts of each and every major city of the world.

- Dr Madan Kataria - founder Laughter Yoga, India

I see a world where there is room for all people and all stories. Where the media is full of diverse languages and cultures and pop culture is as diverse as the streets of our cities. When the media and the stories we see and hear are as diverse as we are I imagine a world of greater tolerance and celebration of diversity.

- Alex Kelly - media/arts practitioner and producer, Australia

I dream of a world, in which everyone is allowed to develop his or her full potential. In which the basic necessities of life are available for human beings from their birth right to their physical death, and nature—including plants and animals—is allowed to flourish and bloom, providing room for the dance between all living beings. Social interaction happens spontaneously and without fear between men and women, different age groups and different races, nationalities and species. Diversity is appreciated and supported by rules and regulations, which have shrunk to the bare minimum. Everyone gives what they can give best according to their talents and skills and receives what they need. Money is no longer necessary in local surroundings. For intercommunal trade there exists medium of exchange, which is stable, inflation proof, and promotes long term thinking. War has become unthinkable as everyone understands that we are all ONE.

The earth—after having gone through a major upheaval—is the paradise, which it was meant to be from the beginning. But now people have learned what it takes to keep it this way and are consciously working together like the healthy cells in our body looking after themselves, the organ (or group) to which they belong, and—as a third level belonging—the whole "body of humanity" on this planet called "Earth".

- Dr Margrit Kennedy - founder Money Network Alliance for Research and Development of Complementary Currencies (MonNetA), Germany

I envision a society where each person is valued regardless of gender, race, cultural background, sexual identity, ability or disability, or access to wealth.

This society would provide adequate shelter, food, education, recreation, health care, security, and well-paying jobs for all. The land would be respected and sustained, and justice and equal opportunity would prevail.

Such a society would value cooperation over competition, community development over individual achievement, democratic participation over hierarchy and control, and interdependence over either dependence or independence.

What is your vision?

- *Paul Kivel - educator, mentor, social justice activist, author You Call This a Democracy? Who Benefits, Who Pays and Who Really Decides*

My Dream World:

Human scale communities: People who wish to can live in walkable communities where they have a wealth of face to face human contacts and interactions.

Cultivation of human potential: People will, as they feel called to, have the time and opportunity to participate in activities that cultivate their spiritual, artistic, and intellectual capabilities.

Freedom from fear: People live without fear: fear of want, fear of violence, fear of rejection.

Slow travel: People who wish to travel long distances can do so slowly and in such a way that the journey takes the traveler to places with authentic and distinct characteristics, e.g. architecture, dress, customs, language. The slowness of travel will give the sense that one has genuinely broken connections with what is familiar and moved into something truly foreign and distant.

New frontiers and new Others: Since this is a dream world, here I give myself permission to include elements of the fantastic. My dream world includes portals to other worlds. These portals are scattered throughout the world, and this ties back into slow travel. One might spend weeks or months traveling at the speed of horse or sailing vessel in order to reach a specific portal, and when one passes through the portal, one takes only one's body, memories, and skills, and emerges naked on the other side.

Return is possible, but again, all one can bring back are accounts of one's travels.

Competitive outlets: People can, as they feel called to, participate in competitive activities and even violence in a controlled and consensual context. Entrepreneurial spirits will be able to express their competitive gifts in a market economy and benefit off the community in the process. Those with Transhumanist ambitions are free to edit "atavistic" impulses for competition and violence from their own psychological make-up, but those who want to run the old school human operating system will have outlets to do so that respect the right of non-participants to live without fear.

High technologies: The pursuit of worthwhile human goals will be aided by the implementation of genuinely "high" technologies. These technologies will not require the sorts of energy and material inputs that industrial technologies demand, and their use will advance the goal of living in harmonious inter-dependence with the biosphere.

Acceptance of "human nature" as it is: We will order our social institutions around the general principle that the psychological needs that we refuse to acknowledge consciously will seek expression and satisfaction in unconscious and destructive ways. The very fabric of society will include an acceptance of all aspects of the human psyche including the needs of the "shadow" elements that our current societies refuse to acknowledge and accommodate.

- *KMO - founder C-Realm Podcast*

I strive to imagine what it would be like to live in relationship with the world, where the human possibilities of freedom are endless and everyone can wake up to a new day with joyous expectancy rather than stifling expectation. I strive to imagine what it would be like to live in a world where we have an appetite for truth, compassion, and tolerance and believe that everyone has something to contribute. I strive to imagine, because if I can imagine, I can believe; and if I can believe, it can happen.

- Sarah Koch - dreamer, believer, co-founder Development In Gardening (DIG)

Overview
My dream world is a place characterized by beauty, spirit, wisdom and harmony. An intentional community, with a high level of individual and group consciousness, where ever greater degrees of elegance and insight are sought in all endeavours.

Skills & Knowledge
Education is an engaging, inspiring and lifelong process. Beginning as an infant, with fun, integrated perspectives on play, nature, learning and creative expression—right through the course of one's life, with apprenticeships and specialist guilds to develop and master the particular and diverse natural gifts of all. Guilds exist for all key human activities including: craftsmen, builders, cooks, gardeners, artists, musicians, counselors, martial artists, teachers, scribes, healers, shamans, alchemists. All opportunities and resources for developing skills and knowledge are open to everyone, young and old, male and female. Time and energy are channelled into specific areas through the on-going and collaborative balancing of an individual's natural talents and propensities.

Spirit & Discovery
Spirituality, philosophy, psychology, mysticism, science and the arts are seen as different facets of the same jewel. Each to be

explored and experienced to help formulate the most graceful expression of the harmonic convergence of the different dimensional planes. Emphasis is placed on felt experience, rather than on pure theory, as the most enlightening and fruitful means of discovery. The interconnectedness of all things is deeply comprehended and the illusion of separateness is recognized as a transient imaginative manifestation of form. This underpins all disciplines, removing hard boundaries between areas of study and promoting an integral approach to the expansion of knowledge and wisdom.

Scale & Organization

A natural, healthy population level is understood to be the foundation for abundance, sustainability and a flourishing community. A well-defined optimal harmonic population level is calculated and adhered to, plus or minus 10%. It is understood by everyone that to shrink or grow too much brings disharmony and therefore discontent to all. A key factor in acknowledging this, is the appreciation that to live on the land is to live *with* the land. Respect and light-footedness are thus highly valued. An assembly of wise representatives from each guild looks after wider community affairs such as resource management, community permaculture, events, archives, administrative processes and communications. Administrators undertake their role in addition to their real work. All assembly processes are completely transparent and open to observation and improvement.

Aesthetics & Architecture

Rather obligingly, the aesthetics of my dream world have already been envisioned by JRR Tolkien, in his imaginal manifestation of the beautiful Elven outpost, Rivendell. Rivendell lies at the edge of a gorge, nestled in the moorlands and foothills of a vast mountain range. Waterfalls flow from the mountainsides, with streams and pools weaving through the ancient woods and soft grasses that cover the hillsides and plateaux. The striking pale rock of the mountains is prevalent in the building materials — with every ornate tower, arching bridge, restful dwelling and graceful balcony serving to complement the natural majesty of the land itself. It is as if the mountain had made Rivendell of its own accord. Seasons are well defined, with warm lush greens in the summer, breathtaking scarlet and ochre in the fall and exquisite snow-flecked landscapes in winter.

What It Doesn't Have

There is a notable absence of money, politics, dogma, religion, poverty, pollutants, toxins, crime, hatred, mental illness and immunological disorders; these all being symptoms of unintentional and disharmonious communities.

- *Neil Kramer - writer, speaker & researcher. Navigating the ancient pathways of gnosis, esoteric knowledge, consciousness and the divine. UK*

History works its will on us and the best we can do is heed what Lincoln called "'the better angels of our nature." Our present predicament is managing a transition through the end of the fossil fuel fiasco. I believe we have the capacity to remain civilized and move into the next chapter of the human adventure.

- *James Howard Kunstler - lecturer, author The Long Emergency*

My dream is a knowing that human consciousness will awaken to realize that there is only One, appearing as many, revealing itself as Love.

- *Dr Leonard Laskow - physician, holoenergetic healer*

A perfect world to me would be one where there is only

compassion and caring for other human beings. A world in which everyone followed their passion for one common goal and that is to make this world a place where everyone was happy for others'achievements and had compassion for others' failures. A perfect world would be one where there was no jealousy or hatred - just the willingness of everyone to lend a hand to those in need and the ability to put others needs in front of their own when necessary. If everyone expressed the love, patience, compassion and pride that a parent has for their children for every other human being in this world just think of what a perfect and loving world we would have.

- *Anthony Leanna - founder Heavenly Hats Foundation, Inc.*

Glen Canyon—The Place We Knew

"Lucky you," is what the young'uns say to us old farts who knew Glen Canyon before it was sloshed off the maps under Powell Reservoir. After which act of vandalism we were not lucky at all—except for what it gave us to remember for the rest of our lives. That exception is what keeps us on track to help you see and feel some of the same magic we knew.

The Colorado River there, locked in the embrace of over one hundred side canyons, drew a cluster of people who sought the beautiful, peaceful, untamed and lonely. Of those it drew, it kept a few who learned to communicate with it and with each other. It taught us love for a place—love far beyond the ability to express our emotion to others. Despite all efforts to the contrary, no words, no photographs, no sound could do justice to our feeling for The Place. We took pictures; we wrote, we sang, we talked; shared stories, adventure, and discovery with one other. But in the end, we'd look into each other's eyes with palms up, words stopped in mid air, mouths agape, unable to explain the final mystery of The Place We Knew—a place that swelled our hearts to breaking.

The Final Mystery.

Can I explain it now, forty- six years later? No. That Canyon with its River became my harbor in a storm, my spiritual alcove, my teacher, and finally my mate. What it made me realize was that others following in my wake could not only use, but would need, the same kind of harbor for their spirit; need it even more than I; what with the frantic population acceleration and creeping destruction of such havens as The Place We Knew.

Where will you go? What will you find? Whatever it is, and wherever, keep it to yourself. The sooner someone else finds your sanctuary, the sooner it will be gone, and for reasons you cannot accept or even fathom. Somehow you may find one of Mother Nature's treasures, one she has allowed you to share. Accept that you've been chosen; go lightly, observe intently, ingest the wisdom of the rock, the stream, the trees, the lichen, the sand, the river. Fight to keep it for yourself, for those who care and for those who come after you. But remember, if it is destroyed (maybe because you did nothing to help save it) you may still have it locked in your soul where no one can touch it. You have taken that special place with you, absorbed it through all your senses and it is yours forever.

Then...and only then, can you tell the despoilers to go to hell!

The Place We Knew. In a way that makes us sound like we had the very best of something the rest of you will never know. And it's true...up to now. I don't expect it to be true in half a century. Glen Canyon and its living river are returning sooner than many of us expected. So if you are in your twenties or thirties, more than likely, you could come to know The Place We Knew in your lifetime.

Lucky you!

- Katie Lee - author, singer, filmmaker, lecturer, activist

In the world I envision, people are inspired to take care of the earth and each other. Cities that were once unsustainable are literally life-giving. People have woken up to their power. They give their energy back to the ecosystem that sustains them. They consciously choose to make every action one of healing.

- Andy Lipkis - founder TreePeople

Imagine....

"If you could imagine your world into being,

What would it feel like?..."

SahRa squinted in the late afternoon sun. It was hard to see who was coming, the dry red dust of the road kicked up by their passing in the late afternoon heat, brittle red motes filled the air like an aura of fire in the sun's long gaze. Whoever it was, they were coming from the westward road, a path little used these days. SahRa stood up on tiptoe, focused as a kestrel preparing to dive down on her prey, for this was her first day to serve as lookout.

It was rare indeed that anyone came down from the holy mountains these days, through the old forest to approach this village from the west. For long and long those lands were held sacred by all who knew of them. Those who dared enter the forest rarely came out. If they did they were forever changed choosing to live there rather than return to the village. It was a mysterious place, the home of the most ancient forest, and one best left alone. Another reason why SahRa was as attentive as the stranger approached for it certainly was a sign of changes to come.

"Someone's coming from the West," she called down from the tall rock pile on which she stood. "Who?" Andrew replied. Her older brother wanted to make sure it wasn't just a trick of the light, a mirage caused by the late afternoon haze.

"I don't know but they will be here in a few minutes," SahRa said. So Andrew quickly took off, running to the village center crying out as he went, "Stranger coming from the west, all gather at the meeting place."

The children, the young sprouts, sprinting quick-quick like small deer before a hungry mountain cat hunting. They arrived first with much giggling and whispering for this was news of the best sort. Followed were they by their older brothers and sisters, the young saplings, willowy teenagers frisky in their liveliness, all the while trying to look unexcited while asking: "Who is it?" and "Can you see who it is?" SahRa shook her head for she could not see who it was for the glare.

They all wondered, for it was rare to receive visitors from that direction. Everyone knew that it foretold changes for the village, the place they all called Heart's Home. Ever since the Great Shift, the one that changed everything and everyone forever, had it been called thus for it was a place of living from the heart in harmony with the land and all who lived there. This community was a resting place, a haven for everyone.

The adults who worked to sustain the village, the strong trees, the hunters, growers, makers, and creators came swaggering in from their tasks of the day. Wiping their brows, they laughed and greeted each other in the old way: "Well met. How goes the day?" and responded "Blessed." Happy folk for the most part were they, robust and gentle in their ways of working. Reciprocity was the way of giving and receiving amongst them, in this way they maintained the cycles of sustenance for the community. Those who had given generously to those with less so all lived well. Such was the way of things in these days; a far more gentle way to live that ensured that everyone cared for each other.

Finally, the wisdom keepers, those serving as Elders, the towering trees, came two by two dressed stately they came, these keepers of memory many-layered and radiant, exuding harmony and peace. Last, yet not least, walked the pair of flowering hearts, the lord and lady responsible for carrying that most sacred bundle of mystery that nourished the heart of the village. When they arrived at the old Grandfather Tree, they greeted him, giving an offering and prayer of thanksgiving as they knelt and gently wiped clear a resting place at the base of the tree to receive it. There they placed it reverently snuggled close within the exposed roots twisting out across the green like snakes seeking sunlight in the dawn of a day. There, the heart of the village waited like a baby snoozing in swaddling to be fed with sacred food for the spirit so the village could thrive.

This Grandfather Tree, was older than old, no one knew how long he'd stood there collecting the stories of the village like an ancient old man all ears for news after a long hard day. So old it was that its tough skin trunk seemed made of many trees rolling and rippling around, providing comfortable places to lean into. This old tree's ancient arms reached up high up into the violet sky, giving refuge to many a bird, some branches so heavy they spread out along the green ground like benches. It was the time of New Green, the quickening time, so he was covered with succulent green growth, with large orange trumpet flowers calling out to the buzzing bees under the heavy weight of the season. Some of the black-coated sisters, the crows, peeked out from under the eyebrows of green, laughing like children, yes indeed, for they loved gathering old tales and bright bits of lore more than anything...

For long and long, had this stately tree on the western edge of the village been a gathering place, longer even than the village itself had existed. This Grandfather Tree stood tall and stately towering in the breeze like an old gentleman caller dressed in fancy dress tails. No one knew how long he'd stood, yet everyone knew he was more ancient than old, his spirit born in the first forest of the long ago before the two legged people came to be breathing. They called him Methuselah, the ancient of days, for if you sat beneath him and leaned back relaxing in the silence, you swear he was whispering tales into your heart of hearts, muttering of the here now and the far long ago. You see he was a storyteller tree, a keeper of tales and the history of the people. Oh, how they loved their stories, they did, for they spun them high and low all the same. And in the twilight, if you looked closely enough with an open heart, you could see him step out clearly as he walked out of the tree to ramble among the village listening to life rustle about.

The westward wind sang as it danced through the leaves, whistling of what was to come and what had passed, and the dreamings that might be. One by one they all found places to lie down on the grass-covered earth as they waited for the stranger to come. Yes, they all waited wondering and hoping if it was her, a wandering tree of a woman, a walking legend who carried stories from the westward hills.

The dust of the road began to settle as she approached their meeting place. "It is she," SahRa cried, being the first to see her up from where she stood on the lookout. Although she'd only heard stories, for she was young in her days, they knew of only one who carried an aura of light about her. She came striding forth into the village green, old yet ever young, her eyes flashing with a white light that blazed like lightning crackling across a summer sky before a rain. SahRa sprang down from the lookout, as word spread whisper to whisper to those gathering beneath the old tree. Now she knew beyond guessing that it was a special day indeed for it had been many a season since she'd came down from the mountains to visit them.

The old grandmother had walked a long way to get to this village, over three days on foot on a long dusty open road, traveling as the Sun tells time to the Moon. Her clothes were old style leathers, flexible yet sturdy, dusted with the cinnamon haze of the old dry track for the rains were late this season. She knew the old ways she did, being one of those who lived wild and free. All roads were one road to one such as her, the old ones said, for she knew how to walk the between.

No matter how still the wind, her hair stole out of the braids that held them, gently moving in a breeze no one else could feel. Some said she was born of the westward wind, some said in an otherworld or ever changing borderland, though some said she was born just like you and me, but restless and rambling from place to place. She wandered most of her days following Spirit for she'd learned to twist her hair long ago, braiding it up with the hidden bits of lore rarely heard by more ordinary folk. It was part of the mystery that cloaked her like twilight for no one knew where she came from, nor where she called home.

Indeed she was a mystery to all of them, even the Elders, and some said in whispers, even unto herself. Her memory was so long it went back to the far long ago, the time when the world was born and the first people walked the world into being. Her dark skin was painted in fine wrinkles, weaving like a river delta after a rain, rich with the loam of a life well lived.

She shook off the dust of the road and began unbraiding her hair, so long it was that it flowed like falling water in rippling waves to the sea. When the unruly wind tugged at it, you could see odd bits woven in, old white hollow bones, tri-colored beads, small hag stones, along with many a feather. Sometimes when you looked at her when the light was just right, her head seemed more that of a fox than a woman. Then you'd swear she was one of the immortal ones, the old forest spirits, more spirit than human. Perhaps she was, then again perhaps she wasn't. Only La Madre, our sweet mother earth, knew for sure and she was wasn't telling, for she is a keeper of secrets to those that know not how to court her.

A young sapling, her skirts tinkling with the bells of her flowering, shyly brought her a glass of water from a bright spring sparkling clearly out of the nearby ash-colored stones. The old grandmother drank deep with pleasure, giving the old thanks, "May you never thirst." The dark leaves overhead whispered amongst themselves as she approached the old tree, rustling in the winds of remembering. Even the crows settled into silence eagerly awaiting what was to come. She rested her hand briefly on the old grandfather's bark hide in sweet greeting, silently conversing with him of tales long spent but nary forgotten.

She sighed as she sat down to rest her weary bones against the tough old skin of the ancient tree. It was comfortable there for it was well worn by many a story's telling over the seasons of this world's turning. One by one, the villagers quieted, leaning close so they could more easily hear Abuela speak. No one remembered her name anymore, though everyone knew who she was when they saw her. Her presence was legend among the people for long and long she'd been coming to this village, always knowing in some uncanny way when the people needed her most, when they began to fall into a deep sleep of forgetting.

For such is the way of the wild walkers, the old curanderas, the healer shamanas who walked in and out between worlds as they wandered the old tracks. As they wandered, they walked with Spirit, following the old leys singing the land up into being with their healing songs and stories. Their ways were their own, mysterious and hidden, for they lived differently according to ways unknown to most others. Not unknowable mind you, only unknown, for most were not willing or able to leave behind the comfort of ways more commonly lived. Although most of the walkers stayed in the wild places, on the edges of the border-lands between the worlds, from time to time some still walked the open roads bringing news and renewal to the people.

For the people always had a way of forgetting, of falling asleep when times got tough or feelings too intense, or more often when life got too easy. Such was the way of the two-legged people, forgetting then remembering, then forgetting again especially in times like these when all was plenty. When she'd heard the call from La Madre, sweet mother of all, she picked up her bones, and came to help them remember their relations and the sacred ways of the heart of the earth.

"Do you recall the old meaning of that word, remember, the original meaning of it?" To remember as in to re-member, meaning to put back together again. When one dives deep into their heart of hearts to discover the mystery, to remember who they really are. Those were some of the ways she kept close yet shared with those in need.

For in our heart of hearts lives a mystery, one we each carry, a long record of who we are, or more clearly stated of what we are and why we chose to be. It is a sacred place where we can discover all that we need, the answers to all that we seek. For living is an art, one best practiced from the heart. Most of the people lived that way these days for everyone knew instinctively that all life was sacred and everything that has a form has a spirit living in it.

These people had remembered how to live that way, ever since the Great Shift that changed everything and everyone forever. Oh there had been shifts before this one, at least seven cycles, held in the memories of the people. They always occurred when the people got too big for their britches, too full of themselves, too dependent upon external things of their making for that which could be experienced and known directly within. When it got too out of hand, La Madre cried out "enough", and the cycle was shifted from what was into what is now — a new dawn of a new turning wheel, a reset of life as they knew it.

Abuela spoke gently "Do you remember...?" So softly she spoke with presence, letting the silence hang after her words, waiting for the gift of the present to unfold in the hearts of those who sat around her. For such is the way of the great storytellers, a part of the art where they opened the way in the hearts of those listening to receive the seeds of old knowing. It was an old way of imprinting body memory with stories and lore, an old art of speaking memory into being.

The children cried out, "No Abuela, tell us a story!" It was a time-honored response, it was indeed, an old call and response they delighted in giving. She chuckled, she did, the laughter rippling up from her belly full up with pleasure, for she loved all people. And they all laughed with her for how could they not, so infectious it was, that soon everyone was rolling and bubbling with it bouncing around like rich bits in boiling stew. They all laughed so hard that they eventually wept as everyone came together again. Then one by one, silence descended among them as they wiped their watering eyes and leaned forward, craning their necks to hear her.

And so she began to tell a tale that began in the last cycle, the one right before the Great Shift, the last one before the current turning of this world. It was a tale of a time before the people began to remember themselves again, a time of forgetting.

"Long ago as people used to tell time, before they remembered how to count the seasons in their bones according to the dance of the sun and the moon, everything was different. Do you know how different it was?" she asked.

"No Abuela tell us how different" the little ones chimed in, their bell like voices ringing in the sweet high tones of birds courting as they squirmed with excitement. The older ones nodded their heads to let her know they were listening. She waited while the last stragglers came near, for that was how you weaved a story in the old way, weaving all of the fibers of the village together, from young sprouts to the towering trees.

"Well now, I'll tell you how it was back then and how we came to be where we are today. So listen up. Hear." She said. Silence descended again like a warm cozy blanket of comfort, cradling them all in a cloak of connection. Even the wind seemed to stop its sighing and the ever-present crows rustled overhead as they preened, their eyes bright with a knowing too deep to be seen.

"Long ago before the Great Shift, the last one that changed the face of our mother earth and all of us forever, the people were different. The young ones, as their elders who kept the old ways called them, left their homes in nature to explore and to make things. They left the land of their Ancestors and their ways of living in balance and harmony, moving out over the land like a horde of restless locusts. So many were they that it was hard to see the earth in some places; so ravenous were they that many went hungry. It was a time of pain and suffering for most, though they pretended that they were caring well for themselves. They felt lost and alone in their efforts to hold onto a way of life they'd created that could not be sustained.

"These lost ones, those who left their home in nature, grew to be so many that they covered the face of much of the world. They covered the so called civilized places with cities and hard oily roads criss-crossing and scaring the grasslands and natural tracks. They created toys to play with, machines and many so-called labor-saving devices to distract them from what they were feeling to make their lives easier. They became fascinated with making and owning things, they went even so far as trying to possess the skin of La Madre, she who can never be tamed.

"Yet the more they made and the more they hurried, the less satisfied they became. Day by day, they had less time, less freedom to feel, to touch, to laugh, to share with each other. Oh how they suffered, these lost ones did. This went on for so long, that they forgot who they were, became lost in their senses numb to their links with Spirit and nature. They even taught their young to live their heads, to abandon their hearts where the most precious gift of the present resides.

"During this time, the people were rushing here, rushing there, here, there and everywhere, trying to get things done in a never-ending competition with each other. They created a false god they called Time, a great slave-driver being clothed in watches and clocks, full of deadlines that they forced themselves to meet. It was a game that no one could win, that battle with time; for there were never enough minutes and seconds to get everything done that they wanted to do.

"So they forced themselves to be what others wanted them to be, to listen to others' expectations rather than to their own sweet souls in an ever maddening dash for lessening resources. They created money, which created haves and have-nots, and competitions which made everything worse. And they labeled each other with job names and numbers to indicate their worth. There was never enough no matter how much they acquired. All of it was an illusion they'd made up to entertain themselves, so much they believed it that it became real, the outer world they'd convinced themselves into seeing.

"Oh how they suffered, they did those young ones born into the grand tribe of forgetting. Yes they did, I tell you they did. For in the hustle and bustle to catch up with time, to acquire more things, to be safe in their fear of the future, they forgot what made life worth living. They neglected La Madre, each other, even themselves and their kith and kin. It got so they forgot that we're all related, they forgot how to care for each other, the four-leggeds, winged ones, crawling ones, swimming ones, and the natural green. They even forgot that the Oneness, the source of all life, animates us all in our breathing. They forgot, and in their forgetting, lost themselves to themselves if you catch my meaning. Like a plague of forgetting it was and all of the people felt it.

"So they forgot who they were and fell into a sleep of forgetting, into a dream more nightmare than real. Such was the world back then, before the Great Shift, a world of harsh angles and rules and complex meanings. The consensual world became so complex that Fear became huge, bigger than Life, stomping its way across the hearts of the people. Then Loneliness, Rage, Envy, and Greed sprung up like contagion in their minds, eating away at their essence, leaving Grief, Sorrow, and Pain in their wake. Many fell sick with disease and soul loss as they tried to be who they were not to avoid feeling their feelings. As things got more and more complex and false Time sped up, many began to notice that life had become like a house of cards, one that could collapse in the gentlest of breezes.

"Yet in hard-to-reach remote places, the old ways of harmony and joy still flourished. Ways of wisdom that offered a healing balm to all people, handed down from mouth to ear through the nighttime of our world. The Elder wisdom keepers saw what was happening in the so-called modern world. They saw how La Madre, the people, all living things suffered under the burden of it. One by one the light of those who remembered went out in the night of our sweet mother earth until only these few pockets of remembering remained. The Elders cried out for guidance and healing for all of the people as the prophecies came into being."

She paused in her story to allow time for reflection, a gathering of attention for what was to come. And the people of Heart's Home grew sad as they recalled how the young ones suffered back then. Yes, they reflected how sometimes even now, they'd watered the corn of similar things in their own hearts of late, comparing themselves to each other, creating hurts with their words rather than joyous connection. Some of them shook their heads as they reflected on this, resolving to turn away from fear of lack back to practicing love and kindness. Abuela continued to speak, weaving a tale of memories easily misplaced.

"When many thought all was lost, that the young ones would never awaken, fearing that La Madre might collapse under the burden of all of this excess, just when the night was darkest and all seemed to be lost, miracles happened, as some of the young ones began to wake up. The Elders in their wild places saw lights of awareness coming up like new candles to shine in the vast darkness of the world's dreaming. The young ones began to question what was happening, what life was about, who they were and why they existed. But rather than running around lost in their heads, they decided to dive deep inside to discover the wisdom that lay waiting, like bright jewels in their hearts along with everything they needed.

"By then, the time of the great purification had begun and La Madre was shaking and writhing in her birthing pains to bring forth a new expression. The young ones began to notice what their actions had done, the hole in the sky that burned the land, the absence of life in the oceans, the dirt growing less than before, and the air stagnant with fumes from the oil they'd released. The old grandmothers did what they could to stave off the Great Shift of her rebirthing, to allow more people to awaken. For they knew from cycles before that if enough woke up then all would wake up and the world would renew in her being.

"Still many of the young ones refused to listen, to take note of what was happening; stubbornly thinking they were fortunate for having more money, more things, that they were isolated somehow from what was coming. Yet they grew ever more fearful of what they might lose; no matter how much they gathered, there was never enough for them to feel safe and secure. There was never enough to satisfy the hunger of the Fear that ate away at their minds. So they spun, yes they spun around in their heads chasing their tails like a squirrel spinning in circles, ever more stressed than before in fear so great that it was almost their undoing."

Abuela paused in her story to take another sip of life-giving water. So pure it was now that one could hardly remember how barren of life it had been before the Great Shift. What a difference love and gratitude make, she reflected. What a difference it makes to simply focus on creating a positive dreaming. The leaves rustled overhead as the crows shifted their feet to gain a better view point. A beautiful orange flower the color of sunset fell into the hands of a small one who caught it in wonder, a promise of renewed hope and healing.

"Back then they were unhappy. The funny thing about unhappiness is that when it gets too deep, then things start happening. Well, La Madre continued to shake, and the people began to quake. Some of the young ones, those with souls older than old, began to question, to point out the heart that was missing in a lifestyles focused on material greed. So they chose different roads, yes they did, as they took a decision to live differently and dream a new gentle dream. Then here and there, more and more began to awaken, to quicken with that mystery called life. To the Elders watching as a new dawn approached after eons of darkness, the light of awareness was beginning to come on again in the world. This wave of awakening was contagious, passing from one to another as more and more turned inward to listen and follow the soft voices of their souls.

"Enough, they cried, enough. Like a seed cracking wide open, they each began to transform, to change from who they were not into what they are. They began to follow that still quiet voice speaking from the source within them. And they opened their hearts to help each other and began to take care of each other, coming together in clans to support each other's dreams. As more and more began to awaken, the outer world began to change to reflect their new dreaming.

"The grandmothers and elders kept helping our sweet mother earth and all who lived on her to keep living. They began to open their ways to outsiders among the young ones, those whose spirits were more suited to preserving old ways, passing on their wisdom to those whose hearts were wide open and listening. Those hearing the call went deep in themselves to listen to the silence growing within. And in listening, they changed more and more as La Madre kept changing along with them. They chose to live from love and not fear. As time went on, they became bridges between the elders and the modern day people as wave after wave of spiritual energy flowed transforming the world."

Abuela sighed, this time with sweet satisfaction for the people were listening, remembering the gifts they'd been given since the Great Shift that changed all creation. They remembered the sweet gentle rains, clear breezes, rich food, and loving relations, the peace that blessed their minds and the love that filled their hearts. They recalled more deeply what really matters—not things, but each other and nature. They remembered our world is a mirror reflecting the choices we hold in our hearts expressing an ongoing creation.

Oh how precious life is, what a sweet and rare gift, this world that we live in, a place unsurpassed in its beauty. A wondrous place where each one experiences exactly what they choose to experience moment by moment. The choices we make in each instant determine our fate in this perfect reflection, this green holographic garden we call mother earth.

SahRa smiled as she thought of those times they'd all shared, kind words, gentle touch, joyous singing sweet free expression in the gift of the present moment. Feeling that precious thing beating, back and forth, the heartbeat of life connecting all people and the lands. Through all of the changes, they'd never wavered in their faith; trusting La Madre to provide for their needs, and El Padre, the sun to keep shining the light that guided them onward.

The villagers hugged one another and laughed, recalling their folly of forgetting back in those days before the Great Shift, for they were the young ones reborn. They chose to let go of old hurts as they relived their joyous translation from young ones to a people with hearts wide open, present and feeling.

As the sun dipped down low in the sky, they stood and helped each other stroll toward a magnificent feast that was waiting. They laughed and they sang and the wise ones knelt down to pick up the sacred heart of the village, that grew tender and tearing as they lifted it up to receive the light of a rainbow steaming down from the light of the sun. Their change had been great, from young ones lost in forgetting to a people who cared now for all their relations.

Abuela stretched as she reflected on what had occurred before and since the Great Shift, of how our mother earth and all life had utterly changed. Yea, what would it feel like if we could dream our world into being? That with each breath we take, we can choose to feel peace and love for all our relations.

Well now, we've remembered before and we're remembering again. We are awakening what we are and how precious life is for all nations.

"So what would it feel like...?"

- *Wendy Luckey - traditional healer (curandera)*

The world started and remains perfect, it's just littered with "improvements".

- *Ian MacKaye - musician, aberrationist, founder Dischord Records*

In an interconnected world, we are all empowered to make the world a better place. I dream of a world free of disease and human suffering; a world where economic status does not relegate one to a life of suffering and disease; a world where we can use the convergence between health and technology to bring good health and prosperity to all, irrespective of their geographic location. I believe that good-quality health care is a right and can be accomplished everywhere in the world and can be made affordable and accessible to all of mankind. Wealth alone should not determine who lives and who dies. The quality of health care available in developed countries can be made possible, accessible and affordable in low-resource nations by smart design, careful choices and appropriate adaptation of culturally relevant technology.

- *Dr Ernest Chijioke Madu - founder, chairman, chief executive officer Heart Institute of the Caribbean, West Indies*

Love Letter to the World

When we wake up each morning, do we give orders for the sun to pass over the sky, for the birds to start singing, for all the creatures to awake and go about their business? Do we send instructions for our breathing to change its rhythm, for our pupils to bring in the correct amount of light? Do we increase our heart rate so we can be more active? Do we signal for the tide to turn, the moon to wane, the seasons to pass? No, it's obvious that we don't. But if we're not doing it, what is? What is taking care of it all? When we stop to consider the world around us, even if we just look at our own body, we see that life is full of unexplained miracles. Taking place every single second of every single minute. And not just the odd one or two. Thousands of them. Something's taking care of it all, and whether we're conscious of it or not, it's doing it so consistently and so precisely that we have come to rely on its delivery.

I often like to imagine exactly how much brilliance goes into each tiny facet of life. If someone asked you to come up with a design for a warm energy source that was the exact distance from the Earth for life to flourish, for the seasons to be possible and for all the processes of nature to exist in symbiosis—would you be able to come up with the Sun? Not the idea of the sun but the actual sun itself! What about designing, and making, a being that is connected at all times to a life-giving energy source (which is invisible) but the being also simultaneously appears to be an individual unit (which you can see but which is actually a temporary illusion). Not only that but this being has to be able to think, feel and move. The thinking part has to be invisible, the feeling part can be discerned in the body but not seen by the eye and the movement part has to use the previous two elements to judge its effectiveness. OK. And what's more the being has to have the faculty of knowing, a level of communication beyond thought, emotions and actions. And while you're at it, can you make the physical body, although temporary, to be full of complex processes, both seen and unseen, which are synergistically perfect and at the same time, age. Uhmmm! Mind-boggling isn't it? We're already stumped and we've only outlined the basics!

So whatever came up with the design and working of the human being is not only intelligent, it's able to sustain complex systems and structures simultaneously and effortlessly. And we could go through every facet of life on Earth and find the same story. Flowers, insects, bird migration, whales. An overwhelming display of precision and intelligence. The interweaving of seen and unseen threads in an endless dance. We don't need to look far in nature to see that one of the strongest qualities of this energy is beauty. Left to its own devices, it lends itself to beauty. The shine on a horse's coat, a sky ablaze with colour, the metallic shimmer of an insect's armor, the smell of orange blossom, dew drops hung on cobwebs. And not just things, thoughts can be beautiful, emotions can be beautiful, smiling can be beautiful.

How much does it cost to have access to such an incredible environment? What is the price for such a system. It's free. It's given freely in every moment. The energy source of life is abundant. We can fashion it into whatever we choose. It's not stipulated that we must create one form over another. It is completely without preference. So in addition to its intelligence, precision and consistency, we can say that it is also benevolent. It gives without end and it gives without expectation. If we consider the created world in this way, it is of course, incredible. And there's a sense of wonder and appreciation that naturally arises. A sense of connectedness. No matter how difficult our challenges can be, no matter how much we might struggle with life, contemplation of the beauty of life can lift our hearts and minds. It can reconnect us to what is real and true. Once we connect with this sense of appreciation, we wonder how we ever felt grumpy or ungrateful. Of course, there'll still be income tax and rainy days. There'll still be mothers-in-law and traffic jams.

There'll still be bad hair days and toothpaste tubes squeezed the wrong way. But is that where we want to put our focus, when we're literally surrounded by beauty and intelligence and knowing what we know now about how this energy works?

When we're looking at the bigger picture, what happens? Our experience of life changes. Nothing on the outside has to change. It all happens on the inside. And with this shift, we start to see beauty everywhere, we start to see intelligence everywhere, and reliability and precision and benevolence! We start to love life, we start to love the very same life we were just complaining about. And then something very magical happens—and this is where I feel the greatest awe and reverence—life loves us back. And that is when we realise that in addition to all the qualities we have identified, this energy that we are, The Sea of Awareness, is also sentient. Sentience is conscious knowing. It is bringing our world into being and our being into the world. The more we know the sea of awareness, the more it knows us. For there is only one and we are all of it.

This is my love letter to the world. It is my appreciation for all we have and all we are. May we smile often.

- Jeddah Mali - spiritual mentor, author Godkind: The Residents of Heaven on Earth, UK

I have therefore come to the opinion that the most reasonable recourse for the humanization of society and its institutions is to abandon them and begin again to build a society with a just, equitable and compassionate economy with justice, equality, and reverence for all life insured by the goals and forms of all its institutions....

In order to have a truly happy life we probably need to address three areas, at least, that affect our well-being. We need to feel good about ourselves, about our relationships, and about our society.

We need to feel good about ourselves first, to believe we are living our lives to the fullest, using all our potential talents and creativity toward some worthwhile purpose balanced with fun, learning, and growth—a sense of always becoming more than we were.

We also need closeness with other human beings, relationships that are supportive and caring, in which we continue to learn and grow and expand our horizons. For myself, I discovered twenty-five years ago that the tool of co-counseling contained all I needed to work both on myself and on my relationships. It has also been easy to teach others and perfectly fits my world view of a benign Creation in which all of us can learn to live in a good way.

We also need to have a pride in our organized society, which exerts powerful influence over our lives and fortunes. The majority of people believe they have very little control over the organization of that society, and they just try to get along in it without calling attention or injury to themselves.

I want to tell you about my way to change the society.

What's wrong with society, in my view, is that it is organized as a pyramid, with power coming from the top down and the fuel that makes it function is fear. We who were raised in this society do not find that remarkable. Like goldfish raised in a bowl, we cannot imagine another possibility. The bowl gives them order, definition, safety. Anything beyond is unknowable, hazardous and threatening.

A society without a hierarchical power structure conjures chaos to our minds. Without an executive authority and a military or police to enforce that authority, we would live in continual fear of encroachment by others, of the loss of possessions and even of life or limb. But throughout history and before it, and down to this present moment, there have been innumerable cultures and societies that lived and live now in freedom, equality, and safety. Our problem has been a 10,000 year history of violence and greed that informs all our culture, our public and private institutions, our education, and tells us our only options are conformity or ostracism and isolation. So we escape into the culture's diversions, into reading, viewing films and television, playing electronic games, drugs, shopping, isolating ourselves further. We even go on vacations alone, or with only our nuclear family, never really getting close to other people.

But human beings are tribal by nature. People need closeness to other people. The greatest crime of our culture is to make us suspicious and fearful of each other. The importance of human beings in our lives is reduced to what goods or services we can buy or sell each other.

I saw that the society of my ancestors was fundamentally different from that of the dominant culture of today. It was a more human society. Its basis was in respect. Respect for life, for the earth, for all the earth's dependents including the family of humankind. Native American society was rooted in the family and in our relationship to all beings. The extended family was the heart of the tribe and its attitude of respect and caring for all.

Most importantly, I saw that this tribal society based on respect which supported the family and all its members was a society that worked. It was a system that worked well for over a million years, whereas the civilization of today, only a few thousand years old, was clearly not working. It was coming down around our ears in violence and alienation.

The reasons for this became quite clear to me. They were centered in the concepts of fear and domination that characterize the motivating forces of this society. Societies that worked well for all people were societies based on trust and mutual respect. The dominant culture of the world, whether capitalist or socialist, is dominant because it dominates. I don't know which came first, the fear or the domination, but they feed each other. The institutions of society protect the domination of the earth and its resources by a few people. Every social ill we suffer is a result of that fundamental fact.

If we are going to fulfill our potential for love we must at the very least put an end to every form of human beings harming human beings. We must agree and be admitted to a simple, obvious moral necessity—that every child born to woman is entitled to a fair and equal access to the resources of the planet we all share.

These goals are what I have derived from the teaching of my elders about the Original Instructions for human beings, to live respectfully in a circle of equals and devote ourselves to the care of our children, our elders, and all people of earth, including our plant and animal relatives, our Mother Earth, and all the coming generations.

By grouping together in cooperative, sharing communities, people can satisfy all their basic human needs with a fraction of the income it takes to survive individually, and these communities can be further strengthened by bio-regional networking and trading. The more self-sufficient we become the less we contribute to the military and prison industrial complexes and to the oppressive economic injustice of obscene wealth and wretched poverty and the destruction of the environment by our consumerism.

The notion of living together in more communal closeness has been growing in the past decades, after a temporary revulsion from the chaotic confusions and dissolution of many of the communes of the 60s. New, consciously designed communities are flourishing. Ecovillages are appearing everywhere. Networks of communication among all these are broadening.

This is the area I feel has the most promise for changing the world. Unless society changes utterly from its foundation in power, in punishment, violence, in the amassing of hegemony through the wealth of the few in the oppression of the many, unless we can breathe freedom, equality and fellowship in every breath we take, we will not be all that we long to be in human creativity, love, and joy.

I have therefore come to the opinion that the most reasonable recourse for the humanization of society and its institutions is to abandon them and begin again to build a society with a just, equitable and compassionate economy with justice, equality, and reverence for all life insured by the goals and forms of all its institutions.

Human beings stay human in their relationships to the extent they are close and know one another, which is possible only in groups small enough for each individual to be heard and known to all members. Such groups, agreeing to respect equality for each member, will be sure to look out for the welfare and happiness of all.

The way for large groups in society to provide for the welfare and happiness of all individuals is for those groups to consist of active small groups which have the power to safeguard their own interests. For a city that would mean many small neighborhoods consisting of even smaller circles, like the circles we call clans in this village vision, which would meet often and actively address the concerns of its members. A circle of representatives of these clans would oversee the governance of the neighborhood, and a circle of representatives from the neighborhoods would oversee the governance of the city.

Many, probably most of the responsibilities of municipal government could also be handled within the neighborhoods, which would be like small villages. Education, recreation, sanitation, health, law enforcement, and all the other functions that villages manage could be largely managed within those neighborhoods, with municipal departments facilitating cooperation among the neighborhoods and handling matters beyond their scope.

The important thing is to keep as much of the ordering and decision-making as possible in the smallest units where power is vested directly in the people. But more important even than the functional organization is the coming together of the people to open and follow their hearts together. In this way I believe even cities may become human and friendly, free from fear, corruption and injustice—villages that are concentrated together sharing resources and culture.

My book *Changing the World* is a vision of a village of the future, functioning tribally, where each person of any age is a member of a smaller circle, or clan, which guides the whole and in which every voice is equal. Basic human needs of food and shelter and fuel and health care, as well as education and creativity, are supplied self-sufficiently within the community.

For many years we have been making summer camps which explore and function under this "Circle Way" system, and the response has been uniformly positive. The common comment at the end of camp is, "This is how human beings are meant to live together, how can we live this way for the rest of our lives?"

We need to get closer. You and I—all of us. We need to take back control of our lives, our society, our earth. We need to communicate and open our hearts and minds to each other. We need places on the earth where we can get closer to each other, to our families, our children, to be safe, to relax and slow down and get away from stress, to live simply without harm to others or to the earth, to play, have fun, create, get close to the natural world. Without having to join any religious or political movement, follow any particular tradition or creed, but allow and respect and appreciate all the diverse ways that others engage in. It is such a beautiful world we have been given, we are endowed with such fantastic capabilities, and every baby born is a miracle, a delight, a shining star of hope for the future.

We have begun to approach the next step. We are having conferences in Europe now to begin to build our first Circle Way Village. (Contact us at circleway.org)

So I daydream now of this first Circle Way Village, and then of another and another and another, proliferating throughout Europe and spreading to other continents, around the world. I dream of a network of Circle Way Villages that will communicate and learn from each other, help and trade with each other. There are already networks of various kinds of communities, spiritual communities, egalitarian communities, ecovillages, for instance, and I would like to see our Circle Way Villages join with them and bring all networks together to broaden and strengthen the tribal movement.

What is special about the Circle Way is how it helps us get closer to each other, to deal with emotions of all kinds, to encourage and appreciate the best in all of us, to listen to each one and work together to solve our problems, and to keep our children free from more of the patterns that oppressed us when we were young. I would like, as we have in the past, for people from our villages to be available to teach the Circle Way, to any group or community that requests it.

Here is an excerpt from my book *Changing the World*:

"This is certainly nice," another of the group says, "But part of your vision here is to be a model for the world of peaceful cooperative living. You are only a thousand here, and there are, what — another thousand villages like it around the world?"

"Some are larger now, but none larger than 3,000."

"So maybe they could amount to three million or so in a while."

"We have more visitors all the time, and more villages keep sprouting up."

"Say more villages might grow the number to six million eventually. But there are ten billion people in the world today — and growing."

"Our idea is that when people notice how happy, how relaxed and safe we are here, and how much fun we have, creating instead of consuming, they will want to give up all the stress of the rat race and join us. With all the villages in every part of the world having more and more visitors, we figure the growth will be exponential at some point in the future and transform all of society's notions. But we need to be growing slowly in order to learn and make it right. A lot of society's problems have come from moving too fast and not seeing where we were going."

"So the Circle Way grew quite slowly?"

"Naturally it didn't happen overnight. We started from nothing but a dream and figured it out as we went along. Building homes, planting and harvesting, creating businesses for everything we need little by little. Slow growth—but that's the easy part. Human beings are builders. It was the excitement of creating our own world as we want it that carried us over the lean years. By sharing everything and inviting people to come and help we got by and it just kept getting better and better. Because we kept to the circle, stayed close to each other, kept on listening and caring and helping each other.

"And to the children. You know, whenever your energy gets a bit frayed, whenever you may feel a bit low, discouraged, wondering if it's worth it, all you need to do is go hang out at the playground. Watch the little ones and restore your faith in the human race. Then join them, let them teach you to let go of your seriousness and just play. You will get your hope refill. And then you'll be able to lose yourself in creativity and find your purpose again. We need the children to remind us who we are."

Climbing onto the wagon we could hear the shouts and laughter from the playgrounds and the sport fields. We are all quiet. Thinking perhaps about when we might come back or visit another Circle Way Village, perhaps even join one and change our lives. Change the world. A whole society of fun and play and creativity, of closeness, friendliness and love.

As we pass under the gate and look back one more time we notice another sign with a quote from Manitonquat who long ago had a vision of a Circle Way Village:

Together There Is Nothing We Cannot Do
- *Manitonquat* - *Assonet Wampanoag elder, philosopher, author Changing the World*

On my perfect blue planet not one thing would be more important than another.

No one person or group of people would be more valued than another.

Each individual's capacity to explore, challenge and question would be encouraged, embraced and valued. Together this would build a better, more productive, harmonious and empathetic world.

We will have finally learnt from past mistakes, that if the rivers become dry, plants fail to grow, the seas turn barren and animals vanish, that the real value of our money and possessions will be nothing.

The only welcome extinction would be our consumptive society.

We will look up to Mother Nature, use her enduring wisdom and be guided by her on how to live a sustainable existence. We will work with nature and not against it.

Our ability and willingness to be as one with our environment will determine what we are able to keep and what we will become.

- *Sheree Marris* - *environmental communications consultant, documentary filmmaker, author KarmaSEAtra: Secrets of Sex in the Sea, Australia*

"Humanity is asleep, concerned only with what is useless living in a wrong world. Believe that one can excel this only habit and usage, not religion. This 'religion' is inept....

Do not prattle before the People on the Path, rather consume yourself. You have an inverted knowledge and religion if you are upside down in relation to Reality. Man is wrapping his net around himself. A lion (the man of the Way) bursts his cage asunder."

Sanai 1131 A.D.

"Between stimulus and response there is a space. In that space is our power to choose our response. In our response lies our growth and our freedom." Viktor E. Frankl

"We must deliver ourselves with the help of our minds...for one who has conquered the mind, the mind is the best of friends; but for the one who has failed to do so, the mind will remain the greatest enemy." The Bhagavad-Gita

"A human being is a part of the whole, called by us the universe. A part limited by time and space. He experiences himself his thoughts and feelings as something separated from the rest. A kind of optical delusion of his consciousness. This delusion is a kind of prison for us restricting us to our personal desires and to affection for a few persons nearest to us. Our task must be to free ourselves from this prison by widening our circles of compassion to embrace all living creatures and the whole of nature and its beauty." Dr Albert Einstein

Love
Love is never alone.
Love is always crowded.
Love is the shared self.
We cannot own our love.
And we cannot teach our love.
The longest breathe of love
is the shortest distance to heaven.
The deepest life is love.
The deepest love is an embrace.
Love is not rest.

Love is peace.
Love is the purpose.

Akiane, age 11 child prodigy

When I was first asked to address the question of my ideal dream world I was quite taken back with the question as to how to answer this. Language does have its limitations and such a question is almost un-Englishable. However, I can say without a doubt that there would be no money or medium of exchange. The strong would not victimize the weak. And the weak would not be enslaved by the strong.

I laughed when first was asked to summarize this question as I replied in my mind that we are all in a huge dream. An illusion addressed by our sensory system trying to make sense of our senses at each moment. So as the days past I found myself trying to awaken further from the dream to construct my perfect dream world within the limits of the technology of language. I suppose many would address that as an individual issue rather than addressing the holographic principle that makes up our collective inter-connectedness of all that is.

I have a dream. A dream world would be one whereby the value systems of the planet would be based on higher principles of consciousness and money and medium of exchange would be obsolete. Our collective humanity would place its most cherished values on our children. Children from all cultures would be earth's most treasured assets as keepers of our world. Our inner worlds of our future selves would be the primary area of focus for all of humanity as it is there that all of our tomorrows will reside. The children would be parents and the parents would be children. There would be no division between them as it would be up to the elders of a world to supply the higher levels of consciousness that would allow for man to re-align itself with the bio rhythms of the planet, nature and our animals. It is the care of our inner world, which will change our outer world. All of man's dreams would be united with the inherent value system that we are one. That humanity can no longer see ourselves as separate from each other or that of any species. All of our techno- logical advances would be aimed to liberate man rather than to enslave our modality from growth. The synchronization of time that man has so aptly post-suggested himself into would no longer exist. Time itself would mean something else as this dream suspends our ideas of time and suggests that our inner worlds determine our outer worlds from the moment we are born. There would be no organized religion in any culture. Religion as a term would no longer need to exist. Man's need for religion would no longer exist as humanity would be self- realized and wouldn't find it necessary to seek something outside of themselves for truth.

- James Martinez - radio talk show host Cash Flow

The immutable biological and physical principles governing the world function perfectly, whether we understand them or not, whether we accept them or not—for example, change is a constant process (which equates to the impermanence of all material things), every cause has an effect (which is the cause of another affect, and so on, and so on, ad infinitum), and entropy (whereby energy spent in use cannot be regained in like measure). In the sustainable world I envision, we humans would practice the humility to consciously accept these principles and live within their social-environment constraints as trustees of Planet Earth—our biological living trust. We would, therefore, care first and foremost for the biophysical processes that maintain the functional integrity of the ecosystems that provide us with Nature's free services, such as fresh air, clean water, and fertile soil. In this way, we would maintain the land's productive capacity and thus its life-serving choices for all generations.

We would nurture our children with wisdom and give them a voice in current affairs, as if their desire for a dignified future really mattered. We would teach our children in the positive so they could articulate what they want their life to be like and not become stuck trying to move away from what they don't want, which is a physical impossibility. And we would allow our sons to mature with the same emotional sensitivity as we do our daughters.

Women would be honored for their sense of viable relationships and multitask labors and would be accorded equal seating *and* voice at the communal table of civil governments and ceremonial religions, from the various oppressive sects of Christianity to those of Judaism and Islam. Moreover, women— all women—would be the keepers and controllers of their bodies and the ultimate determiners of how many children to have and when. With respect to the necessity of controlling our human population, men would do their part and have vasectomies.

As for the world's ceremonial religions, many of which have sought social control through armed conflict, as some still do, they would put true spirituality where it belongs—far ahead of male egotism and domination. The lust for power would be supplanted by compassion for the divine essence in all things and would culminate in the international cooperation necessary to ensure the greatest integrity of the global commons as the uncontested birthright of every creature in all generations. Then, and only then, would the legacy we bequeath future generations be worthy of them because it would be an unconditional gift from physiologically mature adults to their children, their children's children, and beyond.

- Chris Maser - lecturer, international facilitator, environmental consultant, author Earth In Our Care: Ecology, Economy, and Sustainability

I see a world where the carbon dioxide concentration in the atmosphere is back below 350 parts per million—and hence the icecaps have ceased melting, drought spreading, mosquitoes proliferating. I like, in other words, the world we were born into, the one that worked pretty much as it had worked since the start of human history.

- Bill McKibben - co-founder 350.org, author Fight Global Warming Now

There is a powerful but often overlooked (or concealed) fact of life—that when enough people really care enough to want something to happen, it happens! The good news is that millions have, in recent years, begun to realize that the world is rapidly approaching a tipping point. Many are also awakening to the fact that while the possibility of "Armageddon" is certainly one possible outcome, an equally dramatic, but *positive* future, is now possible. Many people believe that if enough of us really want that future, we can have it. The question is whether or not enough of us will have the courage to hold such a positive vision. My dream world looks like this:

Species-wide Self-respect and Self-esteem: Compassion and authentic respect for the uniqueness, preciousness, spiritual essence, and intrinsic value of each human being. The true meaning of healthy self-esteem has been realized and is reflected in the respect and dignity for every human being that has become the norm.

Transformed Healthcare: All human beings have access to holistic healing tools (those that address mind, body, emotion, behavior, and spirit) and skilled practitioners. A human approach to health care that includes the use of modern scientific and technical advances is universal. The collective resources of the world's healing wisdom and knowledge are available to every human through purposeful use of modern communication technologies. People are to employ the self-care and wellness approaches that prevent 80% of the illnesses we now see.

Humanity-Centered Wedding of Technology and Art: Technology and Art have been brought together to create powerful models, inspired guidance, and rich imagery for Deep Healing, personal development, and collective evolution, at all levels of system, in dramatically effective ways. The vision articulated here is that of LIGHT, the Leadership Institute for Global Healing and Transformation. http://drmiller.pinnaclecart.com/

Unity in Diversity: Humanity has awakened to a planet-wide awareness of the intrinsic beauty of all living beings; hierarchical social models of control and dominance have been superseded by distributed leadership models that are based on justice, equality, respect, love, and community. Our cultures have turned away from a focus on acquisitiveness and things—and toward honesty and integrity in authentic relationships. We have realized that what we share is so much more than what divides us.

Love: We have discovered Love as the positive attractive force of affiliation that brings people and things together in harmonious ways. We have achieved understanding of the experience of Love as an intentional state (not something that people fall in). Our notion of Love goes beyond the pseudo-love of neediness, dependence, dominance, and abuse and embraces the qualities of sharing, mutual respect, affection, and appreciation of our common essence. Communication is compassionate and caring, sensitive to others' feelings and needs, supportive and nurturing of the positive and good in others.

Nonviolence: Disagreements are handled in ways that begin with respect for each other's rights, beliefs, and traditions, and end with the application of nonviolent approaches that allow second order change, transformation, transcendence, and subsequent resolution. Armed conflict is no longer an option. Violence in all its forms—child abuse, sweatshops, human trafficking, economic imperialism, corporate abuse of workers and the environment, and crime, are rapidly disappearing. Unconditional positive regard and respect have become the norm in all human interactions, including individual, family, workplace, community, and government.

Community Values: We have recognized the value and potential of our communities, of the collective. Families, education, nutrition, housing, recreation, wise land use, freedom of information, respect for earth systems, spirituality, and sustainability are widely supported with appropriate and effective action. Perhaps all these changes will not, perhaps cannot, occur in any of our lifetimes. But why not get as close to this ideal as we can? Besides, who could have predicted Jesus, or Muhammad, or Moses, or Gandhi?

You may say I'm a dreamer,
But I'm not the only one.
I hope some day you'll join us,
And the world will live as one.
– John Lennon

The "Serenity Prayer," made famous by Alcoholics Anonymous provides some guidance, "God, give us the grace to accept with serenity the things that cannot be changed, the courage to change the things that should be changed, and the wisdom to distinguish the one from the other." Clearly, what is needed most these days is wisdom. Our treatment, then, must be designed to awaken the wisdom we need, to awaken the leader within.

Ah, but a man's reach should exceed his grasp, or what's a heaven for?
– Robert Browning

- Dr Emmett Miller - physician, poet, musician, storyteller

Dream of Awakenings

Imagine a world where unconditional love is the guiding force, where the unique gifts that each individual brings receive honor and respect, where all are nurtured in allowing their gifts to blossom, to manifest the joy of living in each moment....

Imagine a world where all of nature is also honored, so all may live in harmony and share an increasingly vibrant and beautiful environment....

What we imagine we can create, starting in this moment. This vibrant world will come into being as each of us empowers ourselves to live the dream now and share it with others. Playing a part in the creation of this dream is the mission of Awakenings.

- Drs Phillip & Jane Mountrose - co-directors Awakenings Institute, holistic coaches, ministers of holistic healing

My Vision of an Ideal world

is one where human individuals use every scrap of potential that they were born with. As an astrologer, I would call this "living through the center of the chart." The phrase refers to that state of perfect balance we attain when we see all the myriad facets of our being as existing for a reason: each skill, each talent, each challenge and seeming imperfection is understood to be an invitation to refine the awareness. In this view, the whole chart is a statement of one's integrated Self; an entity that is aligned with cosmic intelligence and is therefore far more meaningful than the personality-based self. To identify with this level of ourselves leads to an effortlessly balanced state of mind. This vision is not limited to astrology, of course. Many spiritual systems use a similar model, and similarly propose that when we come from this place, we will know what to do, no matter what the circumstance. An ideal world would be one in which every human being—or even a critical mass of them—lived at this level of consciousness. Then the world as a whole would be able to come up with the perfect responses to the daunting crises of our era. Collectives follow the same Natural Laws as individuals: when we are connected to the core of our being—on the personal level, on the societal level, on the level of all sentient beings—we intuitively attract into our reality whatever external event or outside aid is needed to solve a given problem, rebalance a particular imbalance, or heal a present wound.

  - *Jessica Murray - astrologer, author, teacher*

I dream of a world in which war—and all of the death, destruction and unfathomable hardship that war brings—is a footnote in the history of humankind.

  - *Dr Samantha Nutt - founder and executive director War Child Canada, Canada*

My dream is a blend of dreams: a sustainable world of abundance, clean cheap energy, peace and justice. To that end, Meredith and I created Montesueños (Mountain Dreams) in the Andes of Ecuador to create retreats directed toward a positive future for humanity and nature.

  - *Dr Brian O'Leary - scientist, former astronaut, international speaker, author The Energy Solution Revolution*

Why people don't believe they can live their dreams?

Why people don't believe they can live their dreams? Either people have lived in a cultural environment with a belief system that has them believing they cannot do what they love and earn enough to live their dream.

People are not clear about what brings them fulfillment. Many people don't know what brings them fulfillment, pleasure and how to fall in love with what they do. They go on and on hating doing what they do work/career-wise rather than starting on a more spiritual self-fulfillment path. They live in fear and that keeps them paralyzed.

Many people don't think they have the right to have and live their dream. I truly believe that all people have a dream. Some people keep that dream so air tight within themselves that they don't see it or acknowledge it themselves.

Many people don't believe they can make enough money to live their dream. This is the biggest obstacle I hear from people when they tell me: I would love to go on that Journey with you... It has been my dream to go there. As long as we continue to do the same thing and we don't take a risk to change what we do and do something we love to do we will not be able to create the adventure and go on to fulfill our dreams. People stay doing what they do for the salary and the false sense of job security. Why not at least take a look at your dreams and make a plan for a transition?

People are lazy. I honestly don't believe that all people are lazy. People have become resigned, fearful, and many times depressed about their situation but they are not lazy. People love to see productivity and change in their lives. When you become resigned or stuck on a less than the ideal life, you don't take action towards that which will bring you fulfillment even when you know what to do.

People don't think they have time to think about starting living their dream. Amazing to see how life slows down in India and there is time to do everything. People here are caught up in the rush and business of today's world and don't believe they have time for their dreams. People have to analyze what they must eliminate in order to create more free time in their lives and with that the reduction of stress.

People still believe that hard work will pay off. I am not suggesting not to work hard, but work with the heart and soul in a way that is more smart than hard. Once you passionately fall in love with what you do, work becomes more meaningful to you.

People are afraid. Many people live in fear and in most cases they don't even admit that they do. Fear of failure, of success, of rejection, of relationships, intimacy, sex, of being different, of dancing and being wild and different, of acting childish and demonstrating exuberant joy. We are all afraid of something, and it will only keep us from getting what we want if we allow that fear to become bigger than us and we take no action. What is your fear?

People don't love themselves enough. People don't love themselves enough; to be selfish in a way without going to altered ego selfishness. Why do I deserve to be happy? Why do I deserve to have enough? My parents suffered a great deal... So many people don't have... All of these are limiting beliefs! People don't feel worthy enough to invest in themselves.

People are not ready. Many people are well aware that doing what they do and living their lives in the way they do will not bring them fulfillment, they also know that it will require a significant effort and investment in themselves to get their lives turned around. Many people admit that taking a good look at themselves and their life is not something that they are ready to do at this time.

So here is the question. What is stopping you? Is there anything you can't overcome? Is it self-imposed limitations or a false belief system about you and what you can accomplish? In reality, there is only one thing that will prevent you from living your dreams... YOU

- Ernesto Ortiz - facilitator, teacher, therapist, founder and director Journey to the Heart

In physics, when particle pairs are created, it not understood why one spins in one direction and the other necessarily spins in the opposite direction despite the fact that the particles do not communicate in any evident way. Furthermore, the communication between the pairs is at a speed greater than the speed of light, which is considered impossible. My solution is that these pairs are actually just one particle being viewed from two different perspectives.

If you use your imagination, you can see how this solution could allow a person effectively to be in two places at the same time. Or, put another way, how a person could instantaneously travel from one part of the universe to another. This would change the nature of existence by making time just another dimension through which we move at a speed of our choosing.

Reducing the cost of transportation to nothing would mean nearly limitless access to resources and no longer having to compete for oil, food, or land. War and the nation state would be superfluous.

- Ted Pascoe - executive director Senior Support Services

My Dream World!

I have a friend who wears brightly- colored p.j.'s to bed at night, hoping to trigger colorful dreams. Despite my keen sense of humor, my dreams tend to be serious and, at times, even scary. During one of my nightmares, my husband will recognize my struggle, and gently tug on my ear to "change the channel". What is so magical about this? It works!

On the other hand, while fully awake, when my consciousness is revitalized and I dream (daydream), it's not possible to change the channel. No one controls the outcome. As such, my abstract musings are much more daunting than nightmares because they have more serious consequences with very real horror. What could cause such a chill and be so alarming? The lack of attention to organ donation and its dire impact. The huge gap between supply and demand is costing lives.

My dream for the world is for people to leave behind a meaningful legacy. I would first love every human to indulge in the total freedom of health, to feel the full force of vitality, to embrace and use it. When the fateful moment comes and life is over, it's time for the legacy to be revealed. There is no rush, of course; the time eventually comes for all living creatures. This is such old news we don't give it a moment of thought! Here is the mistake. We need to be prepared before that moment comes when we are being bagged and tagged.

When speaking of legacy, of course, I mean organ and blood donation. Actually blood is the easiest feel good act/legacy in the world. But with organs and other tissue, I would love to see our laws changed to Implied Consent. Why? Right now we have a system of "opting in" where as if you have given this matter thought you must take proactive steps to see it to reality, and frankly far too many well-intentioned people neglect or forget to take even the simple action of signing a donor card. Literally thousands of life-saving organs are going to waste due to simple human error. People simply don't think about dying; either the possibility is too remote for most of one's life or the prospect is too scary; you change the channel and nothing is done.

Our current system of educating and encouraging people to sign up and talk to their family—both of which is required to be organ donors—is not good enough. We are losing far too many precious lives! What I believe to be a better solution is the Presumed Consent law. This means you are automatically a donor unless you choose otherwise. "Opting-out", which is a choice you can make, requires the action instead.

Still, I would add one twist to this Presumed Consent law. In the situation where a person chooses to "opt-out", not be a donor, if this same person needs a transplant, he/she would automatically be placed at the bottom of the list. An example is the lottery; in order to win, you have to buy a ticket. The same applies here. If you are in need of an organ, in order to receive one, you must first be a willing to participate. This is only fair.

Opt-out systems are used in many other countries and they have much higher success rates and smaller waiting lists for people in need of life saving organs than those countries who have the "opt in" system. We are talking life and death here! Nothing could be more important! After all, the human heart is mighty and strong... And I do not have to dream to believe it.

- *Kelly Perkins - author The Climb of My Life, Scaling Mountains with a Borrowed Heart*

The Ecology of Soul

The world is perfect. We only need to be attuned with her. "*To be absorbed in the song of creation is to love the singer.*" I was named by my mother and father: Carol. My mother immigrated to the United States from Nicaragua when she was 23 years of age. My father was born in Tyler, Minnesota, the largest Danish community founded by their ancestors. They found in each other a love of music and an attraction for the opposite in culture for they were both one of seven siblings who married outside of their Maya and Nordic customs. I was born the first of three children in San Francisco, California where the remnants of an ancient civilization can be felt today.

I was a precocious child full of knowing which often caused disorientation in others. I had been blessed with a natural inclination to absorb my senses in the silence of the inner world. I was enchanted with states of energy and often experienced expanded symptoms. As a young adult I began a serious course of meditation. My adventure with being was one of sovereignty. I often felt I lacked spiritual advancement by an inability to attract a teacher and when I did they were often abusive. It was clear to me I was traveling alone prompted to find my soul within.

I continued my adult life seeking those who might help me to progress in understanding what it means to be a human being. I chose Physiotherapy as my vocation and recognized that each client who came to me for healing was my teacher. I practiced for 30 years in three different states until I had a physical injury. I had accumulated an amplitude of knowledge. I was to integrate and purify the consciousness of those whom I served as myself.

I took refuge in the Mojave Desert where I live far from major cities. I learned to walk in the culture of nature. I began to have visions which came like a wind and took me to South America and Europe to receive soul impressions of the earth and to experience the vortices. I still had a longing to belong to people of culture. As the first born I was a blend of both on a master course which had me draw the sails of my soul and learn to trust ancestral guidance.

It has been a passion play, one of deep isolation along with a learning, to still the mind for the desire to know the song of creation has been my true north. At the time of this writing I have chosen to fast on liquids one day at a time and there have been 24 days. As the desert crystals sprout green, I delight in the orchestral opera of the birds. They are mating and as I draw to me the beloved breath of life they are also competing with their song.

Where I sit the sun shines opening my heart and this is the vision for the future taking form in the dream of good men and women. Humanity's crisis has been mine. Consciousness is the mediator of compassion and drives one to explore human relationships with Mother Nature. For one to know our creator is to be immersed in the beauty of creation. A planetary lake of compassion is the soul of the environment where the weather is our ally. Generally speaking humanity's lost connection to the environment is in effect a threat of the weather. It is our mutual folly and focus on survival that separates us from the affinity nature has with the evolution of one's soul. The seeker refrains from conflict which arises from an attitude of surviving, then casts their reflection into the lake of compassion, therein the soul sustains love of creation and the body, mind and spirit are in harmony. All that is spiritual is born of Mother Nature. Global warming is an opportunity to spiritually align with the planetary soul.

We are metamorphosing, while our Earth is adapting to celestial weather. With the lessons from materialism, we have been given a challenge to return to the Earth to understand the need for protection from the elements as well as to protect our natural resources. The evolution of Earth continues and we must adapt. This is our genius to become caretakers of the physics of the universe the ancients call Sacred and Natural Law.

The government as we know it today will change from fifty states to states combining lands of bordering states and bordering countries to form Preserves. The Preserve will have a three-fold governing body. The outer territorial preserve will protect the integrity of the boundaries of the Preserve. The central territories will protect the natural resources such as forest, rivers, water sheds, and wild life. The center of the Preserve will have the duty to regulate sustainable energy, and agriculture. Each Preserve will have representatives from the communities that form a council. The governing councils of the Preserve are founded on environmental laws. Each Preserve has a unique biosphere and to that biosphere education, research and development to the native soils, minerals, plants and wild life are protected.

Co-opting Preserves for environmental reclamation and restoration will dissolve corporate debts and begin an era of a sustainable exchange of technologies. The Constitution of the Preserves will favor the rights of the farmer over those of the bankers as the weather determines the ley of the land, flora and fauna. The wealth of a sustainable future in cooperation with native culture is the end of the White House and the beginning of many Green Houses, a Federation of Global Preserves.

The future of tomorrow is adapting to evolution. We have entered an eon for the architects of consciousness. Awakening to the current, we are dreaming collectively the solution to the environmental poisoning of our species and creative life as we know it. A new culture is rising, the culture of womankind, a culture of water, wind and soil. The future generations are harvesting a rebirth of sustainable ecology. Global gardening is to tend to the soul's need for embodiment. The earth is the heart of our universe. When first lady Mrs. Michele Obama put a spade in the ground to overturn the soil for a garden at the Capitol, all cameras were poised. Then she spoke, "My girls like fresh vegetables because they taste better," America listened.

- *Carol Petersen - traditional Elder, creation singer*

The future—if we get it right—will flourish with the rich biological and cultural diversity that existed in the world into which we were born.

- *Mark J. Plotkin, Ph.D. - ethnobotanist, author, president Amazon Conservation Team*

The Dream World

The optimist claims we live in the best of all possible worlds, and the pessimist fears this is true. - James Branch Cabell

I was reminded of this quote when asked to describe a dream world, because one's spiritual perspective determines whether one would agree with the pessimist or the optimist. Judeo-Christian idealists would describe a dream world as one without its current flaws, most of which stem from human nature. In our present world, people lie and manipulate out of selfishness, greed and/or lust; despite exposure to spiritual teachings that advise against these behaviors and feelings. In a dream world these problems would not occur, because people would act out of a higher state of consciousness.

Achieving higher states of consciousness has another important effect. Eastern spiritual traditions teach that our perception of the world is an illusion. By reaching higher states of consciousness, we can experience bliss and love. We can also see that the world is already a perfect and unified whole. The human imagination cannot dream up a world that surpasses the one described as the "real" world by mystics who have experienced this state of consciousness. If we were all similarly stripped of our egos and their attachments, we would find that we do live in the best of all possible worlds...the true "dream world."

- *Diane Hennacy Powell, M.D. - activist, psychotherapist, psychopharmacologist, author The ESP Enigma: The Scientific Case for Psychic Phenomena*

The world of the enchanted flower

They have asked me to speak about the "dream world" a world that resides in the virtual reality, yet just about to be manifested, a world where the cause and effect meet.

The ancient world that many tribes had known, the world where the ancestors went to bring the teachings and the songs, the world where all is one... This world is now....

A new world is awakening inside of the true human, a world that has been encoded in the true human being's DNA since the beginning of time, a world that the ancestors called the world of the enchanted flower.

Inside of human being resides the key to open that world within the self, that world has been visited many times, sometimes without realizing... It is the place where the hemispheres meet.

In this world, many of the concepts and ideas of reality are obsolete, for in the world of oneness there is no separation concept. There is no pain that created that separation, there is no money, for the cause and the effect are happening instantaneously, there is no government, for human beings know how to relate, there is no time as the third and fourth dimension knows it, for the time was an invention of the "dark lords" as the Chilam Balam said, the concept of time in the world of the enchanted flowers is not based on process that created the illusion of separation, it is based on a cosmological way of thinking. In the world of the enchanted flower, there is nothing separated; it is a world of unity.

The cosmic way of thinking is awoken in the world of the enchanted flower, for human beings recognize her-his-self as an entity of a higher order, the divine order, where all is a big family, for the worlds are part of the one as one is part of the all, all is a beautiful orchestra happening with completely divine order, in a perfect harmony.

In this beautiful world where the true human being has always been, all is bonding into one, for it is the one that unfolded, the one that understands where you have always been, for you are being integrated into a higher version of your own self. There is one single language that resides in the outside as well in the inside, for communication happens in a very direct form, there are no filters that create a process, it is a communication that is unfolding instantaneously, and is happening with everything that exists, at the same time, for time equals zero, love is the energy that connects in the purity of the essence, and the connection is the way of living.

In the world of the enchanted flower, there is no separation of the chakras, no divisions between conscious and subconscious, no separation of mind, body emotions, spaces or dimensions, for all the dimensions are contained in the one. This means that there is no world separated. It means that there are worlds inside of worlds inside of worlds, all is completely integrated, all is one, for through the essence of all vibrations communication is taking place, for the root of the tree of life has always been one, for the one is contained in the whole as the whole is contained in the one.

As the sun enters in the center of the galaxy, the connection intensifies, through that connection authenticity comes into being. The authentic human being embraces peace by nature, by their own nature. True human being is a peaceful entity, for human beings know that nothing can harm them... Human being will be conscious of that connection with the spirit from the heart, for all connection is sacred and every single life form is connected one to another. Through that connection, freedom will come into being; freedom comes through recognition within... For human beings are free. Freedom is everywhere, for there are no boundaries in the inside as well as the outside, in the world of oneness freedom is a natural state of being human as it has always been. It is the world of the absence of fear.

The world of the enchanted flowers is being awakened when you know that you are being observed, senses are open..., feel it, and face the fear by just observing that you are being observed. By what? You are being observed by your own higher self-God-Goddess-mother-matrix (womb), or whatever you want to call her-him. It is a grid, a grid that was built by communications, in your own connection with the spirit that you are(!) by that connection. Meaning that if you can see the flowers, the flowers can see you, if you can see the creation as you call it, then the creation can see you, through that observation and recognition of being observed, you will begin to use the part of the brain that contains the connection and a new way of perceiving reality, and then creation of a better place has been made. Your behavior, thoughts, way of perceiving yourself will change, for you will be in alignment of that one that is observing you.

You are aligned then to the divine order, in perfect harmony with all around you, perfect harmony with the multiverse... All in perfect synchronicity, all in perfect movement, the perfect sacred dance of a cosmic way of thinking... Then human beings will realize where they are and be comfortable with the self, meaning pain is gone, separation is gone, all that doesn't belong in the world of oneness is gone. Changes come from the inside to the outside.

The world is in deep changes. The "new world" is about relationships, the way the true humans relate to each other, the environment, and to the self, for all relationships are sacred. The web, in all life forms is sacred, the connection is sacred, and all life forms are sacred.

The ancestors didn't disappear. They are here, in the golden city as many call them, the golden ones, the shiny ones, and they have many names... Human beings have all the assistance, there are beautiful beings waiting for human beings arriving into the world of the enchanted flower, they are rejoicing, they are celebrating....!

In the world of the enchanted flower, you will find many possibilities for many worlds; you will uncover all the worlds inside of yourself, and when you think that you have them all, a new one will appear, for it is infinite. Human beings cannot take things that belong to the third and fourth dimension into higher worlds, for the laws are different in each world - just don't look back... Human beings know in the inner core, that they carry the history of the multiverse within the self; they carry the map of a multidimensionality being that he-she is, for they know deep inside that they have access to the libraries of the cosmos, anytime.

The first door is the union of polarities which means, that you are finally using the feminine side of your brain and your male side of your brain together; you are using 100 percent of the brain! Use your brain.

The relationships are happening inside of yourself, and through that you create a reality according to that perception, according to that belief, your truth, but indeed, I am telling you that you have all the relations inside of yourself. This means that whomever you see is a mirror of you, it is your other you, which means that you are all the relations happening at the same time inside of you. You are in the other side of the mirror.

Human being is the ancient one, human being can never die, only transform, you are just going into a higher dimension, in your time, into the world of the enchanted flower as we call it. Being Human is being a multidimensional entity, with many worlds inside of the self, many realities happening at the same time, Human being is so beautiful! ... and another thing to consider is the Great Spirit does not age....

The kingdom of heaven is on earth, the kingdom of earth is on heaven....

I Am You

In lakesh

Magdala

- Magdala Ramirez - medicine woman, speaker, author I Am You

The World I Dream Is Illumined

My 17 year old son, Eben, graduates from high school in a few months. His sister, Sayre, brings her first year of college to a close. This is an exciting time of new beginnings for my children. But Sayre and Eben, along with their sisters and brothers around the planet, embark into a world no other young people throughout human history have faced. Unrest spans the globe. The biosphere teeters. Our children walk into the future of a species seemingly gone amok. Yet as dire as this appears for my own, and all the Earth's children, the dream for harmony with each other and our planet has never been so strong. And in my dreaming, this reality has never been so close.

In looking through habitual eyes it's easy to see and fear everything wrong in the world today. But in looking through the eyes of our heart, we begin to see differently. Supporting this alternate view are indigenous teachings across the globe which point to this time on the planet as heralding a new age of Light. A higher human consciousness spawns, they say, in which heart and mind will meld as one. Of the many promises this alchemy portends, most important is the recreation of the world according to higher values; in relation to one another, to nature and Spirit.

I feel that Heaven already exists on Earth, we just need to wake up to perceive it. The Earth is abundant with ecstatic life forms and expressions. Ponder waterfalls and oceans. Look up at a starlit sky. Remember mountain vistas. Think of the structure of cells, the scent of flowers or the softness of an infant's skin. Magic can be ordinary yet it's omnipresent. All we have to do is remember to look for the beauty, mystery and intelligence of life to see that it's everywhere. In doing so we glimpse what Heaven on Earth could be; and we fuel its possibility. Why live as we do when our sentient planet can bountifully nourish body, heart and soul? In my dreaming I see that our human family is capable of greatness yet untapped. We can live in harmony with each other and our planet in ways beyond imagining now. Every moment breathes potential. We just need to wake up to it. I dream this reality to be very close at this time in the evolutionary cycle of humankind. In the face of unprecedented personal and global challenge, our Universal aspects now pressure to the surface.

I envision a world where humans are illumined. How we experience reality, what we desire and create is different. In this world, interconnection is valued over separation. We live respectfully and in balance with our planet. Doing so makes our communities wholesome and we're aware that doing otherwise doesn't make any sense. In knowing we're parts of the same whole, we live harmoniously with each other. War doesn't exist because we feel complete in ourselves and know our connection to all things. There are no foreign threats because nothing is seen as separate. The desire to dominate others and nature has dissolved. The incentive to amass wealth, territory, power has fallen away. In letting go of self-serving values we are spiritually lifted and gain esteem through compassionate action. Suffering, famine and disease are vanquished. Problems that were once insurmountable have either instinctively disappeared, or solutions have come to light. We depend on few physical resources to survive. As we're fabricated more of energy in this world, what was physical and solid prior to our awakening, has changed. We select foods for their energetic vibrancy yet have less need to eat. There are some of us who breathe in life force from the atmosphere, or absorb it from sunlight and nature, with such efficiency that we don't require food at all.

Some of us live in urban areas but there are much smaller numbers of people concentrated in cities and they have different qualities than before. They're quieter, calmer, and are healthy places to be. We use natural power sources that are unlike any alternative methods we knew. In understanding ourselves as energy, we've tapped our natural ability to move about in this world and explore others, without external vehicles. These are natural human capacities of teleportation that until current times were only remembered by Eastern yogis and spiritual adepts. Illumination has caused what was previously hidden or veiled from perception to be seen for what it is. This includes innate human capacities. Energy transfers also propel visitors from other places in the Universe who come and go, some living with us here on the Earth. Balls of light frequent the skies and the larger Universal community is now an intimate point of reference. We've rejoined with stellar families, whose existence we had forgotten, and they share many things with us including advanced technologies. The Universe is more expansive and loving than we ever could've dreamed. Old ways of knowing and fears have transformed. The nature of reality has not changed, our acuity has expanded to see its true patterns. We realize now how limited we were, how compartmentalized was our experience; the life we knew was but a small slice of what's possible.

We've awakened from a nightmarish slumber and consciously dream our lives. We direct energy and intention to effortlessly manifest what we desire and need, in consonance with all living things. Many more of us live simply and closer to the Earth in small communities. Nature invigorates, balances us and our communities thrive because we're in harmony with the perfection all around us. The natural world is translucent and individuals relate as intimately with the elements and animals as they do with other people. Humans are also luminous. Spiritual centers in the brain connected with pineal and pituitary glands called Nodes of Luminaria have lighted, opening inner faculties. We emanate light, much like the halos in the renderings of Christ and sanctified beings. In times past a human being's sense of self was focused on sex, survival and on mental projections. Today, we're in balance with all aspects of our humanness, with more of our energy focused around the heart center than it was before. This enables some of us to keep the thymus functioning throughout life. In others, immunity remains robust despite any physical evidence of the gland. This is one reason we're resistant to disease, but primary is that we know only oneness. As heart and mind are one, life force suffuses us unobstructed.

Much of our communication these days is telepathic, which is not simply a mental transfer of thoughts as people used to define it. Telepathy is an empathic exchange projected from, and felt within, our hearts and bodies. This is intimate beyond what language could ever be. Because mind and heart are inseparable, we think and converse differently, through feeling and vibration. We understand one another instantaneously and with a depth that words could never convey. As we share, we extend energy and love as humans are fulfilled by the goodness they radiate. As these changes occur, pollution problems on the Earth impulsively clear. Everything physical is awake to its energetic quality and the higher frequencies renew form to its perfected state. In waking up to our own, and the world's, true character we've created new options for living. In awakening to the dream that is life, we've recognized that we can co-create it. We use light and sound waves to heal, yet serious illness only rarely occurs and previous medical paradigms are seen as archaic. We choose when to stop living in human form. Those who awaken first, help others open to the grace that is our world. This is a reality of wholeness, union with nature and the Divine.

In my dream world humanity is boundless; who we are is consciously entwined with the infinite potential of the Cosmos. I dream this as coming about more naturally than what one might ponder. Think of the symbol for infinity, the figure eight. Imagine that Universal Intelligence, or Source, travels a path of Becoming and Returning as portrayed by the figure eight. The center point of the eight is pure, dynamic consciousness. This consciousness expands out from its own center in a primordial longing to create, a path of Becoming. The Universe's expression is ecstatic as worlds, planets, galaxies, star systems, life forms, come into being. Separation is the vehicle through which form manifests. Separation isn't a problem, it's inherent to the anatomy of generation. But as a result, form isn't conscious of itself or its beginnings. As manifestation peaks, forgetting is most prevalent—on our figure eight this point in the journey would be the outer curve of the first loop.

Yet Source longs to know itself through creation, affecting the Cycle of Return—calling all that It has manifested, back to Itself. In moving closer to its origin, pure consciousness, creation quakes. Polarities exaggerate because all is called back to know itself as Source, light as well as dark. In my imagined world, this would be the time period within which we now live. Nearing the hub of the figure eight, the Cycle of Return approaches completion. In reaching Its heart, as Universal Intelligence remembers Itself through form, all of creation is illumined. All that is manifest now knows itself as Source. The Universe embarks on a fresh journey of Becoming, a new world is born.

Indigenous shamanic peoples of diverse cultures say we and our world are an interconnected dream. We are one with everything, all is one with us. As in sleeping dreams, this dream of who we are is malleable. We and our world can transform. We can reshape at anytime. Prophecies from all over the planet point to this time in human history as one of monumental change. As Universal Intelligence is ecstatic, its repertoire, infinite; the time is ripe to dream ourselves freshly. In doing so we can realize our true potential and create a new world—for our own, and all the Earth's children.

- *Llyn Roberts, M.A. - teacher, spiritual ecologist, director Dream Change, Inc., author Shapeshifting into Higher Consciousness*

I yearn for a world where funerals for the young have been replaced by funerals for the old.

- *Hans Rosling - professor, director Gapminder.org, Sweden*

Since my youth, I have been blessed with a very active imagination during my waking time and an interesting and active dream world during sleep. I am aware that things existing in my dream state often become reality during the day.

My perfect place would have two major aspects that would be a part of it. First would be an environment where my wishes, fantasies, dreams, visions and thoughts would instantly manifest to allow me to experience what I have perceived. The key word here is instantly. From a philosophical standpoint, we create our reality on this earth plane based upon that which we most often have within our thoughts, desires and wishes. My dream world is the possibility of experiencing this in a quicker time than our normal earth sequencing. A famous quote from the past says, "We do not see things as they are, we see them as we are." I believe that is from the Talmud. If there really were more to our existence than just our own creating then I would love to have the ability to see things true as they are without my influence. My life philosophy is based on the ancient Greek concept of The One, The Good and The Beautiful. To this, I dedicate my life and to the service of others, I dedicate my time in this world. In my perfect world, I would ask that the highest and best, that is possible to manifest, for each person in my sphere, manifest for them.

- Steven A. Ross - researcher, lecturer, philosopher, chief executive officer World Research Foundation

The world I see is a world in which people have realized that contentment comes not from what they have or do. Contentment is an essential quality of the mind in its natural state, untarnished by need or concern. I see a world in which people are free from discontent. Free to experience things as they are, without fear or attachment. Able to be at ease in the moment. I see a world where we are no longer controlled by a self-created sense of lack. Where we can respond to situations with compassion and understanding.

The world I see is so close—closer than any of the worlds we seek out there. Can we live in this world? That is up to us. We each must set our own mind free.

- Peter Russell - author, speaker, personal development consultant, philosopher, futurist, UK

The World I See.

Actually, I can see various different scenarios playing out, from the intensely positive, to the profoundly negative. The world I would personally wish to be in is one where the physical world and society reflect a respect for deeper values of the natural world. First of all, a world in which we humans have suddenly learned to respect the Creation and have stopped exterminating all the biodiversity that has taken millions of years to evolve. That, quite suddenly, we have become respectful of life forces that are much more complex and wonderful than our own narrow greed and arrogance. A world in which we respect life as a process; where we respect that which we cannot duplicate. I frankly have my doubts that industrialized consumer society can actually reach this level of understanding and respect, however.

If we can learn to respect other life forms, then we can respect other human beings and the creations of those human beings. By seeking the common bonds that make us human, we can hopefully reach across cultures to achieve a better understanding of the positive achievements of those cultures. This would be a tremendous evolution from the present US/Euro-centric view of culture, which has become global and which spreads noxious non-culture through the media. I am extremely proud of Western Culture up to the early 20th Century, but am ashamed of most things we have done since then. Not only have we destroyed our own culture in the West by branding it as outdated, but this global non-culture has decimated the cultural basis of the rest of the world. Thus, I would like to live in a world where people have woken up to the value of their own individual culture, their artistic, musical, architectural traditions, and who have belatedly recognized that what the global commercial machine sold them was worthless consumer junk.

The world I see radically revises the role of "experts" by instituting simple criteria to weed out impostors, of which we have hordes. In the sciences the role of the expert is to maintain correctness and integrity, but in non-scientific fields, so-called experts are most often promoters of some or other ideology, or tools of a global marketing machine. Those persons are terribly destructive. A world in which people exercise their own intuitive criteria about non-scientific matters could become more honest. It will take a generation to rid ourselves of conditioning through the marketing of useless and even harmful goods, and to rediscover a truer value closer to the heart.

None of this is possible without some sort of return to a higher order of values. Many people in this world have open, healthy, or suppressed religious convictions, and I hope that those can be oriented towards an understanding of nature, humanity, and the best fruits of human creation. They often are, but religious sentiment can either be extinguished by marketing, consumerism and propaganda, or otherwise turned towards harmful ends. Religious sentiment gave us many of our greatest works of art, music, architecture, etc. all around the world. It is a universal phenomenon not due to the specific culture nor the specific religion, but an intensely connective process that binds us to the universe and allows us to create. I wish to see a world in which people value the creations of nature along with those of human beings genuinely trying to reach beyond their own physical limitations. I believe this is achievable through the notion of the sacred.

Going up to a bigger scale, I wish to live in cities of the future that closely resemble the most human-scaled cities of the past. Where walking is made possible once again, and where one can enjoy the company of nature and one's fellow human beings without the terrible stress of mechanization. Where mechanization is truly the servant of humankind, not its totalitarian master. Many energy-intensive movements can be replaced by electronic transfers so that people can be induced to stay closer to home. All of that has been predicted repeatedly until we are now weary of hearing it, but I see it finally being implemented. Of course, I realize that much of suburban sprawl in the industrialized world represents a vast problem because it is built according to a defective geometry. By the time we can get around to retrofitting suburbia, it may not be worth doing at all, since the quality of all that recent building stock is too low to warrant salvage.

In architecture and urbanism, I see a wonderful new appreciation of forms, structures, and textures that express the type of complexity which nourishes us humans. I see a new type of built environment that gives the same emotional nourishment as the most loved parts of historical architecture and urban places. I would like to see a recycling of all those hostile fashionable forms that actually make us ill, just like junk cars are recycled for their parts. I see a world where people have woken up from a massive deception that built monstrous buildings and inhuman cities while proclaiming them miracles of progress. I see a world that has undergone genuine progress in judging what is healthy and what is not, as far as how architecture and urbanism affect our well-being.

The world's poor could benefit from some emerging technologies that will allow them to build their own houses with relatively inexpensive materials. I hope that we can persuade governments to support self-building by providing the correct infrastructure, instead of trying to impose top-down high-rises that make some companies very rich. There are other ways to make a vast profit, like actually building infrastructure, so there is no need to build inhuman blocks for the poor. I hope that the revolution in Peer-to-peer urbanism really takes off so that we can see a new paradigm of people helping each other and circumventing an often rigid or corrupt system. In this I am quite hopeful, since the internet has made a Peer-to-peer society possible as never before in the history of humankind.

What I don't want to see is a world that is left scarred and radioactive. But I am worried of a totally crazy consumption of non-renewable fuel resources coupled to an exploding population. Those nations who run their economies on oil will simply take it from those who have it, and fight with others who also want it. It just so happens that many players in this dangerous game possess nuclear weapons. This is not a very reassuring scenario. My concerns are intimately tied to urban development in both the industrialized and developing worlds. Some countries that have subsisted on a fairly sustainable way of life are now changing it for a petroleum-based one. That does not bode well for their future, and I mean not only the ability to afford to run their society: I actually mean the prospects of keeping their society intact. It is not difficult to imagine that nations who were left behind in the great "modernization" towards unsustainability will probably survive the coming clash. Those who have been modest will have a better chance for the future.

- Dr Nikos Salingaros - mathematician and polymath, urban, architecture and complexity theorist, design philosopher

Utopia is a state of consciousness in which each seeming individual Knows: that he or she is One with every other seeming individual and All That Is; that we are all holy, eternal, unlimited, courageous souls; that we are Love.

- Robert Schwartz - author Your Soul's Plan: Discovering the Real Meaning of the Life You Planned Before You Were Born

Mind-Body and the Social Dimension

Sheila, a tough-minded New York career newspaperwoman turned magazine writer prided herself on her cynical view on life, and her ability to not be taken in. She got an assignment from her magazine to do a story on Mother Teresa, and welcomed the opportunity.

"I thought she was a fraud, a genius at public relations maybe, but I disliked her conservative theology, which I thought demeaned women, and I found her constant involvement with the rich and famous very suspect. I arranged to join her and spent more than a week traveling with her and watching her at one of her hospices. My first impression never changed. I disagreed with almost everything she had to say about religion. I found her views about God depressing, and her vision about the place of women in the church almost medieval. At the same time from the very first moment I was in her presence, I had this overpowering urge to call the magazine and tell them that I wasn't coming back; that I wanted to give myself to Mother Teresa's work. It left me confused and ecstatic."[1]

Beingness can not be quantified, yet everyone who encounters it knows exactly what is meant. It is with beingness and its impact that we cross from the individuality of the mind-body relationship, to the social generality. Others have written at length about the individual mind-body connection, describing such things as the psycho-physical self-regulation processes that produces placebo response, and hypnosis reactions. There is a great, and growing, amount of research telling us how strongly our emotions and mental activities affect our happiness and wellbeing. And gaining insight into the relationship of consciousness and matter will surely help resolve humanity's most enduring great question, about who we are and how our consciousness and our physical reality relate to one another.

I want to suggest, however, that there is a second domain of the mind-body linkage: the social manifestation. And that this mind-body expression powerfully determines how the society of which we are a part thrives, and how our own personal lives are happy and fulfilling. It seems to me highly consequential that we learn how the mind-body linkages that create culture operate.

One thing is clear from the start: As at the individual level there is both a local and a Non-local component and, at the social level this linkage exists as well. A portion lies within space-time, but there is also a portion that exists in the non-local energetic information domain.

As Nobel Laureate physicist Wolfgang Pauli put it, "The only acceptable point of view appears to be the one that recognizes both sides of reality—the quantitative and the qualitative, the physical and the psychical—as compatible with each other, and can embrace them simultaneously."[2]

It may surprise you how much science can contribute to understanding how this social process moves from the individual to the nonlocal to the culture that is the manifestation of this marriage.

Chemist Douglas Dean and parapsychologist Karlis Osis showed that different experimenters, carrying out the same experiment, got different results.[3] Psychologists Gertrude Schmeidler and Michaeleen Maher made videos of well-known researchers conducting experiments and then played them for students with the volume turned so low as to be inaudible. The students were asked to describe the researchers, assigning them words like "friendly," or "cold." Estimates were then made as to how experiments conducted by these researchers would turn out. Those with "cold" type responses were estimated to have respondents who produced lower scores; the converse was true for researchers described as "friendly." The actual results of the experiments were then compiled. Those with "cold" type adjectives did in fact have informants who scored lower.[4]

Psychologists Paula Hazelrigg and Cooper Harris, et al. examined "personality moderators of experimenter expectancy effects" and focused on five and looked at them from the perspective of both researcher and the participant. They reported, "Experimenters with stronger interpersonal control orientations, more positively evaluated interpersonal interaction styles, and greater ability to encode nonverbal messages are believed to be more likely to produce expectancy bias."[5] They also looked at subjects with greater need for social approval and greater non-verbal decoding ability, and hypothesized that such individuals would be more susceptible to bias.

They reported two "moderators" mattered: "the experimenter control orientation and subject need for social approval hypotheses. There was also evidence for a boomerang effect—subjects low in need for social approval gave ratings opposite to the experimenter's outcome expectancy. Finally, effects appeared stronger when positive expectancies were communicated than when expectancies were negative." [6,7]

In 1961, in a set of rooms in Linsly-Chittenden Hall on Yale's old campus, psychologist Stanley Milgram, began an experiment that has come to haunt all scholars studying how evil arises in seemingly cultured societies, and it has much to say about the power of beingness, both locally and non-locally as it expresses itself socially.

Prompted by his experience of the trial, a year earlier, of Holocaust war criminal Adolph Eichmann, and the banality of the man and his explanation for what he had done—I was following orders—Milgram decided to explore the question of a normal person's obedience to authority. In essence how we react to the beingness of an individual in an authoritarian mode.

His protocol was very simple. He put in a newspaper ad, offering participants $4.50 for an hour's participation in what was ostensibly a learning study. Using actors who posed as "learners" he had a stern authoritarian "experimenter" wearing a white lab coat ask "teachers" recruited through to the ad—who were the real focus of the study—to help the learners learn, by giving them a shock when they made a mistake. The experimenter explained to the teachers that they were to read word lists of coupled words, which the "learner" was to repeat back. When the learner made a mistake, it was explained they would get a shock. This was supposed to aid in memory retention. During the sessions the "teachers" had before them an impressive apparently "scientific" shock generator that had 30 switches each carefully marked and advancing from 14 to 450 volts. Each also had a label, they went from "slight shock" to "danger severe shock" to the last two which were simply marked "XXX."

To make sure the teachers understood the shocks, each was given a 45 volt jolt as a demonstration. The learner in the presence of the teacher was then escorted into another room, and strapped into a kind of stereotypical electric chair, all done to impress the teacher with the seriousness of the experiment. The teacher then returned and sat in front of the shock generator and the session began. The actor-learner deliberately made mistakes and with each one the increment of voltage went up 15 volts.

Before he had begun the experiment Milgram had "sought predictions about the outcome from various kinds of people— psychiatrists, college sophomores, middle-class adults, graduate students and faculty in the behavioral sciences. With remarkable similarity, they predicted that virtually all the subjects would refuse to obey the experimenter. The psychiatrist, specifically, predicted that most subjects would not go beyond 150 volts, when the victim makes his first explicit demand to be freed. They expected that only 4 percent would reach 300 volts, and that only a pathological fringe of about one in a thousand would administer the highest shock on the board."[8] These were, after all honest Americans.

What actually happened was rather different. As the learner's mistakes mounted, and the voltage increased, the learners were ostensibly (but not actually) shocked with increasing intensity. "At 75 volts, he grunts; at 120 volts, he complains loudly; at 150, he demands to be released from the experiment. As the voltage increases, his protests become more vehement and emotional. At 285 volts, his response can be described only as an agonized scream. Soon thereafter, he makes no sound at all."[9] When teachers quavered and asked whether the experiment should continue they were admonished by the experimenter to continue, and told the experimenter accepted full responsibility for whatever happened. Did they continue? Indeed, they did. Sixty five per cent of them went all the way to the lethal end. Not one teacher stopped before 300 volts. If you stuck your finger in a light socket you would experience 110 volts. It could kill you.

Milgram went on to try various scenarios. In one series at 150 volts, the actor learner would plead that the experiment should end. The experimenter would instruct the teacher to "go on." And so they did, at least 62.5 per cent of them. In another series he moved the sessions into an ordinary office room off of the Yale campus, and discovered in this less authoritarian setting on 47.5 per cent would go all the way to 450 volts. If the "experimenter" was not actually in the room with the teacher but gave instructions this dropped still further, by just by voice command 20.5 per cent of the teachers were still willing to continue.

In an article he wrote for *Harpers Magazine*, Milgram gave his own assessment of his study.

"The legal and philosophic aspects of obedience are of enormous import, but they say very little about how most people behave in concrete situations. I set up a simple experiment at Yale University to test how much pain an ordinary citizen would inflict on another person simply because he was ordered to by an experimental scientist. Stark authority was pitted against the subjects' strongest moral imperatives against hurting others, and, with the subjects' ears ringing with the screams of the victims, authority won more often than not. The extreme willingness of adults to go to almost any lengths on the command of an authority constitutes the chief finding of the study and the fact most urgently demanding explanation."[9]

Have we changed in the four decades since Milgram carried out his research? Sadly we have not, as Jerry M. Burger, a professor of psychology at Santa Clara University in California, discovered.[10] In 2006 using 70 paid adult volunteers recruited from ads in newspapers, and Craigslist, as well as flyers, Burger essentially replicated Milgram's work. Although, since it made people in the research community queasy, even in mime, to administer 450 volts, Burger's research capped out at 150 volts. Burger found that "70 percent of the participants had to be stopped from escalating shocks over 150 volts, despite hearing cries of protest and pain."[11]

Burger's view is "the conclusion is not: 'Gosh isn't this a horrible commentary on human nature,' or 'these people we so sadistic.'" Instead he felt, his work showed, "the opposite—that there are situational forces that have a much greater impact on our behavior than most people recognize." he said.

It is easy to see why Abu Ghraib happened.

Albert Speer, Hitler's favorite architect and, later his Minister of Armaments and Munitions, was considered a genius of organization, even by his enemies. The only member of Hitler's inner circle to plead guilty at the Nuremberg Trials after the war, he was imprisoned until 1966 in Spandau Prison. Interviewed after he had been released by Gitta Sereny he said, "I ask myself time and again how much of it was a kind of autosuggestion.... One thing is certain: everyone who worked closely with him for a long time was exceptionally dependent on him. However, powerful they were in their own domain, close to him they became small and timid."[12]

Goring supported Speer's point. He is reported to have told Finance Minister Hjalmar Schacht: "I try so hard, but every time I stand before the Führer, my heart drops into the seat of my pants."[13]

If we cannot measure beingness in any objective way, what

can we say about it? The individuals who seem to be the seed crystal around which the zeitgeist centers have a single-minded intentionality, a form of genius, whose intensity others find irresistible. The pattern is the same for good or ill, and consistent with the patterns of other more conventionally recognized genius events, like symphonies or laws of physics. Once again, there is a leap into the unknown. The communist vision of Stalin and the race based national socialism of Hitler, took their countries and the world through changes that were violent breaks with the past, leaps into the unknown similar in essence, but far more powerful than any genius effect in science or the arts. Drawn to the social realm by the seductive temptation of power, dark geniuses live out the relationship between their numinous beingness, and its social context, and societies tremble.

Historians have debated for centuries what forces produce what they call "The Great Man," or "The Man on Horseback," leaders like Napoleon who arise from the mass, and with astonishing rapidity achieve positions of unchallenged power. How does a misfit like Hitler become the leader of one of the great European peoples at a time of high civilization? The answer may be found in something Carl Jung said: to appreciate how Hitler came to power it was necessary to realize that "Hitler did not lead the German people, Hitler was the German people."[14] He was the personification of a popular critical consensus, as Speer agreed. "It remains a mystery," he said, "but the fact is that it is impossible to explain Germany before 1933, and from 1933 to 1945, without Hitler. He was the center of it all and always remained the center."[15]

At the time Jung made this statement the full import of what he meant could not be appreciated, because it was thought that most Germans did not really know about the "The Final Solution." Recent research flatly contradicts that assumption and supports Jung. Historian Robert Gellately: "The mass of ordinary Germans did know about the evolving terror of Hitler's

Holocaust. They knew concentration camps were full of Jewish people who were stigmatised as sub-human and race-defilers. They knew that these, like other groups and minorities, were being killed out of hand.

"They knew that Adolf Hitler had repeatedly forecast the extermination of every Jew on German soil. They knew these details because they had read about them. They knew because the camps and the measures which led up to them had been prominently and proudly reported step by step in thousands of officially-inspired German media articles and posters."[16] As a peculiarly sensitive resonator, at that moment in history, Hitler personified and gave voice to the dark pool of anger and humiliation felt by that portion of the human race self-defined as German. This is the power of dark genius, and the results that flow from the linkage, both local and nonlocal, when collective cultural beingness springs from the shadow.

It matters that we understand, far better than we do, how these linkages occur, and how to neutralize or enhance them. And it may surprise you to learn that we have gained some insights there as well.

We have learned, for instance, that one aspect of the individual mind-body linkage is that "a happy heart just might be a healthier one."[17]

Between 2002 and 2004, Andrew Steptoe, a physician at University College London led a team that studied whether "positive affective states are associated with favorable health outcomes. A population of 2,873 healthy British men and women between the ages of 50 and 74 participated. During the course of a single day six samples of saliva were collected from each of these individuals and analysed for their cortisol levels and the inflammatory markers C-reactive protein and interleukin-6. After each collection the men and women were asked to record their emotional state at that time—the extent to which they felt "happy, excited or content."

The study concluded, "Salivary cortisol averaged over the day was inversely associated with positive affect after controlling for age, gender, income, ethnicity, body mass index, waist/hip ratio, smoking, paid employment, time of waking in the morning, and depression (p = 0.003). There was no association with cortisol responses to waking. The adjusted odds of C-reactive protein >/=3.00 mg/liter was 1.89 (95% confidence interval: 1.08, 3.31) in low- compared with high-positive-affect women, and plasma interleukin-6 was also inversely related to positive affect in women (p = 0.016). Neither inflammatory marker was related to positive affect in men. These results confirm findings from smaller studies relating cortisol with positive affect while suggesting that in women, positive affect is associated with reduced levels of inflammatory markers."[18]

In an interview Steptoe was asked what his findings suggested. He replied, "These findings suggest another biological process linking happiness with reduced biological vulnerability."[17]

When he was asked, "But if happier people are healthier people, the more difficult question remains: How do you become happier?" he answered, "What we do know is that people's mood states are not just a matter of heredity, but depend on our social relationships and fulfillment in life.

"We need to help people to recognize the things that make them feel good and truly satisfied with their lives, so that they spend more time doing these things."[17]

In Buddhism, there are four "immeasurables" which must be understood and integrated into one's being for true happiness and spiritual growth to occur: Love, Compassion, Joy and Equanimity. To a sincere Buddhist the definition of love is wanting others to be happy.

In Matthew 22:37-40, Jesus makes essentially the same statement

"You shall love the Lord your God with all your heart, and

with all your soul, and with all your mind. This is the great and foremost commandment. And a second is like it, You shall love your neighbor as yourself. On these two commandments depend the whole Law and the Prophets."

These sentiments are echoed in most of the other great spiritual traditions. The ethnohistorical record is very clear about linking happiness, wellbeing, and love, and all these paths to self-awareness, enlightenment if you will, acknowledge both the local and non-local aspects of these processes.

So let's take those research findings, and these great traditions and see what this looks like when it is extended to the social domain.

As Rob Stein wrote in the Washington Post, "Happiness is contagious, spreading among friends, neighbors, siblings and spouses like the flu, according to a large study that for the first time shows how emotion can ripple through clusters of people who may not even know each other."[19]

"You would think that your emotional state would depend on your own choices and actions and experience," said Harvard medical sociologist Nicholas A. Christakis, coauthor of the BMJ paper presenting the research.[16] It does not. Rather, as the paper concludes, "People's happiness depends on the happiness of others with whom they are connected. This provides further justification for seeing happiness, like health, as a collective phenomenon."[20]

This conclusion is based on studying 4739 individuals for two decades, from 1983 until 2003. And its conclusions go well beyond generalities.

The study reports, "Longitudinal statistical models suggest that clusters of happiness result from the spread of happiness and not just a tendency for people to associate with similar individuals. A friend who lives within a mile (about 1.6 km) and who becomes happy increases the probability that a person is happy by 25% (95% confidence interval 1% to 57%). Similar effects are seen in coresident spouses (8%, 0.2% to 16%), siblings who live within a mile (14%, 1% to 28%), and next door neighbors (34%, 7% to 70%). Effects are not seen between coworkers."

Equally as important, the paper notes, "The (happiness) effect decays with time and with geographical separation."[17]

Like so many things in our society, when we let data drive policy, not ideology, or bias, we discover we know more than we thought we did. We know expectant mothers need sufficient nutrition, particularly during the 19th and 23rd weeks of pregnancy, so that the brain of the child they are bearing will develop properly. If it doesn't we know that that child will be a maimed human being all their lives. We know that early childhood development is critical if we want our children to grow to be productive, functional, socialized adults. We know that happy people are healthier, that happiness spreads, and that happy people make healthier choices that produce a healthier happier society.

We know a lot of things about the mind-body connection, but we don't seem to know how to muster the will to put what we know in action. And we don't like to look at, and take responsibility for, what happens when we don't act on what we know, and the shadow emerges.

Stanley Milgram saw the essence of the problem clearly, "ordinary people, simply doing their jobs, and without any particular hostility on their part, can become agents in a terribly destructive process. Moreover, even when the destructive effects of their work become patently clear, and they are asked to carry out actions incompatible with fundamental standards of morality, relatively few people have the resources needed to resist authority."[19]

It's time to change this.

- *Stephan Schwartz - remote viewer, founder Schwartz Report, author Opening To The Infinite*

There is no shame in facing difficult times. But there *is* shame in taking advantage of those facing difficult times.
    - *Molly Secours - writer, filmmaker, speaker, activist*

Every so often, the question arises: what would a more perfect world look like to me? There are many ways to answer this question. On a more integrated and pragmatic level, I would have to say that in this world, animals are no longer killed for food, but are treated with love and respect. That rivers are pristine and flow freely into healthy oceans. That there is a deep respect for our planet—for the trees, the air, the soil, and a universal benevolence for all beings, no matter their shape, color, size, etc. In this world, there is a tremendous appreciation and regard for Beauty as one of the highest laws of the land—a virtue unspoken and held dearly and inseparably—ingrained deeply into the core of our beings. This Beauty would express itself in every aspect—music, architecture, landscaping, art, everything. A place where Love overflows and where communication is deep, real, and seamless. In this world, we take care of one another as an expansive sense of One Self.

I could take this vision even further and imagine travel between different planets, all designed around different manifestations of Beauty.

Though I believe sincerely in the world I've described, I'd be lying if I said that this was my real answer. Because when that question arises, the answer that consistently comes to mind is something altogether different. What comes to mind is simply a state of Magnificent Bliss or Ecstasy so profound that it literally BLOWS THE MIND. And with no mind, there can be no wish for pristine rivers, care for one another, nor rainbows. In the world I imagine, there is no longer a world—only a state of Perfectly Divine, Eternal, Glorious and Supreme Nirvana. :)
    - *John Silliphant - artist, servant, lover of life, founder Seva Café,*

India

My vision of an idealized world is one which all organisms are respected as the evolutionary successes of our times. If there was the United Organism of Organisms—UOO (pronounced Uh-Oh) and each organism had a vote—would we be voted on the planet or off the planet? I believe the vote is being tallied now.

If ecosystems continue to decline, species diversity will plummet, with humans not only being the primary cause, but one of the victims. Investing and respecting biodiversity provides us with a natural form of resilience to catastrophia, enabling adaptation to ever-changing circumstances. Life support systems are based on interrelating bio-networks, with fungal mycelium joining them. Fungal networks in the form of mycelia are the essential fabric for creating soils, budgeting nutrients, and influencing the equilibrium of populations. Mycelium offers powerful solutions to critical issues—from hunger, pollution, water purification, carbon sequestration, biofuel production, disease control and habitat sustainability.

By respecting and supporting nature, we help the organisms upon which we and our descendants all depend.

We need to develop language skills to communicate with other biological residents—so they can advise us with their collective evolutionary wisdom.

Honoring Nature is not only a daily spiritual practice—it is an act of survival. We are in control of our own future. We must take a thousand-year view of our actions—to do otherwise is to commit ecological suicide.

- Paul Stamets - mycologist, speaker, author Mycelium Running: How Mushrooms Can Help Save The World

I want us to build a civilization that will allow humans to thrive in an endless variety of ways forever.
- *Alex Steffen - co-founder and executive editor Worldchanging*

Half the vehicles in the U.S. are powered by hydrogen or biofuels (gasoline and diesel made from crops or waste materials) and California becomes the first state to ban the sale of any new vehicle that burns petroleum. China, India, and several other emerging economies have leap-frogged into a biofuels and hydrogen economy, much as nations have who jumped right to cell phones instead of first building massive hard-wire communications systems. As a result three quarters of the vehicles in those nations are clean, efficient, and running on domestic energy.

American automakers are in solid fiscal health. Ford burst into the future first with internal combustion hybrid hydrogen cars, making them the market leader in the eyes of consumers. Ford's use of hydrogen fuel in familiar automotive engines pays off around the world, as other nations are quick to embrace the alternative to scarce, expensive, polluting oil. GM took a few years longer, but grabbed market share with high-tech products using fuel cells and drive-by-wire technology. Both companies also built millions of vehicles in the past twenty years that run on batteries, natural gas, and biofuels as a transition to hydrogen-powered vehicles. Foreign automakers are still a dominant force though, offering consumers home hydrogen and natural gas fueling appliances along with their cars, making a growing number of consumers truly energy independent.

Since the U.S. invasion of Iraq in 2003, no further wars were fought over oil, saving thousands of lives and billions of dollars. As a result of these changes, the U.S. economy is strong, the deficit erased, few terrorist actions have taken place, and the global fleet of oil tankers are systematically being converted to move scare supplies of fresh water around the globe. Although these tankers still routinely leak, because it's only water it no longer matters. The sky is bluer again and the water is cleaner, with the end of human-made pollution from petroleum products not many years in the future.

- Terry Tamminen - a vision for the year 2025 from his book, Lives Per Gallon: The True Cost Of Our Oil Addiction

A world I would dream of would be a world of **abundance**.

Abundance without guilt: There is plenty, of everything, for everyone.

Abundance without waste: biological and technical materials flow through their various cycles and are re-directed to their maximum social, economic and creative profit. Abundance without destruction: where all industrial and productive processes are at harmony with their local environments and not only respect but also promote natural diversity and systemic health.

A world I would dream of would be a world of **variety**. A world of diversity—full of originality.

A world immensely and intricately interesting.

A world you could travel through and never cease to be amazed by the richness and peculiarity of local craft and nature, surrounded by ever newer colors, tastes, languages and designs.

This world I would dream of would be a world of **community**: a world of caring for each other, of exchanging gifts, sharing talents and confronting opinions.

A world of nourishment and togetherness, but with much room for singularity.

A world where every human being would be not only allowed but also encouraged to express themselves critically and creatively, and to live according to their personal values and true desires.

A world I would dream of would be a world of **meaning**. I can only wonder... What would it be like, to live in a world where every object and every action was soulful and cultivated and *meaningful*?

Any world I could dream of would be a world founded on **Love**, and filled with appreciation for life. **Life**: within and without, **life**: human, animal, vegetable or ethereal... **life**: sacred, beautiful and overwhelming.

A world I could dream of would be a world of **Joy**, full of dance and celebration.

In this world I could dream of there would also be **Death**, and pain—for who am I to extricate those from our experience, even in dreams? Pain and death must remain... but our way of relating to them would be entirely different, and altogether wiser, so our actions needn't be motivated by so much suffering or fear.

This world I can dream of would be a world of **imagination**, where wild and mythical creatures could roam free. A world that is Human, in what Human does best: producing new **forms**, new **stories**, new **metaphors**, new **understandings**, new **shapes**, new **rhythms**, and new **realities**.

A world I would dream of would be a world of **Art** and creativity.

I suspect that a world I could dream of already exists in some level... intricate patterns, a web of lives related. There are worlds of incredible beauty and delicacy in our planet... even though most of those are currently threatened by forces that thrive on homogeneity, waste, meaninglessness, and power over others. There are, however, a myriad of possibilities of resistance (or re-existence?), that I dare say are in themselves more diverse, seasoned and imaginative than they ever were. We are the recipients and co-creators of an amazing legacy of art and knowledge. What a privileged time to be alive, when we are so forcefully called upon to discover more benign or fruitful ways of relating to ourselves, to each other, and to our planet.

A world we could dream of exists, around and within us, as a finer, subtler, and more luminous possibility, that silently but surely claims for our dedication.

- *Carla Tennenbaum - artist, artisan, designer, history graduate, Brazil*

Honoring our Differences and Building a Positive World for the Children of Humanity

The foundation for the future of humanity is in our children. In Lakota thought and philosophy it is said that our children are "Wakanyeja" (sacred beings or sacred gift) meaning children are the closest human beings to the spiritual world.

We also share a simple belief as Lakota people that "We are not human beings on a spiritual journey but rather spirits on a human journey" our purpose on this earth is to fully live out our human experience. My personal interpretation of these traditional Lakota teachings is that it is our duty to the next generation of children to co-create a world that will be safe, a world of equality and justice. Not the justice of "an eye for an eye or a tooth for a tooth" but a world where we focus on our commonalities as human beings rather than our differences.

Thus said it's important that we honor our differences because as children of humanity we are made up diverse cultures, histories and spiritual beliefs. Being diverse is what defines us as humanity, owning this diversity is what the foundation for the future should be built upon.

Thus far in the history of the world and in the evolution of humanity we have built systems of oppression where power and privilege prevail. These systems have divided the people of this world. They have been the foundation of injustices, war, greed and violence. Leaving our children a world with little hope and endless despair. The knowledge meant of these systems of oppression is our first step in creating a world of peace and equality.

The strategy that we should collectively work towards as human beings is using the existing systems to change where power and privilege comes from. Once we have recognized our own individual powers and privileges then we can use them to create unity amongst all of humanity.

The vision I hold in my heart is a world where every innocent sacred child has equal access to food, shelter, safety and genuine love. When a child has basic necessities in life then hope can be instilled in them. It will take a generation of children that feel safe, that have hope, that don't carry fear in their hearts but love and compassion.

With love and compassion for humanity and all living things we will prosper in this world and will accomplish many things for our people and for this world. Getting the most out of our human experience will only insure that we will continue this work once our time on this earth is complete. We will always work for beauty, equality and love for the next generation weather we are still in human or spirit form. It is a continuation of these beliefs that will see a world of beauty, love and hope. We owe it to ourselves, to our unborn children and to all living things. It is not essential that everybody share these beliefs immediately, but that humanity makes a conscious effort to work towards them.

- Nick Tilsen - community organizer, executive director Thunder Valley Community Development Corporation

Whose Dream World?

A million years ago our biological ancestors, on the plains of northern Africa, lived a stable and enduring life, with persons, families and tiny communities succeeding each other for thousands and thousands of generations. We don't know what they were like, but they had a continuing relationship with the physical and biological world upon which they depended and of which they were a part. They were around for a very, very long time. One thing we do know: they had babies, and enough of their babies had babies to send their genes into the future year after year, millennium after millennium. To us.

What was their dream world?

Over a long time, perhaps three hundred thousand years, small groups of these people began to travel north, adapting to new ecosystems. They were able to adjust to the cold and the new life forms they encountered. We don't know why they did this, although it was probably the most important process in all of human time. Their numbers began to grow very slowly, as they did in Africa. They evolved, and their descendants changed color, grew larger and smaller. There were surely other changes, of which we know little or nothing. Most of all, they had babies, and their babies had babies, and they sent their genes into the future. To us.

What was their dream world?

For reasons we don't understand, although genetic mutations may have played a part, about ten thousand years ago some of our ancestors quite suddenly increased their control over plants and animals, inventing ways to grow more food and defend themselves against disease and predation. Their babies had babies, but now many more of them survived. In a blink of an eye human population began to grow rapidly. Nothing would be the same after this, not for us nor for all the life forms on earth.

Did they invent a new dream world?

Farms and empires arose. People clustered into cities, harnessing new sources of energy. They overcame disease, starvation, even a tendency (rare in most other organisms) to kill their own kind, until they covered the earth with themselves—us. We will soon have a human being for every acre of arable land on the entire planet. We are everywhere. Natural selection has continued, but to it we have added survival and reproduction managed by human choice. Some of us now have fewer babies, others have more babies. The ones who have more babies, and whose babies survive to have more babies, dominate the genes we send into the future. To them.

The world of ideas—the noosphere—began to grow rapidly as humans clustered, communicated, and used leisure time to ponder the world and themselves. Ideas began to have babies, and their babies had babies, evolving in parallel to the humans inside of whose heads (and machines) the ideas lived and evolved. Natural selection continued to influence the biological changes in human populations. But memetic selection became more dramatic and important as the noosphere itself grew even more quickly.

Can we have a dream world?

This won't stop. The only way to think about the future is to understand that change is always underway. The evolutionary crystal ball is foggy and unclear, but it is the only one of any importance. No dream world that imagines a steady state of any kind will be anything but a temporary concept, valid for only the tiniest moment of time. By nature, we destabilize.

And the pace of change is accelerating as the taking of the earth becomes complete. We know exponential growth cannot continue. We know, too, that we are already approaching the top of the s-shaped curve in the growth of almost everything related to human demographics and the resources we rely upon. We cannot forever have increases in population, resource extraction, biosphere depletion and ecosystem contamination.

How this stabilization plays out is the most important question and problem for the dreamers of our time and, probably, future times. No dreamer can plausibly imagine that the growth we have experienced for ten thousand years will continue, and no dream can fail to address the forces that have driven us up the curve. It is true that ideas, and the technology built upon these ideas, have made it possible for some of us to slow this growth even in the face of plenty. Put differently, memetic evolution has begun to interact powerfully with biological evolution, raising at least the possibility that dreamers can imagine a world in which exponential growth can be stopped by means other than food shortage, predation and self-destruction. In 500 years we may have no Japanese at all, or even Italians. Yet we may have a world made up of 20 billion descendants of those, mostly in the poor countries of the world, whose babies do have more babies.

But can this transition be managed by humans as we are? Growing scarcities and the human ability to hate and kill other humans, along with our ability to convince ourselves that a diety of some form condones and even promotes such behavior, may create such conflict that the planet will be overcome with warfare and human self-destruction. This is the ghost that haunts all of us who worry seriously about the future. It is the end of dreams. It may be that these predispositions, clearly genetic in nature, contributed to survival a million years ago—unless we acquired them more recently. But not anymore. Anyone tracking the emergence of nuclear warfare capabilities is aware that modern political history is a chronicle of relentlessly increasing jeopardy—to cite but one of the threats we face.

And will we, as we are, be part of the dream world?

So, what is my dream world? Can it be different than the dream world of earlier human times? We have intimations of what life was like for so many hundreds of thousands of years drawn from the lives of the social isolates we have studied in Africa (e.g. the Khoisan) and elsewhere who (until recently) seem to have maintained the life of our ancient ancestors? My greatest fear is that that is the only realistic dream world for us, but one that we can not imagine recreating because we are so many. Or can we?

In sum, the most important obstacle in setting forth a plausible dream world is the genetically imbedded attributes of human "nature" that carry over from the times in which we lived in tiny isolated communities on the African plains. It is the unavoidable litmus test of any vision of the future that it be compatible with human genetic makeup as we know it. Or—and this is the big one—the vision must posit a fundamental change in our biological character such that the babies that have more babies are genetically better than we are at loving, caring, and respecting life, and are less inclined to follow to others who seek welfare for themselves by promoting hatred.

If we must live with ourselves, genetically unchanged, will our inventions—the products of new ideas and technologies— create new ways in which we can coexist under conditions of growing scarcity and inequality, despite these traits? If so, memetic evolution may in then become the most important in the transition of our earth, dominating (and, ultimately, perhaps, guiding) biological evolution in the shaping of the future. If so, how will it come about? There is no evidence yet that social and cultural constraints have been effective in achieving this. This does not mean it is impossible. But what it does mean is that we must invent institutions and social constraints that are new and powerful, and lasting and accepted (or imposed)—very, very quickly. These will be the most important part of the dream world, without a doubt. Give me no dreams that don't explain quite clearly how we will constrain our destructive tendencies under conditions of scarcity—we have thousands of years of failures to draw upon for lessons. And give me no dreams that posit changes in human genetic characteristics but do not tell us how we get to those changes.

In the long term, we will not be what we are now. If we survive, we will evolve, as will our ideas. It is certain, then, that there should be no single dream world, but dream worlds that fit the time and the products of genetic and memetic evolution. Should we suggest a dream world for people who will not be like us, but will be biologically different and whose ideas will have evolved rapidly? Will memetic evolution and artificial intelligence produce other beings—biological and made of electrons—with physical and ethical claims to life, respect, and a dream world of their own?

Here is my dream.

My ideal dream world is one in which, in a thousand years and on into the far distant future, the inheritors of our genes (and the new genes that will join or replace the old ones), and the new creatures that arise from our ideas, may have babies, who have babies, who are themselves able and eager to ask what their dream world might be.

- Frank Tugwell - president and chief executive officer Winrock International (nonprofit global development organization)

Oneness and Unity should not only be viewed as concepts and ideals to strive towards, but can and should be lived daily through our actions. Only then will we truly embody our full potential and create a more just and sustainable world.

- Emmanuel Vaughan-Lee - founder and director Global Oneness Project

Living As Self-Conscious, Self-Learning Souls

I believe the universe is intrinsically conscious throughout its multiple dimensions, destined to explore its potential within and beyond space and time through all its aspects and living species. The consciousness that animates all life forms is transcendent and seeks full self-realization through its cycles of learning, rest and reflection, and new levels of creativity. When humans recognize this, the world I dream of will have become manifest. Where do the processes studied in quantum physics, evolutionary biology, genetics, neuroscience and consciousness studies merge? I suggest that occurs in study of the phenomenon of reincarnation. This is where "life and death," "mind and matter," "past and present," "potential and manifest" all merge in the spiral of creation's conscious evolution.

My book *The Soul Genome: Science and Reincarnation* reports on an experiment to evaluate verifiable evidence related to an integral model of the apparent natural process of reincarnation. *In this book, soul or psychoplasm means a genome-like, energetic and information biofield that embodies a single being's knowledge, feelings, and behavior patterns that transcend space-time.* If validated, the psychoplasm as a concept has the potential to reconcile the physical and psychical dimensions just as Einstein's concept of special relativity appeared to reconcile Newton's law of motion with the electromagnetic field.

www.reincarnationexperiment.org

You may be surprised to learn that many verified life histories cannot be as logically explained by other theories as they can by a 'general reincarnation hypothesis.' You may also be amazed to know that if it is real for people like the Dalai Lama, it is equally likely that you and all other humans are reincarnations of people who have lived before. Simply giving consideration to the possibility of reincarnation may change the way you think about all aspects of human behavior.

To contemplate that most of what you are today might have come from knowledge and experience gained in many lifetimes may shock you. Consider that whom you marry, or not, what you study in school, where you live and work, how you spend your free time, who your friends are, and what you feel about it may reflect the influence of events in centuries past. What difference would it make (in your life) if you learned that how you interpret global, national, neighborhood, and family affairs may be based on more than you learned since birth?

Much thought-provoking evidence suggests that your physical appearance, the way you think, how you react emotionally to events, the way you interact with other people, and the creative activities and vocations you choose may be predisposed by the experiences of one or more humans who lived in the past. Even if you don't know who they were, you may find what appears to be their 'soulprints' in the person you are today and the manner in which you live.

Why do I suggest these radical possibilities? The facts are that credible researchers have thousands of cases where people recall or intuitively act on knowledge and traits that seem to come directly from the private lives of individuals who lived before they were born. When other hypotheses attempt to explain this irrefutable evidence, I believe they cannot measure up to some as-yet-unknown form of reincarnation. By "reincarnation" I mean the linear "carry-forward" of all this inherited data from lifetime to lifetime in a kind of a nonmaterial soul.

Though opinions about what it means may differ widely, the corpus of evidence stands on its own. For those whose worldview depends on rationality, the compilation of correspondences— links between the past and the present—points to a "genome of the soul." If the existence of a mechanism along the lines of the soul genome is sustained by more research and experimentation, the study of human consciousness may have fully entered the quantum era.

While I cannot yet say how, I believe the evidence suggests that—in some form or the other—the learning from previous lives provide each of us with an innate legacy to build upon. It does not matter who or what we might have been in a previous life. We cannot change that. What really matters is to consciously develop in this world the legacy each of us would like for his or her soul genome to energetically transfer to the next generation.

- *Paul Von Ward - interdisciplinary cosmologist, author The Soul Genome: Science and Reincarnation*

The world I see in my dreams.

This is a home where everybody, young and old, women, men and children, leaders and common men all live satisfied, with clean water, sufficient food, clean and renewable energy in plenty and the environment taken care of with regard to the coming generation yet to be born. This is the world I need and I dream of everyday.

Currently, in the underdeveloped countries like Kenya where I live, children go hungry without food, prices of essential commodities goes up every day and over 70 % of Kenyans cannot afford Unga (Maize flour) which is our staple food in Kenya. Over 82% of the country's population has no access to energy. Use of undesirable farming practices has created change in climate, produce has been lost in floods and droughts, people go hungry and hunger is already taking a toll on this population since people succumb to hunger. The National grid only connects 18% of Kenyan and energy sources that are currently used destroy the environment every time by emitting a lot of CO_2 to the atmosphere. Farming practices, like the use of chemical fertilizers, harm the environment more and depletes the soil with time. The ruling elite do not seem to look at the poor. These are all problems.

I am looking for a country which inspires everybody to realize his/her own potential, a world free of inequalities, and a world that can feed children, women and the most vulnerable. A world where energy supply is locally originated, renewable and clean. Food production and society development done by all members. Where clean water availability is for all and people look forward to saving their environment.

Remember "free is the sun." With connecting everybody to

this natural grid and using locally available resources to get energy, the world will be able to purify water, meaning clean water to cook, produce sufficient food, and light their houses. Dependence on some part of the world with a fossil fuel that destroys the environment will be over.

This is self sufficiency and that is my dream and my drive.

- Zablon Wagalla - founder Trees For Clean Energy Network, Kenya

Homeward Bound

What a dangerous and exciting raft ride we're on! To finesse these rapids of constant, accelerating change, we must continuously improvise new ways of life, because genetic change is far too slow. "Protect your territory," say our genes. "But our territory is the Earth, we see that now," our expanding paradigm replies. "Store material goods in case of drought and infestation," instruct our genes, but our culture-mind knows that some store far too much. "Win the respect and trust of your community," say our genes, but technologic takes a devious, irrelevant shortcut: big houses and fast cars rather than generous lives.

In the only kind of future that can work, nature and culture will fit together like hand and glove. We'll have loftier, more humane goals and more satisfying ways of meeting them. "Success" will always be the prize, but its definition will be radically different: health and wellness rather than wealth and "hellness." By slowing down to the speed of life, humanity can still save the pieces, just in time to regain our balance. Because of resource shortages; a reduced capacity of the environment to clean up after us; an epidemic of debt and doubt; and a deep-seated instinct for ecological stability, we'll invent a lifestyle that is materially leaner but culturally richer, as many civilizations have before us.

The secret of success has never really been a secret; it's in plain sight: moderation, an elegant middle way of life. We'll get more value from less stuff and better stuff by tapping into riches like quality, nature-based products; brilliant design and redesign of cities and towns; cultural and aesthetic greatness; curiosity and fascination about how nature really works; cooperation with co-workers and neighbors; and generosity, just because it feels right. Like former addicts who walk victoriously away from the cliff, we'll choose to experience and embrace life rather than try to dominate it.

Although the pace and density of our world are often frightening and confusing, we are very certain about the need for a new direction: we want more meaning and purpose in our lives; and we want to use logic that's based on reality rather than obsolete rules and legends. We've always loved the idea of rising to the occasion, of being heroes in the last minutes of a game. We've practiced heroism for many thousand years in our myths and scriptures. We're ready, in these most critical times, to continue the transition—individually and culturally—from the "love of consumption" to the "love of life."

- David Wann - father, gardener, filmmaker, futurist, author Simple Prosperity: Finding Real Wealth in a Sustainable Lifestyle

I will consider our world to have progressed when I can no longer walk or drive into a neighborhood and know, even without seeing a single person on the street, or in their yard, or on their stoop, the race of those who call the community home. When I cannot tell, by merely observing the physical condition of the surroundings, the race or ethnic background of those who live there, this will suggest that the institutionalization of white supremacy—and the systemic praxis that keeps it in place—has either ended or is well on its way out as a key organizing principle of society, whether in the United States or globally.

- Tim Wise - writer, speaker, anti-racist activist

The world as I see it is perfect just as it is. It has always been perfect. We who tend to take action in the name of the world or planet are just fooling ourselves if we believe that our actions will change the world.

Our actions must be for ourselves. It is we who need to change and learn to become aware of the world's perfection. It is we who need to learn more and see that our actions can either harm ourselves or benefit ourselves. The world doesn't really care one way or the other. We do. Time to get wise.

- *Fred Alan Wolf, Ph.D. - physicist, lecturer, author The Yoga of Time Travel: How the Mind Can Defeat Time*

I am a pragmatist who focuses on the here and now and respects the mystery of a future driven by collective free will.

- *Machaelle Small Wright - author, researcher Perelandra, Center for Nature Research*

I hope there will be a world where all human beings can live in harmony with each other, and our time, energy and resources are not being put into international counterwork but into the things that have advantages to all human beings, such as scientific research, the work of art or welfare for the poor.

- *Quanzhi Ye - undergraduate student, discoverer of Comet Lulin*

A culture guided by an unwavering principle of justice for *all* living things. A culture that wittily embraces the subversive pleasure of critical, independent thought. A culture with far more questions than answers...and all those answers remain permanently open to debate (and maybe even laughter).

- *Mickey Z. - author No Innocent Bystanders: Riding Shotgun in the Land of Denial*

I dream of a world in which my job is not necessary. A world in which my lens captures the red of sunsets and not the red of blood.

I dream of a world that understands that war creates enemies, not eliminates them. A world in which soldiers are never asked to do what they are trained to. A world in which the loss of human life comes as a last resort.

I dream of a world in which the most powerful nations lead by example and not by intimidation. A world in which leaders lead with grace, intelligence and forgiveness: not ego, greed and vengeance.

I dream of a world in which education is paramount and is held as the most priceless commodity. A world where the educated are able to cure illness, stop hatred and heal a planet that has been injured by years of indifference.

I dream of a world in which the gap between rich and poor is measured in centimeters and not kilometers. A world in which we do not turn our backs on our neighbors and they in turn do not turn their backs on us.

I dream of a world in which art and beauty are of greater value than profit. A world which measures achievement in numbers of friends or experiences and not numbers of possessions.

I dream of a world that is not impossible to obtain, but one that is merely a few decisions away from the one in which we currently live.

I dream, and yet I wake up every day and work toward that dream.

- *Zoriah - photojournalist, war photographer*

Biographies

Adisa, Opal Palmer

Writer, performer, photographer and storyteller, hails from Jamaica, which she deems as the perfect, physical world; however, as a society it, Jamaica, needs to return to a harmonious unity with nature and all people. Her latest collection is *I Name Me Name*, poems and stories that draw on historical and biographical information. Visit her website:

www.opalwriters.com

Aggrey, Isaac

He holds a City & Guilds United Kingdom qualification in General Mining Engineering obtained from the University of Science and Technology Ghana, and has 6 years experience in Training and Coaching relating to businesses.

Isaac developed his social development skills when he opted to teach science and mathematics in a remote rural school during his national service.

He had most of his experience from SIFE, BMF and CENCOMM where he had the responsibility to provide entrepreneurship, leadership and basic supervisory skills respectively.

Isaac has given students and community members an opportunity to grow and make a difference in the environment in which they live. He has also set a pace for young disadvantaged individuals to converge to share their innovative ideas and accomplishments with top business leaders of today to foster a better future for all.

His expertise and mentorship has empowered young adult women, unemployed youth and graduates which has propelled them to far-reaching results thereby creating sustainable enterprises within marginalized communities in South Africa.

Isaac has answered the call to support youth entrepreneurship in South Africa and has been honored with prestigious awards.

He has a passion, strong ethical values and a sense of community development in South Africa and has participated in different forums that seek to alleviate poverty and unemployment. His inspiration lies in helping others to succeed.

As the demands of the global economy place increased pressure on societies to become self-sufficient, the importance of providing opportunities to those who lack the necessary education and financial resources has become increasingly apparent. The emotional and material support generated by projects such as those initiated by Isaac is integral to promoting efficient markets and thus helping to alleviate poverty.

Well-known for the numerous roles he plays in youth entrepreneurship, Isaac has pledged his support in empowering and developing young Managers and Leaders in institutions.

The role entrepreneurship plays in the growth of a developing country, such as South Africa, is undeniable. Through the success of his entrepreneurial endeavors, Isaac has recognized the amenability of the South African entrepreneurship and is ready to associate himself with all those willing to embark on entrepreneurial ventures in marginalized communities.

Isaac is determined to further open the doors for those in need to find ways to help themselves and sees the "teach me how to fish" method of disseminating information as key in countries such as South Africa where resources are often limited.

Isaac believes promoting gender equality and empowering women is the only powerful weapon to address unemployment, poverty alleviation, reduction of crime, restoring the moral fabric and rebuilding of family lives in the long run.

Women Business Center -

www.womenbizcenter.wordpress.com

Agnivesh, Swami

This unusual swami (religious teacher) has been consistently doing battles on behalf of the poor, the weak and the defenseless of India. Agnivesh's campaigns have led him to *fight alcoholism, female foeticide, bonded labour, child labour as well as struggle for the emancipation of women.*

He looks like a sadhu (holy man), talks like a politician and — most importantly — voices the case of the underprivileged millions of India. Swami Agnivesh is a strange man by all counts. He puzzles and provokes at once, and is loved by the masses.

Unlike the politicians who mouth religion between the teeth of communalism, Agnivesh participates in politics as an outworking of his spirituality. He bridges politics and religion with the plank of social justice. In a way parallel to the liberation theologians of Latin America, the swami has been waging war relentlessly on behalf of the poor, the weak and the defenseless of India.

He preaches. But preaches only what he practices. His words catch fire in the heat of his involvement imprinted with the zeal of compassion. He leads and inspires. His date with the oppressed and passion for social justice are as old as his political career which goes back many years to his entry into the Haryana Assembly in 1977.

'My saffron garb,' you will hear Swamiji say, 'is my uniform for socio-spiritual action, a call to battle on behalf of the oppressed.' Saffron is the colour of sacrifice, commitment and purity and he believes it helps him in his work of love, truth, compassion and justice. He says with utmost realism: "If my clothes come in the way of this, I won't mind renouncing them. It matters little if you call me "Swami Agnivesh" or simply "Agnivesh". All that matters is that the fire inside of me, the presence of the divine in the inner temple of my being, should continue to blaze till the end.'

He narrates a tale of how during a visit to the island of Mindanao in the Philippines to be with the rebels encamped there, he was told that his saffron garb would make him highly conspicuous. 'Then, I quickly switched over to jeans and a T-shirt,' he says.

Sixty-year-old Agnivesh is easily the most distinguished leader of the Arya Samaj. Last year, he was appointed the Chairperson of the UN Trust Fund on Contemporary Forms of Slavery. He is better known across India for his campaigns against bonded labour, and is founder-head of the Bandhu Mukti Morcha (Bonded Labour Liberation Front). Recently, he has been appointed the President of the World Council of Arya Samaj (Sarvadeshik Arya Pratinidhi Sabha).

So far, his campaigns have led him to *fight against alcoholism, female foeticide, bonded labour, child labour, and for the emancipation of women.* His current 'mission' includes fighting the *consumer culture and the Western model of development in India, opposing Western cultural imperialism, and battling casteism, obscurantism and communalism.* www.swamiagnivesh.com

Allan, Sterling D.

Sterling is the primary driving force behind PESWiki.com, NewEnergyCongress.org, FreeEnergyNews.com, PESN.com, and PureEnergySystems.com, which have been growing consis-tently, with increasing team participation.

PES, which stands for "Pure Energy Systems", is a news and directory service whose mission is to find and facilitate the best renewable energy technologies. It is aided by the New Energy Congress, which is an association of energy professionals from around the world who review the most promising claims to existing and up-and-coming energy technologies that are clean, renewable, affordable, reliable, easy to implement, safe, and legitimate. From this ongoing review, they generate a Top 100 Clean Energy Technologies listing. They also endeavor to facil-itate the emergence of some of the more promising exotic technologies into the marketplace.

His passion is to see clean, affordable, reliable, safe, and practical energy solutions proceed from research and development into market penetration. He has made the term "free energy" more acceptable by relating it to solar, wind, geothermal, and other well-understood technologies; while also making the more exotic approaches not seem so crazy.

Sterling is the founder of a dozen-plus organizations whose functions range from preparedness and alternative energy development and promotion to defining, teaching and researching better ways to live as a society. He has proven experience in creating, managing and sustaining organizations, as well as in using websites as a way to teach, publish and disseminate information. He has long been interested in alternative energy systems, and has established a positive reputation in maintaining a news service and an extensive directory of energy solutions that are friendly to the environment. http://pureenergysystems.com

Allen, Laura

Laura Allen is a Bay Area educator and greywater activist. She has a BA in Environmental Science from UC Berkeley, and a teaching credential and Masters in education from the New College of California. She is a co-founder of The Greywater Guerrillas and co-editor of *Dam Nation: Dispatches from the Water Underground* (Soft Skull Press, 2007). She presents about ecological sanitation and leads hands-on workshops to re-plumb houses to recycle their greywater.

Alvarez, Ana Maria

Ana Maria Alvarez grew up in the south, the daughter of two labor union organizers—a unique childhood experience that she draws from in the creation and performance of her work. After receiving a BA in Dance and Politics from Oberlin College, Alvarez moved to New York where she became the Dance Specialist at The Center for Family Life in Brooklyn. There she taught, danced and choreographed for several years, before moving to Los Angeles in 2002. In 2005, Alvarez received her MFA in Choreography from UCLA's Department of World Arts and Cultures, where she started her renowned dance company CONTRA-TIEMPO. She has toured the company all over the country and the world. The company will be returning to Cuba in July 2009 for the second time and have shared their work in Mexico, Puerto Rico, NY, GA, NC, WA, CA, AZ and Washington DC. At UCLA Alvarez collaborated with teachers and researchers to create a dance program at UCLA's Lab Elementary School, which became the foundation for CONTRA-TIEMPO's arts education program. CONTRA-TIEMPO is currently partnering with many schools throughout Southern California, integrating dance in their educational curriculum. In 2007 Alvarez was hired by the program SmART Schools Program to run (and continues to run) professional development institutes for elementary and middle school teachers on integrating movement into their classrooms and curriculum. Alvarez was also recently approached by the Skirball Cultural Center and will be running teacher trainings on their sight in 2009-2010. Currently Alvarez is a finalist for the Echoing Green Fellowship for Social Entrepreneurs and has recently been nominated for two Horton Awards for dance. Alvarez has received numerous awards and recognition from the arts world and beyond, including Brooklyn Arts Exchange's Artist in Progress Award and from The Association of Performing Arts Presenters Emerging Leaders Institute, The Los Angeles City Council of District 11, The Durfee Foundation, The Flourish Foundation, Festival Internacional de Teatro de Los Angeles' (FITLA) and Instituto de Cultura de Puerto Rico, among others. Recognized as a "Rising star of the dance world" (Backstage NY 2002), Alvarez is inspired to continue to develop and share her artistic vision with the world through CONTRA-TIEMPO's dynamic work. Her choreographic work is processing meaning for and by the communities from which this dancing originated, yet pushing those same communities to question and think critically about their own realities and circumstances. Choreography inspired by and based on those whose story she brings to life on stage gives her work an authenticity and energy that no audience member or critic can deny. The work feels real—it is real—and therefore allows each audience member to relate to it as such.

Anderson, Ray

The story is now legend: the "spear in the chest" epiphany Ray Anderson experienced when he first read Paul Hawken's *The Ecology of Commerce*, seeking inspiration for a speech to an Interface task force on the company's environmental vision. Fourteen years and a sea of change later, Interface, Inc., is half way towards the vision of "Mission Zero," the journey no one would have imagined for the company or the petroleum-intensive industry of carpet manufacturing which has been forever changed by Anderson's vision. Mission Zero is the company's promise to eliminate any negative impact it may have on the environment by the year 2020, through the redesign of processes and products, the pioneering of new technologies, and efforts to reduce or eliminate waste and harmful emissions while increasing the use of renewable materials and sources of energy.

In 1997, Ray described his vision for his company, then nearly a quarter-century old, that stands true today: "If we're successful, we'll spend the rest of our days harvesting yester-year's carpets and other petrochemically derived products, and recycling them into new materials; and converting sunlight into energy; with zero scrap going to the landfill and zero emissions into the ecosystem. And we'll be doing well ... very well ... by doing good. That's the vision."

The once captain of industry has eschewed a luxury car for a Prius and built an off-the-grid home, authored a book chronicling his journey, *Mid-Course Correction*, and become an unlikely screen hero in the 2004 Canadian documentary, "The Corporation" and in the 2007 film by Leonardo DiCaprio, "The 11th Hour." He was a master commentator on the Sundance Channel's series, "Big Ideas for a Small Planet" and was named one of TIME magazine's Heroes of the Environment in 2007, with a similar honor from Elle Magazine that year. He's a sought- after speaker and advisor on all issues eco, including a stint as co-chair of the President's Council on Sustainable Development during President Clinton's administration.

Ang, Bernise

Bernise is an avid social entrepreneur who is passionate about empowering and activating young people to realise their potential, and to bring about positive change in their communities. She has a deep interest in building human capacity and social capital, international development; participatory decision-making; and the empowerment of youth for social change.

In her university days, she was heavily involved in social activism, advocating for the dignity of minority groups such as international students & culturally/linguistically diverse groups, women, and queer students.

Now, Bernise is the founder of Syinc, which works to connect young Singaporeans and build their capacity to engage in their community more effectively and seek innovative solutions for social change.

She has since been appointed to the Advisory Board of Youth Action for Change, which works to engage youth to empower youth through ICT for positive social change.

She also served as the National Focal Point in Singapore for the Global Youth Coalition on HIV/AIDS, involved in an initiative to build a national network of HIV/AIDS actors in Singapore.

In Nov 2007, in recognition of her efforts, Bernisebecame the first Singaporean to receive the YouthActionNet Award & Fellowship from the International Youth Foundation. In her term as Global Fellow, she will be connecting with schools, NGOs, youth groups, public and private stakeholders, to further her work.

Most recently in 2009, she has been voted to the Board of the International Youth Foundation, where she will serve a 3-year term. www.syinc.org

Ardagh, Arjuna

Arjuna Ardagh is the author of seven books, including the 2005 national bestseller *The Translucent Revolution*, and his latest book *Leap Before You Look*. He has trained more than 800 facilitators of awakening since 1995, and has been working with people, both individually and in organizations since 1983. Ardagh has been a speaker at conferences all over the world, including the International Conference on Business and Consciousness, the annual conference of the Omega Institute. He has coached leaders of many international companies in the art of Awakening Leadership, and has appeared on TV, on the radio and in print media in twelve countries. He is a member of the Transformational Leadership Council. www.awakeningcoaching-training.com

Baba, Sunny

Sunny Baba is "a man of nature" and a "natural man." Having built four self-sufficiency communities, he has lived his entire adult life in remote wilderness areas, living and teaching a natural lifestyle of simplicity, harmony, and conscious stewardship of the Earth. Sunny builds his own homes, grows his own food, and makes his own clothes. He is "an artist in all areas" of his life. Simple pleasures and simple things that come from the earth bring him joy. Sunny walks and talks the philosophy of Oneness. Together with his "heart mate," Brook Medicine Eagle, Sunny is building retreat facilities at Earth Heart Sanctuary, "an exquisite place to experience an ecologically-sound lifeway of simplicity, beauty, harmony, and sustainability." He offers private phone consultations, wilderness camps, and sacred relationship counseling for men, as well as ceremonial clothing and moccasins. www.bluediamond-pachamama.com. He is the author of *The Realization of Divine Oneness* (Outskirts Press). For more information go to www.medicineeagle.com

Baraniuk, Richard

Richard Baraniuk is the Victor E. Cameron Professor of Electrical and Computer Engineering at Rice University and the founder of Connexions (cnx.org). His honors include national research awards from the NSF and ONR, the Rosenbaum Fellowship from the Isaac Newton Institute of Cambridge University, the ECE Young Alumni Achievement Award from the University of Illinois, several best paper awards, the Eta Kappa Nu C. Holmes MacDonald National Outstanding Teaching Award, the SPIE Wavelet Pioneer Award, an MIT Technology Review TR10 Top 10 Emerging Technology award, and an Internet Pioneer Award from the Berkman Center for Internet and Society at Harvard Law School. Dr. Baraniuk is a Fellow of the IEEE and was selected as one of Edutopia Magazine's Daring Dozen Education Innovators in 2007. Connexions received the Tech Museum Laureate Award from the Tech Museum of Innovation in 2006.

Barsody, Sister Carmen

I've been privileged and grateful to see and act upon the glorious absurdities of our world as I was born and raised in Minnesota, studied Theology and Pastoral Ministry at the College of St. Catherine in St. Paul, MN; ministered in a predominantly Hispanic parish in Chicago, and then spent seven years ministering in Nicaragua.

Now from the streets of San Francisco I see yet other expressions of our world's glorious absurdities and feel moved to action, together with other faithful fools.

I entered the Franciscan Sisters of Little Falls on April Fool's Day. Nothing is coincidence! www.faithfulfools.org

Beautiful Painted Arrow, Joseph

Joseph Rael - Beautiful Painted Arrow - is an internationally respected author, artist, visionary and master storyteller of the Ute and Picuris Pueblo Indian traditions. He holds a Masters Degree in Political Science and has devoted his life to the understanding of vibration and its role in the creation of conscious reality.

In 1983 he had a vision that led him to the establishment of over 70 Peace Chambers throughout the world—and the number keeps growing. The chambers are specially built for chanting for world peace.

Prayer and ceremony have always been an important part of his life. He was taught by his father's people to pray all the time through his every action, thereby honoring all the principle ideas keeping a continual state of prayer in every single moment of his life.

Although Joseph has retired from his active traveling, you can experience his teachings through his five books, *Beautiful Painted Arrow, The Way of Inspiration, Tracks of Dancing Light, Being in Vibration*, and *Ceremonies of the Living Spirit*. The dances which he inspired still continue through his students. He continues to work on his one-of-a-kind paintings, and some private sessions. The Peace Chamber project is ever growing and new Chambers are being constructed as this vision for World Peace grows. www.peacechamber.com

Benally, Jones

Jones Benally is from the Navajo (Dine) Nation in Arizona. He was taught healing by his grandfathers and uncles at a very early age. He has been the traditional consultant for Winslow Indian

Hospital for over 14 years. Jones is also a world champion Hoop Dancer amongst many other talents. Jones also performs with his family, the internationally acclaimed Native American Dance Troupe the Jones Benally Family and the Native American award-winning musical group Blackfire. www.blackfire.net

Bhatt, Ela

Ela R. Bhatt is widely recognized as one of the world's most remarkable pioneers and entrepreneurial forces in grassroots development. Known as the "gentle revolutionary," she has dedicated her life to improving the lives of India's poorest and most oppressed women workers. In 1972, she founded the Self-Employed Women's Association (SEWA), a trade union with more than 10,00,000 members now. Founder Chair of the Cooperative Bank of SEWA. She is also founder and chair of Sa-Dhan, the All India Association of Micro Finance Institutions in India, and, founder-chair of the Indian School of Micro-finance for Women. She was a Member of the Indian Parliament and subsequently a Member of the Indian Planning Commission. She founded and served as chair for Women's World Banking, the International Alliance of Home-based Workers (HomeNet), and Women in Informal Employment: Globalizing, Organizing (WIEGO). She also served as a trustee of the Rockefeller Foundation for a decade. She has received several awards, including the Ramon Magsaysay Award and the Right Livelihood Award, George Meany-Lane Kirkland Human Rights Award, and Légion d'honneur from France as well as honorary doctorates from Harvard, Yale, University of Natal and other academic institutions. Member the Council of The Elders (2007).

Blackmore, Dr Susan

Sue Blackmore is a freelance writer, lecturer and broadcaster, and a Visiting Lecturer at the University of the West of England,

Bristol. She has a degree in psychology and physiology from Oxford University (1973) and a PhD in parapsychology from the University of Surrey (1980). Her research interests include memes, evolutionary theory, consciousness, and meditation. She practices Zen and campaigns for drug legalization. Sue Blackmore no longer works on the paranormal.

She writes for several magazines and newspapers, a blog for the Guardian newspaper and is a frequent contributor and presenter on radio and television. She is author of over sixty academic articles, about fifty book contributions, and many book reviews. Her books include *Beyond the Body* (1982), *Dying to Live* (on near-death experiences, 1993), *In Search of the Light* (autobiography, 1996), and *Test Your Psychic Powers* (with Adam Hart-Davis, 1997). *The Meme Machine* (1999) has been translated into 13 other languages. Her textbook *Consciousness: An Introduction* was published in 2003 (Hodder UK, OUP New York), *A Very Short Introduction to Consciousness* (OUP) and *Conversations on Consciousness in 2005* (OUP Oxford). Published in 2009, *Ten Zen Questions* is her latest book. www.susanblackmore.co.uk, www.memetics.com

Blincoe, Karen

Karen Blincoe is an educator, designer and environmentalist. She is a Fellow of the RSA and CSD in the UK and a member of DD in Denmark. Karen is currently the Director of the Schumacher College, Dartington, UK, a unique centre for studies in sustainability issues based on Ghandian teaching and learning principles. Karen is the founder/director of the International Centre for Innovation & Sustainability, ICIS, Denmark. She set up the centre in Denmark, (2001) to teach and develop educational models for designers and architects in topics relating to sustainability, professional practice, leadership and business innovation. Karen lectures in sustainability, design and education around the world, and is privately interested in personal development, leadership and conflict solving.

Blum, Dr Arlene

Arlene Blum PhD, biophysical chemist, author, and mountaineer is a Visiting Scholar at UC Berkeley's Department of Chemistry and executive director of the Green Science Policy Institute. Her past research contributed to the regulation of two cancer-causing chemicals that were used as flame retardants on children's sleepwear. Blum has taught at Stanford University, Wellesley College, and U. C. Berkeley,

Blum led the first American—and all-women's—ascent of Annapurna I, considered one of the world's most dangerous and difficult mountains, Blum also led the first women's team up Mt. McKinley; was the first American woman to attempt Mt. Everest; made the first traverse of the Great Himalaya Range of Bhutan, Nepal and India; and hiked the length of the European Alps with her baby daughter on her back.

Blum's current interest is to bridge the gap between scientific research and policy for a healthier safer environment. To that end she is leading policy efforts to reduce toxic chemicals in consumer products and founded *The Green Science Policy Institute* (GSP) to link academic scientists and engineers with policy opportunities as well as provide research to help industries become more sustainable in their materials and processes.

Her first book, *Annapurna: A Woman's Place* was included in *Fortune* magazine's 2005 list of "The 75 Smartest Business Books We Know" and chosen by *National Geographic Adventure Magazine* as one of the 100 top adventure books of all time. Her new memoir, *Breaking Trail: A Climbing Life* tells the story of how Blum realized improbable dreams among the worlds' highest mountains, in the chemistry laboratory, and public policy arena.

Blum's awards include a Purpose Prize to those over 60 who are solving society's greatest problems and a Gold Medal from the Society of Women Geographers, an honor previously given to only eight other women including Amelia Earhart, Margaret Mead, and Mary Leakey.

Arlene Blum is the founder of the annual Berkeley Himalayan Fair and the Burma Village Assistance Project. She serves on the boards of the Society for the Preservation of Afghan Archaeology; ISET, an organization dedicated to solving climate, water and disaster problems in South Asia; and Project REED which builds libraries in Asia.

Borges, Phil

For over 25 years Phil Borges has been visiting and documenting indigenous and tribal cultures around the world. Photographs by Phil Borges have been collected and exhibited in museums and galleries worldwide. His award-winning books have been published in four languages and in 1998 he was presented the Photo Media Magazine "Photoperson of the Year" award. In December, 2003, Phil was honoured with a Lucie Humanitarian Award at the Annual International Photography Awards in Los Angeles. Phil teaches and lectures internationally and is co-founder of Blue Earth Alliance, a non-profit organization that sponsors photographic projects focusing on endangered cultures and threatened environments. Phil's exhibit and award-winning book, *Tibetan Portrait: The Power of Compassion*, focused on the people of Tibet, marginalized by the Chinese occupation of their homeland. In 1998 he joined Amnesty International to present *Enduring Spirit*, an exhibit and book celebrating the 50th anniversary of the signing of the Universal Declaration of Human Rights. His book *The Gift* documents the work of medical volunteers in the developing world. Phil's current project, Women Empowered, focuses on the empowerment and changing role of women in cultures around the world. Phil is Founder/President of Bridges to Understanding, an on-line classroom program connecting children from indigenous and tribal cultures with their contemporaries in North America through digital story-

206

telling. The Bridges curriculum guides students as they examine their own culture and explore the lives of children with beliefs and customs very different from their own. For more information about Phil Borges please visit his website at: www.philborges.com

Bosch, Jason

Jason Bosch is founder of Argusfest. Since 2001 ArgusFest has held over a thousand awareness raising events on human rights, social justice, media, environmental, and other issues of conscience. The ArgusFest Film Series holds weekly documentary screenings around Denver, Colorado. Each screening is followed by an audience discussion where diverse points of views are welcome. The ArgusFest Lecture Series periodically hosts talks by internationally renowned authors and activists. Past speakers have included Dr. Gino Strada, Dahr Jamail, Norman Finkelstein, Robert Jensen, and Kevin Bales among others.

Bostrom, Nick

Professor Nick Bostrom is Director of the Future of Humanity Institute at Oxford University. He previously taught at Yale University in the Department of Philosophy and in the Yale Institute for Social and Policy Studies. He has more than 140 publications to his name, including three scholarly books: *Anthropic Bias* (Routledge, 2002), *Global Catastrophic Risks* (ed., OUP, 2008), and *Enhancing Humans* (ed., OUP, 2008). His writings have been translated into 17 different languages, and reprinted numerous times in anthologies and textbooks. Bostrom has a background in physics, computational neuroscience, and mathematical logic as well as analytic philosophy. Bostrom is a leading thinker on big picture questions for humanity. His research also covers the foundations of probability theory, scientific methodology, human enhancement, global catastrophic risks, moral philosophy, and consequences of future technology. Bostrom developed the first mathematically explicit theory of observation selection effects. He is also the originator of the Simulation Argument, the Reversal Test, the concept of Existential Risk, and a number of other influential contributions. He serves occasionally as an expert consultant for various governmental agencies in the UK, Europe, and the USA, and he is a frequent commentator in the media.

Brown, Adrienne Maree

Adrienne Maree Brown is the executive director of The Ruckus Society, which brings non-violent direct action training and action support to communities impacted by economic, environmental and social oppression. She sits on the boards of Allied Media Projects and the Young Women's Empowerment Project (and just stepped down from the boards of Wiretap Magazine and the Brower Center), and facilitates the development of organizations throughout the movement (most recently New Orleans Parents Organizing Network, ColorofChange.org and Detroit Summer). A co-founder of the League of Pissed Off/Young Voters and graduate of the Art of Leadership and Art of Change yearlong trainings, Adrienne is obsessed with learning and developing models for action, community strength and movement building. www.ruckus.org

Brown, Lester

Lester R. Brown, described as "one of the world's most influential thinkers" by the *Washington Post*, is Founder and President of Earth Policy Institute, a non-profit environmental research organization based in Washington, D.C. Some 30 years ago, Brown helped pioneer the concept of sustainable development. He was the Founder and President of the Worldwatch Institute during its first 26 years. During a career that started with tomato farming, Brown has authored or co-authored over 50 books, the most recent of which is *Plan B 3.0: Mobilizing to Save Civilization*. One of the world's most widely published authors, his books have appeared in more than 40 languages. The recipient of numerous awards, his accolades include 24 honorary degrees, the 1987 United Nations Environment Prize, a MacArthur Foundation "genius award," and the 1994 Blue Planet Prize for his "exceptional contributions to solving global environmental problems." In 1995, Marquis Who's Who selected Mr. Brown as one of 50 Great Americans. In 1986, the Library of Congress requested his papers for their archives, noting he had "already strongly affected thinking about problems of world population and resources."

Caldicott, Dr Helen

The single most articulate and passionate advocate of citizen action to remedy the nuclear and environmental crises, Dr Helen Caldicott, has devoted the last 35 years to an international campaign to educate the public about the medical hazards of the nuclear age and the necessary changes in human behavior to stop environmental destruction.

Born in Melbourne, Australia in 1938, Dr Caldicott received her medical degree from the University of Adelaide Medical School in 1961. She founded the Cystic Fibrosis Clinic at the Adelaide Children's Hospital in 1975 and subsequently was an instructor in pediatrics at Harvard Medical School and on the staff of the Children's Hospital Medical Center, Boston, Mass., until 1980 when she resigned to work full time on the prevention of nuclear war.

In 1971, Dr Caldicott played a major role in Australia's opposition to French atmospheric nuclear testing in the Pacific; in 1975 she worked with the Australian trade unions to educate their members about the medical dangers of the nuclear fuel cycle, with particular reference to uranium mining.

While living in the United States from 1977 to 1986, she co-founded the Physicians for Social Responsibility, an organization of 23,000 doctors committed to educating their colleagues about the dangers of nuclear power, nuclear weapons and nuclear war. On trips abroad she helped start similar medical organizations in many other countries. The international umbrella group (International Physicians for the Prevention of Nuclear War) won the Nobel Peace Prize in 1985. She also founded the Women's Action for Nuclear Disarmament (WAND) in the US in 1980.

Returning to Australia in 1987, Dr Caldicott ran for Federal Parliament as an independent. Defeating Charles Blunt, leader of the National Party, through preferential voting she ultimately lost the election by 600 votes out of 70,000 cast.

She moved back to the United States in 1995, lecturing at the New School for Social Research on the Media, Global Politics and the Environment, hosting a weekly radio talk show on WBAI (Pacifica), and becoming the Founding President of the STAR (Standing for Truth About Radiation) Foundation.

Dr Caldicott has received many prizes and awards for her work, most recently the Lannan Foundation's 2003 Prize for Cultural Freedom, 19 honorary doctoral degrees, and was personally nominated for the Nobel Peace Prize by Linus Pauling—himself a Nobel Laureate. The Smithsonian Institute has named Dr Caldicott as one of the most influential women of the 20th Century. She has written for numerous publications and has authored seven books, *Nuclear Madness, Missile Envy, If You Love This Planet: A Plan to Heal the Earth* (1992, W.W. Norton) and *A Desperate Passion: An Autobiography* (1996, W.W. Norton; published as A Passionate Life in Australia by Random House), *The New Nuclear Danger: George Bush's Military Industrial Complex* (2001, The New Press in the US, UK and UK; Scribe Publishing in Australia and New Zealand; Lemniscaat Publishers in The Netherlands; and Hugendubel Verlag in Germany), and *Nuclear Power is Not the Answer* (2006, The New Press in the US, UK and UK; Melbourne University Press in Australia). Dr Caldicott's most recent book is *War In Heaven* (March 2007).

She also has been the subject of several films, including "Eight Minutes to Midnight," nominated for an Academy Award in 1981, "If You Love This Planet," which won the Academy Award for best documentary in 1982, and "Helen's War: portrait of a dissident", recipient of the Australian Film Institute Awards for Best Direction (Documentary) 2004, and the Sydney Film Festival Dendy Award for Best Documentary in 2004.

Dr Caldicott currently divides her time between Australia and the US where she lectures widely. She is also the Founder and President of the Nuclear Policy Research Institute (NPRI), headquartered in Washington DC. NPRI's mission is to facilitate a far-reaching, effective, ongoing public education campaign in the mainstream media about the often-underestimated dangers of nuclear weapons and power programs and policies.

Caldwell, Gillian

Gillian Caldwell, Campaign Director (Executive Director/CEO equivalent): Gillian is a filmmaker and an attorney with thirty years of experience advocating for social justice in the United States and around the world. She is the outgoing Executive Director of WITNESS (www.witness.org), which uses the power of video to open the eyes of the world to human rights abuses. Gillian led WITNESS' rapid expansion during her decade of leadership and helped produce numerous documentary videos for use in advocacy campaigns around the world, including *Outlawed: Extraordinary Rendition, Torture and Disappearances in the "War on Terror"*, *System Failure: Violence, Abuse and Neglect in the California Youth Authority*, *Behind the Labels: Garment Workers on US Saipan*, and *Operation Fine Girl: Rape Used as a Weapon of War in Sierra Leone*. She is also co-editor and author of a book published by Pluto Press called *Video for Change: A Guide to Advocacy and Activism* (2005). Gillian was formerly the Co-Director of the Global Survival Network, where she coordinated a two-year undercover investigation into the trafficking of women for forced prostitution from Russia and the Newly Independent States that helped spur new anti-trafficking legislation in the US and abroad. Gillian lived in South Africa during 1991 and 1992, investigating hit squads and security force involvement in township violence, and has worked in Boston, Washington DC and New York on issued related to poverty and violence. She is the recipient of numerous awards, including the Echoing Green Fellowship (1996-1998), Rockefeller Foundation Next Generation Leadership Award (2000), Schwab Foundation for Social Entrepreneurship Award Winner (2001-present), Tech Laureate of the Tech Museum (2003), Ashoka: Innovators for the Public as a special partner (2003), Journalist of the Month by Women's Enews (2004), Skoll Social Entrepreneurship Award (2005-present). She received her BA from Harvard University and a J.D. from Georgetown University, where she was honored as a Public Interest Law Scholar. Under her leadership, WITNESS was also honored with numerous awards, including most recently the NY Times Award for Excellence in Communications (2007) and 2007 American Express Building Leadership Award from the Independent Sector. Gillian speaks English and Spanish.

Carter, Dr Majora

Dr Majora Carter simultaneously addresses public health, poverty alleviation, and climate change as one of the nation's pioneers in successful *green-collar* job training and placement systems. She founded Sustainable South Bronx in 2001 to achieve environmental justice through economically sustainable projects informed by community needs. Her work has been noted in numerous books; celebrated with awards from the National Audubon Society, the EPA, the NRDC, and the The Weather Channel among many many others. She is a MacArthur "Genius" Fellow, one of Essence Magazine's 25 Most Influential African-Americans in 2007, one of the NY Post's Most Influential NYC

Women for the past two years, a board member of the Widerness Society, and recording a special national public radio series called "The Promised Land" for 2009 release. Her work now includes advising cities, foundations, universities, businesses, and communities around the world on unlocking their green-collar economic potential to benefit everyone through her role as President of the Majora Carter Group, LLC.

Casey, Marisa Catalina

Founder/Executive Director of Starting Artists, Inc. a non-profit community-based arts center in Brooklyn, NY Marisa Catalina Casey is an artist, administrator, and advocate who has worked almost exclusively in the non-profit sector supporting a variety of constituents and causes from arts advocacy to child welfare to international development work. Ms. Casey obtained her BA in Latin American Studies from Brown University and her MA in Arts Administration from Columbia University Teachers College. Utilizing her artistic and entrepreneurial skills, Ms. Casey has worked as a photojournalist for CARE-Peru, the Alliance for Children, and *The Providence Journal*. Ms. Casey has held positions at the William Randolph Hearst Foundations, Metropolitan Opera, Teen Ink Magazine, Alliance of New York State Arts Organizations, and APERTURE Foundation. Additionally, she co-authored Born in Our Hearts: Stories of Adoption (HCI: 2004), selling over 11,000 copies with proceeds benefiting international orphanages. Her memoir and photo-illustration is included in *Not Quite What I Was Planning: Six-Word Memoirs By Writers Famous and Obscure* (Harper Perennial: 2008). Ms. Casey has received fellowships and scholarships from such organizations as the National Endowment for the Arts, Americans for the Arts, Columbia University, and Congressional Hispanic Caucus Institute. She is an elected Member of the national Americans for the Arts Emerging Leader Council. She has received grants from the Newton Cultural Council,

Production Workshop, and Creative Arts Council. Ms. Casey was a semi-finalist for the 2008 Echoing Green Social Entrepreneurship Fellowship, and is currently 2009 YouthActionNet Global Fellow. www.startingartists.org

Clow, Barbara Hand

Barbara Hand Clow is the author of twelve books including *The Mayan Code: Time Acceleration and Awakening the World Mind*. Her sense of a perfect world comes right out of what she has been teaching and writing for 35 years. When asked to describe a perfect world, she was stumped and thought about it for six months. She attained a great shift in her understanding of what is possible for our planet exactly when *The Perfect World* was completing itself. She was able to write her own description once she saw that what she already teaches is a perfect world, Earth aligned with the eternal laws of Nature and the cosmos.

Cremo, Michael

Michael Cremo is on the cutting edge of science and culture issues. In the course of a few months time he might be found on pilgrimage to sacred sites in India, appearing on a national television show, lecturing at a mainstream science conference, or speaking to an alternative science gathering. As he crosses disciplinary and cultural boundaries, he presents to his various audiences a compelling case for negotiating a new consensus on the nature of reality. Michael is a member of the World Archeological Congress and a researcher in human origins for the Vedic Science Research Center. Michael has a Ph.d. (honoris causa) in science and theology. His work focuses on Vedic perspectives on human origins and antiquity. He has presented papers at meetings of the World Archeological Congress, European Association of Archeologists, and the International Congress for History of Science. He has twice presented papers in the biannual conference series Toward A Science of

Consciousness. He has given invited lectures at the Royal Institution in London, the Russian Academy of Sciences in Moscow, the Bulgarian Academy of Sciences in Sofia, and at other scientific institutions. He has also lectured in hundreds of universities around the world. Cremo is the principal author of the book *Forbidden Archeology,* a comprehensive survey of archeological evidence consistent with Vedic accounts of extreme human antiquity. The abridged popular edition of *Forbidden Archeology,* titled *The Hidden History of the Human Race,* has been translated into twenty languages. Cremo's latest book is *Human Devolution: A Vedic Alternative to Darwin's Theory.* Cremo is particularly interested in examining the history of the archeology and anthropology from the standpoint of alternative worldviews, particularly worldviews with foundations in consciousness-based ancient Indian thought. He has been a member of the International Society for Krishna Consciousness since 1974. Michael lives in Los Angeles, but spends about six months a year travelling for lectures and research. www.mcremo.com

Daoudi, Yannick

A true citizen of the world, Yannick Daoudi was born in 1978 in Morocco, spent his teenage years in the United States, then moved to Canada for over a decade of full-time university studies, all the while globetrotting on a French passport. A life-long student, Yannick is ever-hopeful of completing a Ph.D. in Education. He applies his student philosophy to all aspects of life, always looking for something new to learn from a stranger in an unfamiliar land. His greatest passion in life is travel and adventure. He recently started leading International Cooperation projects in order to encourage such opportunities for young people. Yannick has just launched his first non-profit volunteering project in an orphanage in Uganda. After witnessing the impact of his public conferences, he's now convinced that his mission in life is to inspire people to make a better world through sharing his many travel stories. Some of these are documented on his website, www.postcards-fromtheedge.ca.

Davis, Ron

It took Ron Davis 38 years of struggle to regard himself as a complete human being. Born deeply autistic, he endured daily abuse at home and was labeled mentally retarded at school. Then, against all the odds, he somehow emerged from a void of isolation into the real world at age ten. By the time he was seventeen, his IQ tested at 137.

At age nineteen, speech therapy made it possible for Ron to speak coherently, but sadly he was still unable to read because, he was also severely dyslexic. He remained functionally illiterate until the age of thirty-eight and even though he achieved success as an engineer and businessman in that time, he was hiding from everyone around him the fact that he could neither read nor write.

Then, in 1981, he performed an experiment on his own perceptions that profoundly changed the way he experienced reality. This seminal breakthrough enabled him to correct and control the involuntary perceptual distortions which were at the root of his dyslexia. For the first time in his life, he was able to read a book, cover to cover, without struggling.

Wishing to investigate his personal success in overcoming his life-long reading problem, he experimented with several dyslexic adults who experienced similar immediate relief from their dyslexic symptoms. In 1982, with the help of educational psychologist, Dr Fatima Ali, he researched and developed an intensive one-week counseling program for correcting dyslexia in adults and children, and opened the doors of the Reading Research Council in Burlingame, California. He hasn't looked back since.

Davis's training methods, known as Davis Dyslexia

Correction, are now changing the face of special education and learning disability treatment throughout the world. The unique aspect of his work is a series of perceptual and kinesthetic exercises called Orientation Counseling, which teaches dyslexic students how to recognize and control the mental state that leads to distorted and confused perceptions of letters, words and numerals. In addition, he has developed creative learning procedures called Symbol Mastery and unique reading exercises, which allow dyslexic students to learn how to read.

In 1994, he wrote and published *The Gift of Dyslexia* to answer the continuous demand from parents and educators for a book detailing the Davis Dyslexia Correction methods. By spring of 1995 it was published in English, French, German, Dutch and Spanish. Today, it is published in 18 languages. It is www.amazon.com's number one best seller on the subject of dyslexia.

In 2003, he wrote and published *The Gift of Learning* about his methods for correcting math (dyscalculia), handwriting (dysgraphia), and attention (ADD) difficulties.

Davis Dyslexia Association International (DDAI) was founded in September, 1995 by Ron and Alice Davis. Its goals are to increase worldwide awareness about the positive aspects of dyslexia and related learning difficulties and to present methods for improving literacy. DDAI is accomplishing these goals through Ron Davis's international lecture tours, professional workshops for teachers and therapists, certification and licensing programs, its high profile website www.dyslexia.com and its international quarterly newsletter, *The Dyslexic Reader*. Today, there are more than 400 licensed Davis Facilitators worldwide providing Davis Dyslexia Correction in 31 languages and 41 nations.

Ron Davis is Executive Director of the Reading Research Council and Davis Dyslexia Association International in Burlingame, California, and is internationally known as a leading-edge researcher and advocate in the field of learning disabilities. He is currently researching and writing a book about new methods for addressing autism.

Visit www.dyslexia.com for further information on Ron Davis's techniques

deAngelis, Dr Angela

Systems theorist, social scientist, spiritual guide, psychotherapist, Dr Angela deAngelis, also known as Dr Angela Browne-Miller, is Director of the Metaxis Institute for Personal, Social and Systems Change based in northern California. She is author of some twenty books under her two last names including the innovative internationally acclaimed four volume *Continuity of Life Series*, outlining the next steps in the evolution of the human mind-spirit: Volume One—*Endings Are Beginnings*; Volume Two—*Embracing Eternity*; Volume Three—*Transition and Survival Technologies*; Volume Four—*Healing Earth in All Her Dimensions*. Doctor Angela, as she is called by her clients and readers, earned her two doctorates and two masters degrees at the University of California Berkeley, where she lectured in three departments for over a decade. Doctor Angela's life's work is to contribute to knowledge of the ongoing nature of the life force and the eternal nature of the human consciousness.

de Grey, Dr Aubrey

Dr Aubrey de Grey is a biomedical gerontologist based in Cambridge, UK, and is the Chairman and Chief Science Officer of the Methuselah Foundation, a 501(c)(3) non-profit charity dedicated to combating the aging process. He is also Editor-in-Chief of the high-impact journal "Rejuvenation Research", the world's only peer-reviewed journal focused on combating aging. His research interests encompass the etiology of all the accumulating and eventually pathogenic molecular and cellular side-effects of metabolism ("damage") that constitute mammalian aging and the design of interventions to repair and/or obviate that damage. He has developed a possibly comprehensive plan for such repair, termed Strategies for Engineered Negligible Senescence (SENS), which breaks the aging problem down into seven major classes of damage and identifies detailed approaches to addressing each one. A key aspect of SENS is that it can potentially extend healthy lifespan without limit, even though these repair processes will never be perfect, as the repair only needs to approach perfection rapidly enough to keep the overall level of damage below pathogenic levels. de Grey has termed this required rate of improvement of repair therapies "longevity escape velocity".

de Quincey, Ph.D., Christian

Christian de Quincey, Ph.D., is Professor of Philosophy and Consciousness Studies at John F. Kennedy University; Dean of Consciousness Studies at the University of Philosophical Research; and Director of the Center for Interspecies Research. He is also founder of The Wisdom Academy, offering private mentorships in consciousness; and co-founder of The Visionary Edge, committed to transforming global consciousness by transforming mass media. Dr de Quincey is author of the award-winning book *Radical Nature: Rediscovering the Soul of Matter* and *Radical Knowing: Understanding Consciousness through Relationship*. His latest books are *Consciousness from Zombies to Angels* and *Deep Spirit: Cracking the Noetic Code*. Samples of his writings on consciousness and cosmology are available at www.deepspirit.com, www.TheWisdomAcademy.org, and TheWisdomBlog.

Dickinson, Paul

Founded CDP (Carbon Disclosure Project) in 2000 having previously founded and developed Rufus Leonard Corporate Communications and, more recently, EyeNetwork, the largest videoconference service in Europe. Member of the Environmental Research Group of the UK Faculty and Institute of Actuaries. Author of various publications including 'Beautiful Corporations'. www.sustainabledevelopment.co.uk

Dixon, Frank

Frank Dixon advises businesses, governments and other organizations on sustainability, system change and enhancing financial performance through increased corporate responsibility. For seven years, he was the Managing Director of Research for Innovest Strategic Value Advisors, the largest corporate sustainability research firm in the world. His work overseeing the sustainability analysis of the world's 2,000 largest companies made it clear that systemic issues compel all companies to operate unsustainably by making full impact mitigation impossible. To engage business and investors in driving the system changes needed to achieve sustainability, he developed a new sustainability approach focused on system change, called Total Corporate Responsibility. Before Innovest, he worked in the energy and finance areas. He is advising Wal-Mart and other companies on sustainability. He has an MBA from the Harvard Business School. More information about his work is available on www.GlobalSystemChange.com

dos Santos, Feliciano

Founder and Director of Estamos in Mozambique, he works with villagers to provide clean sanitation, promote sustainable agriculture and development, and to inspire innovative HIV/AIDS initiatives. He uses his music as an outreach for these issues throughout Mozambique. In 2007 his band, Massukos, released "Bumping" and performed at the World of Music, Arts and Dance (WOMAD) festival. dos Santos was the African recipient of the 2008 Goldman Environmental Prize.

Dunbar-Ortiz, Roxanne

Roxanne Dunbar-Ortiz grew up in rural Oklahoma, daughter of a landless farmer and half-Indian mother. Her paternal grandfather, a white settler, farmer, and veterinarian, had been a labor activist and Socialist in Oklahoma with the Industrial Workers of the World in the first two decades of the twentieth century. The stories of her grandfather inspired her to lifelong social justice activism.

Married at eighteen, she left with her husband for San Francisco, California, where she has lived most of the years since, although the marriage ended. Her account of life up to leaving Oklahoma is recorded in *Red Dirt: Growing Up Okie*. She has a daughter, Michelle.

Roxanne graduated, majoring in History, from San Francisco State College, a working class public institution, but was selected for History graduate school at University of California at Berkeley, transferring to University of California, Los Angeles to complete her doctorate in History.

From 1967 to 1972, she was a full time activist living in various parts of the United States, traveling to Europe, Mexico, and Cuba. This time of her life and the aftermath, 1960-1975, is the story told in *Outlaw Woman: Memoir of the War Years*.

Roxanne took a position teaching in a newly established Native American Studies program at California State University at Hayward, near San Francisco, and helped develop the Department of Ethnic Studies, as well as Women's Studies. In 1974, she became active in the American Indian Movement (AIM) and the International Indian Treaty Council, beginning a lifelong commitment to international human rights.

Her first published book, *The Great Sioux Nation: An Oral History of the Sioux Nation and its Struggle for Sovereignty*, was published in 1977 and was presented as the fundamental document at the first international conference on Indians of the Americas, held at United Nations' headquarters in Geneva,

Switzerland. That book was followed by two others in the following years: *Roots of Resistance: A History of Land Tenure in New Mexico, 1680-1980* and *Indians of the Americas: Human Rights and Self-Determination.*

In 1981, she was asked to visit Sandinista Nicaragua to appraise the land tenure situation of the Miskitu Indians in the northeastern region of the country. Her two trips there that year coincided with the beginning of United States government's sponsorship of a proxy war to overthrow the Sandinistas, with the northeastern region on the border with Honduras becoming a war zone and the basis for extensive propaganda carried out by the Reagan administration against the Sandinistas. In over a hundred trips to Nicaragua and Honduras from 1981 to 1989, she monitored what was called the Contra War. Her book, *Blood on the Border: A Memoir of the Contra War* was published in 2005. www.reddirtsite.com

Eisenstein, Charles

I will give you some of my background, although the intense transitions of the last few years have left me feeling like a new person. I was born in 1967 and was a very sensitive, intellectual and dreamy child. I was always consumed by questions like, "Where did I come from?" "Why am I here?" "Where am I going?" so of course, embedded as I was in a culture that sees science and reason as the source of truth, I tried to "figure out" the answers. I graduated from Yale University with a degree in Mathematics and Philosophy, but my development of reason and intellect brought me no closer to any truth I really cared about.

I didn't know what I was searching for, but I knew that none of the usual options life presents a Yale graduate attracted me. I went to Taiwan, learned Chinese, and soon found myself working as a translator. I spent most of my 20s there, educating myself broadly in Eastern spiritual traditions. I also read voraciously: books on health, nutrition, physics, and biology.

Translation led to other business opportunities, and I became familiar with this dimension of the human experience. In Taiwan, I met my dear friend and ex-wife Patsy, with whom I have three children, all boys.

In my late 20s I entered what was to be a long period of intensifying crisis. It started when all my professional work became intolerable. It became excruciating to do work I didn't care about. Even though a million reasons told me why it was irresponsible, impractical, and foolish to quit, I eventually could not make myself do it anymore. An irrepressible feeling, "I am not here to be doing this!" took control of my life. So I entered a long period of searching. I spent time teaching yoga, learning about herbs, and teaching at Penn State's department of Science, Technology, and Society. All of these endeavors have contributed to my present and future, but none were really me.

These last five years have been much like a birthing process. The old world has dissolved, and the contractions birthing me into the new have taken the form of a collapse of all that I once held onto. Crises in health, marriage, and money forced me to let go of a "life under control". In my helplessness, I accepted help, discovering a generous universe that has always met my needs, somehow, in unexpected ways. I have never made much money, but I have become rich in connections to other people. Friends and strangers from all over the world write to tell me how my books have affected them; they sustain my faith and nourish my passion for my work.

Today I am fully devoted to work I love. Before *The Ascent of Humanity* I wrote *The Yoga of Eating*, and my most recent book, really a booklet, *Transformational Weight Loss*, applies the deep ideas of Ascent to a very specific crying need. I also give seminars and workshops. I love to share the gifts I have been given with groups small and large, from tiny informal gatherings to major conferences. My work focuses on two areas: holistic health, and the transformation of human consciousness and civilization. These two areas are intimately related. Many of our health crises today are the somatization of maladies on the civilizational level. I also work one-on-one with people as a healer, or rather, as an agent of their own self-healing.www.ascentofhumanity.com

Mr. Eisenstein will soon be publishing his new book, *Sacred Economics*.

El Ebrashi, Raghda

Raghda El Ebrashi is Founder and Chairperson of Alashanek ya Balady Association for Sustainable Development (AYB-SD). She is currently an Assistant Lecturer of Strategic Management at the German University in Cairo (GUC). She earned her Bachelor Degree in Business Administration in 2004 from the American University in Cairo (AUC), and acquired her Master Degree in Professional Development from the AUC as well in 2006. She is currently writing her PhD thesis on Social Entrepreneurship at the GUC. Raghda has got an extensive experience in the field of community development in various governorates in Egypt since the age of 15.

She is currently working on national and international researches related to economic and social development. She founded Alashanek ya Balady student club at the American University in Cairo in 2002, and she was able to expand it to Ain Shams and Cairo Universities in 2003 and 2004. Raghda founded Alashanek ya Balady Association as a registered NGO in 2005.

In February 2007, Raghda was selected as being one of the most 65 influential social entrepreneurs and future leaders in Egypt by Al Ahram Newspaper, and her profile was published in Nos El Donia Magazine. In October 2007, Raghda was awarded from World Business Magazine (London) and Shell International the award of "35 under 35" for being one of the 35 influential international social entrepreneurs under the age of 35. She received the award in London and her profile was published in

World Business Magazine and Management Today Magazine in London, as well as some national newspapers and magazines in Egypt. In addition, in November 2007, Raghda was selected as being one of the most 30 influential social entrepreneurs in Egypt by H.E Suzan Mubarak, and her profile was broadcasted on the National TV (Channel 1). In November 2007, Raghda was selected and awarded from the UNDP and Microsoft in Malaysia for being one of the influential 100 global young social entrepreneurs. She received her award in Malaysia and attended series of workshops about social entrepreneurship in Malaysia. Recently in February 2008, Raghda was selected as one of the 24 Board of Advisors for the Egyptian Cabinet for a special project named "the Social Contract", which works on the implementation of the Millennium Development Goals of the UNDP in Egypt. In 2008, she earned the YouthActionNet Global Fellowship, where she received the award in USA. In 2009, El Ebrashi was recognized to be an Arab Social Innovator by Synergos. www.ayb-sd.org

Elkington, John
Founding Partner & Director, Volans (2008 to date)

Founder & Non-Executive Director, SustainAbility (1987–2008)

Personal website: www.johnelkington.com

Co-founder of SustainAbility in 1987 (Chair from 1995 -2005), and Founding Partner & Director of Volans, John Elkington is a world authority on corporate responsibility and sustainable development. In 2004, *BusinessWeek* described him as "a dean of the corporate responsibility movement for three decades." In 2008, *The Evening Standard* named John among the '1000 Most Influential People' in London, describing him as "a true green business guru," and as "an evangelist for corporate social and environmental responsibility long before it was fashionable."

Established in 1987, SustainAbility advises clients on the risks and opportunities associated with corporate responsibility and sustainable development. Working at the interface between market forces and societal expectations, SustainAbility seeks solutions to social and environmental challenges that deliver long term value. With offices in London, Zurich, New York and Washington, DC and team members representing more than ten nationalities, SustainAbility works with leading companies, NGOs and influencers around the world. Clients include ABN Amro, BP, Coca-Cola, Ford, Microsoft, Nestlé, Nike, Norwich Union, Shell, Swiss Re, Unilever and Wal-Mart. A global network of experts and partners helps SustainAbility to track emerging agendas, evaluate the market implications and engage business and its main stakeholders worldwide.

Volans, launched in April 2008 aims to find, explore, advise on and build innovative scalable solutions to the great global divides that overshadow the future. Volans is carrying forward John's work with The Skoll Foundation on a $1 million, 3-year field-building programme in relation to social entrepreneurship. Directly linked to this work, John's latest book is on entrepreneurial solutions—particularly on the work of leading social and environmental entrepreneurs. Co-authored with Pamela Hartigan, previous Managing Director of The Schwab Foundation, now Partner of Volans, *The Power of Unreasonable People: How Social Entrepreneurs Create Markets That Change the World*, was published by Harvard Business School Press on 5 February 2008.

Over time, John has authored or co-authored 17 books, including 1988's million-selling *Green Consumer Guide* and *Cannibals with Forks: The Triple Bottom Line of 21st Century Business* (1997), has written hundreds of articles for newspapers, magazines and journal and has written or co-written some 40 published reports.

In terms of other hats, John is a Visiting Professor at the Doughty Centre for Corporate Responsibility at the Cranfield School of Management. He chairs The Environment Foundation and the Aflatoun Impact and Policy Analysis Steering Group and is an Honorary Fellow of The Hub and also the Institute of Green Professionals. John is also a member of strategic advisory boards for, among others: 2degrees Venture Partners; the Dow Jones Sustainability Indexes; EcoVadis; Gaia Energy; the Global Reporting Initiative (GRI), Greenopolis.com; Instituto Ethos; Physic Ventures; Polecat UK and a Cleantech Fund developed by Zouk Ventures. John is also a Senior Advisor to the Business & Human Rights Resource Centre, a member of the WWF Council of Ambassadors, a member of the Evian Group Brain Trust and Council of Global Thought Leaders, the Global Leaders Academy; the Sea Change Advisory Board, Tomorrow's Global Company Inquiry Team; the Cambridge Research Advisory Group for the University of Cambridge Programme for Industry (CPI); and the United Nations Global Compact Cities Programme (UNGCCP) International Advisory Council. John has recently joined the newly formed Cleantech Group LLC's Cleantech Innovation Council. John was a Faculty member of the World Economic Forum from 2002-2008.

Ely, Scott

Scott Ely is **Founder and President of Sunsense Solar Electric and Renewable Energy.** Scott has gained a wealth of knowledge and experience with over 27 years in the solar industry. From solar thermal (hot water) to passive solar design (solar in buildings) to solar electricity, Scott has touched all the bases.

Scott's goal with Sunsense has been to create a business that caters to the curiosity and sensibility of how we use energy. Scott has educated the masses through workshops, display and demonstration systems, hands-on training and numerous articles for national publications.

Over the years, Scott has had the honor of working with many of the solar industry's pioneers and cherishes those long-standing friendships. www.sunsensesolar.com

Feng, Master Li Jun

Master Li embodies the spirit of Sheng Zhen, Unconditional Love, and is the moving force behind bringing the philosophy and practices of Sheng Zhen Qigong to the world.

He is the head of the International Sheng Zhen Society and its main teacher. He is currently the principal qigong instructor at the Academy of Oriental Medicine at Austin (AOMA) in Texas, USA.

Best known as the celebrated former head coach of the world-renowned Beijing Wushu (Martial Arts) Team and the National Wushu Team of the People's Republic of China, Master Li consistently led these teams to victory. They successfully won first place in both national and international competitions for over 12 years. During those years, Master Li also achieved international fame as a martial arts film actor and director.

Today, Master Li serves as advisor to the World Academic Society of Medical Qigong and the Qigong Science Research Association of China. From his base in Austin, he teaches numerous courses and special seminars. He also travels all over the world to conduct weekend workshops, as well as several 10 day Teacher Trainings per year.

To learn more about Master Li and Sheng Zhen Qigong, visit his website, www.shengzhen.org

Fletcher, Jr., Bill

Bill Fletcher, Jr. is the Executive Editor of BlackCommentator.com. He also serves as Senior Scholar for the Institute for Policy Studies. He is a co-founder of the Center for Labor Renewal.

Bill has been an activist most of his life. He has spent most of his adult life involved with organized labor, including as a rank and file member of the Industrial Union of Marine and Shipbuilding Workers of America, Local 5. He also served in staff positions with District 65-United Auto Workers in Boston, MA; National Postal Mail Handlers Union in Washington, DC; Service

Employees International Union; and the national AFL-CIO. In his position at the AFL-CIO he was the Education Director, and later Assistant the President.

Bill held the position of President of TransAfrica Forum for more than four years. This was followed by two years as the Bell Zeller Visiting Professor in political science at Brooklyn College-CUNY.

In 1987 Bill co-authored, with Peter Agard, *The Indispensable Ally: Black workers and the formation of the Congress of Industrial Organizations, 1934-1941*. In 2008 he co-authored with Fernando Gapasin *Solidarity Divided* which analyzes the crisis in organized labor.

Bill is a widely read columnist and commentator regularly published on-line and hardcopy, as well as appearing on radio and television. He can be reached at papaq54@hotmail.com.

Fresco, Jacque

Mr. Jacque Fresco's background includes industrial designer, author, lecturer, artist, architectural designer, futurist, and he is a forerunner in the field of Human Factors Engineering. He has worked as a combination designer and inventor in a wide range of fields spanning the gamut from biomedical innovations to totally integrated social systems. He was a design consultant for Rotor Craft Helicopter Company, served in the Army Design and Development Unit at Wright Field, and as a research Engineer for Raymond De-Icer Corp. He was a technical consultant to the motion picture industry, and also worked on the film *The Magic Eye*, which won the Robert J. Flaherty Award for creative film documentary. He was the creator of Revel Plastics and taught industrial design at the Art Center School in L.A.

Mr. Fresco has invented and patented many different products, which have had wide commercial acceptance in various fields such as aircraft, automobile, prefabricated housing, medical and the motion picture industry. He has authored eight books and numerous articles published throughout the world. He produced and filmed three educational videos about the future that are distributed to high schools, colleges and libraries.

Mr. Fresco has lectured in many universities throughout the world. He speaks dramatically and brilliantly about the urgent transitional problems facing our contemporary society.

A major documentary, titled *Future By Design*, on Mr. Fresco's life, designs and philosophy was produced by Academy Award Nominated and Emmy Winning filmmaker, William Gazecki.

Jacque Fresco is the founder of The Venus Project, which reflects the culmination of his life's work: the integration of the best of science and technology into a comprehensive plan for a new society based on human and environmental concern. It is a global vision of hope for the future of humankind in our techno-logical age. Television and magazine coverage on The Venus Project has been worldwide.

For further information please contact *The Venus Project*, 21 Valley Lane, Venus, FL 33960; Phone: 863-465-0321; www.thevenusproject.com.

Gellman H.D., Dr Alex

Professional speaker, author and wellness guru Alexandra Gellman captivates her audiences with her enthusiasm, energy and the depth of her message.

After building a career in the hospitality industry, working as Corporate Sales Manager (Sutton Place), National Sales Manager (L'hotel) and Director of Sales (King Edward Hotel), Alex turned her considerable talents to developing a healing practice in homeopathy, nutrition and one-on-one coaching. She launched Guru & Associations, Inc. and created a much-in-demand corporate wellness division in order to share her strategies for health and wellness with a larger audience.

Alexandra has appeared on many radio and TV shows, and

has been a presenter and keynote speaker at health and corporate conferences.

She is a regular guest on the show "Style by Jury" and the radio show "From a Woman's Perspective" and many other TV shows. Alex has published several books and various wellness articles. The fourth edition of her third book *Passage Ways to Your Soul* has just been released. Coming soon is her latest book *What Your Eyes Reveal*.

Alex is the Vice President of the Homeopathic Medical Council of Canada. www.wellnessguru.com

Gellman, C.A., C.P. A., Reverend David

David Gellman is director and founder of Universal Oneness United Faith Canada. UOUFC began its mission of building a spiritual community by connecting and drawing upon various faiths in 1996. Its mission is to nurture individual spirit and to foster love. Ordained as a minister of the Universal Oneness United Faith Canada, David offers parishioners an open door to a multitude of religions creating a foundation for the first true interfaith place of worship in Canada. Embracing, respecting, and incorporating beliefs from many religions and spiritual traditions from the present and the past, he offers members an opportunity to embrace greater spirituality in their lives. In addition, he has trained with the Cherokee and Cree Indians in Shamanistic and Native American spiritual practices, as well as ancient Kabalistic wisdom in Safad. David has devoted his life to studying ancient world religions, and incorporates both ancient and modern tools to help individuals make spirituality a corner-stone of their lives. He is committed to helping people find and embrace spirit, and to building a community with a greater understanding of one another.

Glennie, Dame Evelyn

Dame Evelyn Glennie is the first person in musical history to successfully create and sustain a full-time career as a solo percussionist. Evelyn gives more than 100 performances a year worldwide and has commissioned one hundred and fifty new works for solo percussion. Her first CD, Bartok's Sonata for two Pianos and Percussion, won her a Grammy in 1988. A further two Grammy nominations followed. Her successful lobbying led to her government providing £332 million towards music education. In 1993 Evelyn was awarded the OBE (Officer of the British Empire). This was extended in 2007 to 'Dame Commander' for her services to music. To date she has received over 80 international awards. After 20 years in the music business she has begun teaching privately, which allows her to explore the art of teaching and to explore the world of sound therapy as a means of communication.

Glithero, Lisa (Diz)

Education, youth and the environment have been the focus of Lisa Glithero's professional and personal life. With Bachelor of Science, Education and Master of Education degrees, she has taught in Canada, Nepal and has served as the Education Director for Students on Ice, an organization that leads educational expeditions for youth to Antarctica and the Arctic. Through 8 Polar Expeditions, Glithero has witnessed first-hand the impacts of Climate Change, further igniting her passion to connect today's youth to the planet's global ecosystem.

Glithero's dedication towards a 'greener' society led to her establishment of the EYES Project in 2004. EYES is a Canadian not-for-profit organization committed to bringing a sustainability imperative into educational pedagogy and practice. She is currently a Visiting Professor with the Faculty of Education at the University of Ottawa and continues to serve as the Director of the EYES Project, as well as Chair of the Education Advisory Committee for Students on Ice. Glithero is also a board member of the Chelsea Foundation.

In March 2006, she was honored with an international "Women of the Earth Award" by the Yves Rocher Foundation for her work in environmental education and in April 2008 was named by Nobel Peace Prize Nominee (2007) Sheila Watt Cloutier, as one of Chatelaine's "Amazing Canadian Women to Watch."

Glithero inspires audiences to engage in the (re)visioning of society. Her extensive travels and work as an educator and community innovator motivates groups to actively participate in the dialogue and relationship building needed to effect positive societal change. Through personal stories, powerful visuals, knowledge and humor, she addresses such topics as Education and Transformative Learning, Youth Engagement, Sustainable Community Building, Leadership, Vision, and Organizational Change.

Glithero lives in Chelsea, Quebec with her partner Geoff Green and their son Fletcher.

Group, Dr Edward

Dr Group founded Global Healing Center in 1998 and is currently the Chief Executive Officer. Heading up the research and development team, Dr Group assumes a hands-on approach in producing new and advanced degenerative disease products and information. Dr Group has studied natural healing methods for over 20 years and now teaches individuals and practitioners all around the world. He no longer sees patients but solely concentrates on spreading the word of health and wellness to the global community. Under his leadership, Global Healing Center, Inc. has earned recognition as one of the largest alternative, natural and organic health resources on the Internet. www.ghchealth.com

Guevara-Stone, Laurie

Laurie Guevara-Stone is the international program manager at

Solar Energy International. She has a Master's Degree in Energy Engineering from the University of Colorado. She has done extensive work in Latin America with numerous development organizations. Laurie is fluent in Spanish and over the past ten years has conducted projects in Nicaragua, El Salvador, Mexico and Ecuador implementing photovoltaics, solar cooking and water distillation. She began SEI's Women's Photovoltaics program, and organizes and instructs the Renewable Energy for Developing World workshops. Laurie has authored numerous technical articles for publications including Home Power Magazine, Solar Today Magazine and Mother Earth News. She lives in a passive solar straw bale home in Carbondale, Colorado.

Hailes, Julia

Julia Hailes is a leading opinion former, speaker and consultant to industry. She started working as an environmentalist over 20 years ago. Since then she has co-founded both SustainAbility Ltd, a think tank consultancy and Haller, a charity supporting sustainable agriculture and communities in Africa. She also sits on the Food Ethics Council, is a Patron of the Ecos Trust and is working with the Environmental Investigation Agency campaigning to remove halocarbons—which have a huge global warming impact—from supermarket refrigeration and car air conditioning systems. She's written nine books, including the best selling *Green Consumer Guide*, which sold over a million copies world wide. Her most recent book *The New Green Consumer Guide,* was published in 2007. Julia was elected to the UN Global 500 Roll of Honour, for outstanding environmental achievement in 1989 and was awarded an MBE in 1999. www.juliahailes.com

Hairfield, Dr Steven

Steven spent many years as a monk in India and Nepal studying the Tibetan Buddhist traditions with Eastern Masters. He has an

M.A. in Religion and Theology and a Ph.D. in the field of Metaphysics. He works as an intuitive life coach and is an author of many books with the latest one entitled *A Metaphysical Interpretation of the Bible*. www.hairfield.com

Halter, Dr Reese

Dr Reese Halter is an award-winning conservation scientist, father, best-selling author, syndicated science writer, and TV nature documentary host.

Dr Reese's love of Nature began as a child. A springtime tree-planting ritual with his father and brother became his passion. He knew from the time he was a child that he wanted to be a tree scientist and went on to attain three university degrees including a PhD from The University of Melbourne, Australia.

It became clear at a young age to Dr Reese that there was a tremendous lack of basic information on how trees and forests function. He believed that teams of multi-disciplinary problem-solving scientists needed to work together to short-circuit ecological disasters, and identify and protect fragile ecosystems.

In the late 1980s, Dr Reese founded Global Forest Science as a charitable international forest research foundation. He donated the first seed money to the foundation. Today with an international team of over 165 scientists, Global Forest Science is a world leader in forest science research and conservation and has been called the Red Adair of the forest biology world. Global Forest Science has many victories; including the legislation from Ottawa to protect the threatened westslope cutthroat trout of British Columbia and Alberta; protection of the world's largest ant colony in Japan; using trees and forests in Manitoba and Wyoming as a barometer of rising global temperatures; opening an international insect quarantine facility at Simon Fraser University in British Columbia; saving New Zealand's multi-billion-dollar forestry and agriculture industries from the Australian painted apple moth and understanding dieback of the tallest trees on Earth – California redwoods.

Through Global Forest Science, Dr Reese visits schools and encourages children worldwide to embrace conservation, science exploration, and learning.

Dr Reese and his children: "Sharky", Rocket Ryan and Jinji-Jo — and their Chesapeake Bay retriever "Stoot" enjoy hiking, fishing, camping and telling stories around the camp fire. www.drreese.com.

Haramein, Nassim

Nassim Haramein's lifelong exploration into the geometry of spacetime has resulted in an exciting comprehensive Unification theory based on a new solution to Einstein's Field Equations. This groundbreaking theory, which incorporates torque, Coriolis effects and the nonlinear mathematics of fractal systems, has been delivered to the scientific community through peer-reviewed papers and presentations at international physics conferences. His research into a variety of fields including theoretical physics, cosmology, quantum mechanics, biology, chemistry and ancient civilizations has led to a coherent under-standing of the fundamental structure and model of the Universe. This new view leads to an in-depth change in our current perception of physics and consciousness.

Weaving together the sciences of advanced physics, cosmology, chemistry and biology as well as the wisdom and codes of the ancients, Haramein creates an exciting unified tapestry of spacetime which may prove to be one of the most important scientific, philosophical and technological discoveries of our time.

Haramein is the Director of Research at The Resonance Project, a 501(c)3 public charity dedicated to the exploration of unification principles and their implications in our world today. The foundation is actively developing a research park where science, sustainability, green technology and permaculture come together.

Honoré, Carl

Carl Honoré was born in Scotland, but grew up in Canada. After graduating from Edinburgh University with a degree in history and Italian, he worked with street children in Brazil. He has written journalism from all over Europe and South America, spending three years as a correspondent in Buenos Aires along the way. His articles have appeared in publications around the world, including: the Economist, Observer, National Post, Globe and Mail, Houston Chronicle and Miami Herald.

His first book, *In Praise of Slow*, examines the modern compulsion to hurry and chronicles a global trend toward putting on the brakes. His second book, *Under Pressure*, explores the drawbacks of our approach to childrearing—and offers a blueprint for change. His books have been translated into more than 30 languages and landed on bestseller lists in many countries.

Honoré speaks, debates and broadcasts around the world. He has been described by ABC News as "the unofficial godfather of a growing cultural shift toward slowing down." Newsweek called him "an international spokesman for the concept of leisure." He lives in London with his wife, who is also a writer, and their two children. www.carlhonore.com, www.slowplanet.com

Jamail, Dahr

In late 2003, weary of the overall failure of the US media to accurately report on the realities of the war in Iraq for the Iraqi people and US soldiers, Dahr Jamail went to Iraq to report on the war himself.

His dispatches were quickly recognized as an important media resource. He is now writing for the Inter Press Service, Le Monde Diplomatique, and many other outlets. His stories have also been published with The Nation, The Sunday Herald in Scotland, Al-Jazeera, the Guardian, Foreign Policy in Focus, and the Independent to name just a few. Dahr's dispatches and hard news stories have been translated into French, Polish, German, Dutch, Spanish, Japanese, Portuguese, Chinese, Arabic and Turkish. On radio as well as television, Dahr reports for Democracy Now!, has appeared on the BBC and NPR, and numerous other stations around the globe. Dahr is also special correspondent for Flashpoints.

His reporting has earned him numerous awards, including the prestigious 2008 Martha Gellhorn Award for Journalism, the James Aronson Award for Social Justice Journalism, the Joe A. Callaway Award for Civic Courage, and four Project Censored awards.

Dahr has spent a total of 8 months in occupied Iraq as one of only a few independent US journalists in the country. In the MidEast, Dahr has also has reported from Syria, Lebanon and Jordan, and has been reporting from the region for five years. Dahr uses the DahrJamailIraq.com website and his popular mailing list to disseminate his dispatches.

Jensen, Derrick

Derrick Jensen is the author of many books, including *Endgame, A Language Older Than Words, What We Leave Behind,* and *Songs of the Dead*.

Jolivette, Dr Andrew

Dr Andrew Jolivette—Associate Professor American Indian Studies, San Francisco State University. Author of the books: *Louisiana Creoles: Cultural Recovery & Mixed Race Native American Identity, Cultural Representation in Native America*

Kataria, Dr Madan

Dr Madan Kataria, a medical doctor from Mumbai, India popularly known as the 'Guru of Giggling' (London Times), is the founder of Laughter Yoga Clubs movement started in 1995. While researching the benefits of laughter, he was amazed by the number of studies showing profound physiological and psychological benefits of laughter. He decided to find a way to deliver these benefits to his patients and other people. The result is Laughter Yoga, a unique exercise routine that combines group laughter exercises with yoga breathing which allows anyone to laugh without using jokes, humor or comedies. Started with just with just five people in a public park in Mumbai in 1995, it has grown into a worldwide movement of more than 6000 Laughter Yoga clubs in over 60 countries.

Spreading rapidly in USA, Canada, Europe, Australia, the Middle East, South East Asia, China and Africa, this new concept has been widely covered by prestigious publications like the TIME magazine, National Geographic, and the Wall Street Journal and featured on CNN, BBC, US networks and the Oprah Winfrey Show.

Dr Kataria is a keynote, motivational and inspirational speaker for companies, corporations and organizations all over the world. He has done seminars and workshops with UBS and Emirates Bank, IBM, Hewlett Packard, YPO (Young President Association), SAS and Emirates Airlines, Volvo Automobiles, Glaxo Pharmaceuticals, Ministry of Manpower and Social Welfare, Singapore Government, Western Australian Parliament, Dubai (UAE), HRD Congress Malaysia, the Dubai Wellbeing Show. It also includes Management Associations in Australia, Malaysia, Pakistan and India.

He is also a corporate consultant for holistic health, stress management, teambuilding, leadership, peak performance and communication skills to national and multinational corporations in India, USA, Canada, Europe, Switzerland, Australia, Singapore and Dubai.

A popular speaker, Dr Kataria is featured frequently on television and radio worldwide and is associated with a number of research projects to measure the benefits of laughter. Recent studies in the USA and Bangalore, India using unconditional laughter have positively confirmed these benefits. This scientific confirmation of what has been observed in thousands of laughter groups marks a turning point in the acceptance of Laughter Yoga in business world and in schools, hospitals, old age centers and other areas. www.laughteryoga.org

Kelly, Alex

Alex Kelly is a media/arts practitioner and producer who has worked on magazines, film installations, documentaries and community media as well as facilitating arts spaces and large-scale collectively run projects.

After returning to Australia from editing a magazine and presenting films in Europe in 2003, she started working with Big hART. She has since worked on Knot@Home, Radio Holiday, Stickybricks and Junk Theory with the company. In 2004 she moved to Coober Pedy to support the Irati Wanti (The Poison – Leave It) campaign of the Kupa Piti Kungka Tjuta, Senior Aboriginal Women of Coober Pedy. From Coober Pedy she moved to Alice Springs to produce the Ngapartji Ngapartji project, which she conceptualised with Trevor Jamieson and Scott Rankin.

Alex is currently Creative Producer of Ngapartji Ngapartji, Chairperson of Red Hot Arts board. She was the 2007 recipient of the Australia Council for the Arts Kirk Robson award. She is also a 2008 Youth Action Net fellow. http://bighart.org, http://ngaparjti.org

Kennedy, Prof. Dr Margrit

As an architect and urban planner with a Ph.D. in Public and International Affairs Margrit Kennedy was in charge of ecology and energy research in the preparatory group for the International Building Exhibition Berlin 1987. Between 1991 and 2002 she taught as the first professor for "Resource Saving

Building Technology" in Germany and the first woman professor in the Department of Architecture at the University of Hanover. Her interest in ecological building and planning led her to the discovery that within the present money system it is virtually impossible to reconcile ecology and economy on the scale required. As a result of this discovery she wrote two books. The first: *Interest and Inflation Free Money—Creating an exchange medium that works for everybody and protects the earth* was published in 1987 and translated into twenty-two languages. The second: *Regionalwährungen—Neue Wege zu nachhaltigem Wachstum* (*Regional Currencies—New paths towards sustainable growth*) together with Bernard Lietaer was published in 2004. The main thrust of her present work is the implementation of practical examples of complementary currencies in Europe. www.monneta.org

Kivel, Paul
Paul Kivel is an educator, writer, mentor, and social justice activist living in Oakland, CA. His articles, books, exercises and other resources are available at www.paulkivel.com. He can be reached at pkivel@mindspring.com.

KMO
KMO is the founder of the C-Realm Podcast: discussions on topics focused on the coming Vingean Singularity, Entheogenic Exploration, the re-localization of community & agriculture, and Individual Conscious Autonomy.
http://c-realmpodcast.podomatic.com/

Koch, Sarah
I grew up a liberal in the American south, studied art history then ran away to the Peace Corps. I fell in love with West Africa and who I became there. I co-founded and still run an international non-profit organization called Development In Gardening or DIG

where we teach sustainable agriculture to people living with HIV in impoverished nations. There is far more to do and experience in this world than one person has time for, but I am learning that I am capable of much more than anyone ever told me.

Kramer, Neil

Neil Kramer is an English writer, speaker and researcher in the fields of consciousness, metaphysics, shamanism and ancient mystical traditions.

Neil has spent over 20 years on a path of inner transformation and shares his discoveries and gnosis in writings, interviews and lectures, as well as giving one-to-one spiritual teaching. He is a frequent guest on leading alternative radio and internet shows, enjoying international audiences and enthusiastic support. His work is regularly published on cutting-edge web sites, news portals and popular media networks. Neil's acclaimed blog 'The Cleaver' is widely read across the world, attracting a large and discerning readership.

Neil gives interviews, teachings and live presentations on many fascinating subjects including: Paths To Selfhood, The 4D Consciousness Model, Transcending The Control System, Integrated Self-Healing, Synchronistic Awareness and The Dimensional Shift.

Kunstler, James Howard

James Howard Kunstler: Born in NYC 1948. Graduated High School of Music and Art, 1966. Graduated State University of New York, Brockport campus, 1971. Newspaper reporter 1972 - 74 (the Boston Phoenix, the Albany Knickerbocker News). Editor and staff-writer, Rolling Stone Magazine, 1974-5. Dropped out of corporate journalism 1975 to write books and moved permanently to Saratoga Springs, New York. Author of fifteen books, both fiction and non-fiction, including *The Geography of Nowhere*, *The Long Emergency*, and *World Made By Hand*.

Laskow, Dr Leonard

Leonard Laskow is a physician, trained at Stanford as an OB-GYN, who has studied the healing power of love for the past 33 years. He coined the term Holoenergetic Healing, by which he means healing with the energy of the "whole." Dr Laskow found that it takes energy to maintain separation and that as we bring ourselves into wholeness, the energy of separation is liberated. This energy can then be consciously directed to facilitate our body's healing response. Dr Laskow now teaches this process to healing professionals and lay people and is a consultant in Behavioral and Energy Medicine in Ashland, Oregon.

The principles of holoenergetic healing are presented in Dr Laskow's breakthrough book, *Healing with Love* (Wholeness Press, 1992/ 1998). Highly recommended by Deepak Chopra, Larry Dossey, and Dolores Krieger, this book uses ancient and cutting-edge healing techniques, self awareness, energy work, and practical exercises to help one directly experience love as a healing force. In it Dr Laskow describes his laboratory research, which documents the effectiveness of heart-focused holoenergetic techniques in significantly inhibiting the growth of tumor cells in tissue culture and bacterial growth in test tubes. The book, originally published in 1992 by Harper Collins, has sold over 30,000 copies in eight languages. In subsequent research, Dr Laskow has shown that the molecular configuration and properties of water and the physical structure of DNA can be changed by conscious intention, imagery and love.

Dr Laskow is a Life Fellow of the American College of Obstetrics and Gynecology and former Chief of OB-GYN at the Community Hospital of the Monterey Peninsula in Carmel, California. He completed residency training at Stanford Medical Center and took a post-doctoral fellowship in Psychosomatic Medicine at the University of California, San Francisco where he was a member of the faculty. Dr Laskow is a founding member of the Board of Directors of the American Board of Integrative

Holistic Medicine.

Dr Laskow teaches internationally at medical centers, universities, and holistic institutes, including the Esalen Institute, Interface, the New York Open Center, UCSF Medical Center, and the California Institute of Integral Studies. He has appeared a number of times on the "America's Talking" television show, Jeffrey Mishlove's TV series "Thinking Aloud," and numerous other radio and TV programs. He has also appeared before the California Legislative Committee on Self Esteem. www.laskow.net

Leanna, Anthony

My name is Anthony Leanna and I am an 18 year old from Green Bay, Wisconsin. In 2001, when I was 10 years old I started the Heavenly Hats Foundation which donates brand new hats to cancer patients nationwide. Since starting Heavenly Hats in 2001 I have been able to donate over 400,000 brand new hats to patients and hospitals. I decided to start Heavenly Hats after my grandmother Darlene Chartier was diagnosed with breast cancer. I am the son of Glen and DeeAnn Leanna of Green Bay, Wisconsin. I will graduate from Bay Port High School in Green Bay, WI in June of 2009 and will be going to college to study film and photography in the fall of 2009. I plan on continuing the Heavenly Hats Foundation well into the future.

Lee, Katie

Katie Lee has emerged as one of the Southwest's most outspoken environmental activists. Like David Brower and Ed Abbey, Katie has taken up the torch they left burning when they died to sing, write and lecture about the importance of preserving and restoring wilderness refuges; the lonesome characters the West still breeds; and the histories of ancient races embedded in its sinuous sandstone canyons. Today, her unwavering commitment to her principles and feisty eloquence are primarily directed at draining Powell Reservoir and letting the Colorado River once again run wild. (Quote from, "The Place We Knew" Copyright - August 2000) www.katydoodit.com

Lipkis, Andy

Andy Lipkis began planting trees to rehabilitate smog and fire-damaged forests when he was 15 years old. He founded TreePeople and has served as president since 1973.

Across the country and around the world, Andy has addressed groups involved in the linked issues of environment, urban forestry, sustainability, water, and energy use. These include: the United Nations, the U.S. Conference of Mayors, the U.S. Environmental Protection Agency, the U.K. National Urban Forestry Unit, the U.S. Forest Service, the Greenhouse Crisis Foundation, Greening Australia, American Society of Civil Engineers, and many others.

Andy's honors come from groups as diverse as the Baha'i Faith, Daughters of the American Revolution, National Arbor Day Foundation, the California State Board of Forestry and the South Coast Air Quality Management District. Andy and Kate Lipkis were named to the UN Environment Programme's Global 500 Roll of Honour. They also hold American Forests' Lifetime Achievement Award. In 1991, President Bush named TreePeople the 440th Point of Light. In 1998, Andy was honored as Founder of the Year at National Philanthropy Day. In 2007, Andy was named a Durfee Fellow and received the Boeing Crystal Vision Award. www.treepeople.org

Luckey, Wendy

Wendy Luckey, a curandera, traditional healer, and shaman, has spent many years learning about healing from many wisdom keepers from various lineages, including Native American, Latin American, African, Celtic, and Dreamtime traditions. Her practice of the art of healing combines working with traditional natural medicine, along with energetic healing practices, to assist others in their transformational process to support and assist them in fulfilling their life purpose. She helps others deepen their expression of their true essence, to heal themselves and their relationships, and to practice the art of living from the heart. The higher intent of her work is to forward human evolution during these times of great planetary change. Her dedication to learning and passion for medicine work has enabled her and others to deepen their awareness, integrate, and develop their natural gifts. Her interest is in global healing, personal transformation, and cross-cultural communication to facilitate increasing harmony, balance, and growth for all beings on the planet.

Currently, she travels the Americas learning, integrating, and sharing what she's learned about natural medicine and the art of living taught to her by indigenous elders and spiritual wisdom keepers. She facilitates ceremonies and transformational healing experiences, and works one-on-one and with groups of people to help them expand their consciousness and move forward on their journey.

Since mid 2007, she's been a guest speaker at the annual International Amazonian Shamanism Conference in Iquitos, Peru (www.soga-del-alma.org) where she spoke about traditional healing and shamanism while she conducted ceremonies there. Since then, she's been frequently interviewed on the C-realm international podcast (www.C realm.com) and on other radio shows. She is an Advisory Board Member of c3, the Center for Conscious Creativity (www.consciouscreativity.org) in Los Angeles, California where she brings shamanism into the boardroom to facilitate both communication and creativity. She is currently working on a book entitled, *Dancing with Trees*, about working with tree and plant medicine based on her experiences in the United Kingdom and the Americas.

Wendy teaches traditional healing approaches, facilitates healings, and leads ceremonies internationally, as well as leading experiential spiritual journeys to work with elders in their homelands. Contact her directly at wendyluckey2@gmail.com for more information.

MacKaye, Ian

Ian MacKaye founded Dischord Records as a teenager in 1980 with partner Jeff Nelson. Their original intent was simply to release a single to document their recently defunct band, Teen Idles. However, the label has gone on to release music from more than 60 bands, with more than 160 albums over the last 25 years and counting.

As musicians Ian and Jeff went on to form Minor Threat, who along with Bad Brains are credited in the early 80s with introducing the DC hardcore ethic to an audience well beyond Washington, DC.

In 1986, Ian formed Fugazi with Joe Lally, Brendan Canty and Guy Picciotto. Over 20+ years the band has released seven albums and toured the world extensively covering all fifty United States, Europe, Australia, South America, Japan and many points in between. Fugazi is self-managed and maintains a policy of affordable access to their work through low record and ticket prices and all concerts are all-ages. In 2003 Fugazi decided to take an indefinite hiatus from recording and touring as young families and other priorities began to take center stage.

Since 2001, Ian has played in The Evens, a duo with Amy Farina. The Evens revel in short-circuiting the conventions of rock music and perform mostly in non-traditional music spaces—libraries, art spaces, schools, theaters, etc. They have released two albums and have toured extensively in North America, Europe, South America, Australia, and New Zealand. Ian has also been taking on speaking engagements, delivering talks that take the form of informal Question and Answer sessions.

Madu, Dr Ernest Chijioke

Dr Ernest Madu is the Founder of the Heart Institute of the Caribbean and serves as the Chairman and Chief Executive Officer for the center. He is responsible for day-to-day operations, global vision and strategic relationships. Dr Madu served on the Faculty of Medicine in the Division of Cardiology at Vanderbilt University. He is an expert in non-invasive cardiovascular diagnostics, with broad training and experience in all areas of cardiovascular diagnosis. Dr Madu is an internationally renowned Cardiologist that is well respected in the international cardiology community. He has published extensively in well respected medical journals including such journals as Nature Medicine, Circulation, Journal of the American College of Cardiology, Journal of the American Society of Echocardiography and Hypertension.

Dr Ernest Chijioke Madu believes that people in the developing world have a right to world-class health care. At his three Heart Institute of the Caribbean clinics—in Kingston and Mandeville, Jamaica, and in the Cayman Islands—he delivers more than $1 million a year in free or reduced-care treatment, a significant contribution in an area where 56% of hospital deaths are caused by cardiovascular disease.

Now Dr Madu is hoping to transfer HIC's mission and achievements into other low-resource nations. His next target is Nigeria, his home country, where the Heart Institute of West Africa and International Hospital is currently in development as a vehicle to bring high quality, affordable and accessible health care to a region of the world with high disease prevalence but limited access to diagnostic and treatment options. Dr Madu combines clinical experience, technological advances and an entrepreneurial spirit to fulfill his mission to ensure high quality care is available for all. His unique perspective on globalization and its affect on health policy and business development is riveting. Using this as a conduit, he has been able to shape and energize the minds of innovators world-wide.

Dr Madu's views are frequently sought as a Speaker at major international forums. He has recently given major lectures at such conferences as TED Global 2007 in Arusha, Tanzania, United Health International, Florida 2008, Veerstichting, Leiden, Netherlands 2008 and US-Africa Private Health Forum, Washington DC, 2008.

Mali, Jeddah

As a child, I had many unusual (spiritual/extrasensory/paranormal) experiences that taught me how the intention of thought governs differing energy states, which in turn affect the behaviour of matter. These experiences came about unbidden, but even at the age of six I had an innate understanding of their nature. In the same way that a bird 'knows' how to fly without ever having done it before, I 'knew' at an early age that I had an ability to understand, and interact with, the intangible. I also knew that most people were not aware of this potential within themselves, and as a result, it lay largely undiscovered. However, it is always accessible for those who choose to look for it. My own questioning was answered in the form of advanced spiritual masters who appeared to me for teachings and guidance. They have been my constant companions ever since.

Throughout my life, I have experienced a series of awakenings, culminating now in a moment to moment awareness of the source of all existence. I have spent the rest of my life fine-tuning this ability to be able to teach others how to find, explore and realise that incredible potential.

In 1987, at the age of 20, I embarked on a 20 year long journey which led me to Asia to study with some of the world's highest ranking masters: His Holiness the Dalai Lama, His Holiness Ajahn Buddhadassa, Lama Zopa Rinpoche, Master Goenka and realised teachers in the Tibetan, Theravadan and Bhutanese traditions of Buddhism.

In order to understand the concepts involved in these teachings, one must undergo hundreds of hours of precise analysis and exploration through the practice of meditation (this is both in daily practise and in regular 10 day retreats in silence, practicing for up to 16 hours a day). There is little value in reading a book on these subjects. One must practice them in order to gain an experiential understanding. I learnt the necessity of action in achieving a desired outcome. These principles of self-discovery were the foundation for my subsequent understanding and experience of the structure, nature and working order of human consciousness and, of course, its ultimate purpose.

I am particularly interested in how the principles of creation apply to child development. This led me to gain a teaching quali-fication in anthroposophy, the study of spiritual science and its application to child development founded by Rudolf Steiner, between 1995 and 1997. In 1998 I was invited to establish the early childhood department at a school in Australia. Once I had finished my two year contract, I returned once more to my central passion, only this time working with groups as well as individuals.

In 1994, I was given permission from a group of advanced masters to conduct spiritual teachings and healings. I started moving away from a specific philosophical approach towards a more integrated, all-encompassing view of our nature and purpose. Working with the masters, I was encouraged to bring through instruction on how to experience our essence as Source, which had long lay dormant in modern man. I started the mentoring work for which I am best known: helping individuals overcome the limitations of their own thinking and teaching them how to better use the creative capacity of thought to realise Oneness. This has a direct impact on the future of our planet and us as a species.

Since that time, I have been mentoring individual clients and teaching small groups through high level coaching. I have set up and run courses for people to learn about and experience human energy field exploration. I have taken every opportunity to become adept in my field. The extent to which I have achieved this is now available to others.

I have the honor of a hundred percent satisfaction rate amongst my clients. However the real reward lies in helping people gain a better understanding of who they are and how to step into a whole new perception of themselves, thus transforming their reality, and that of our society and our planet, permanently. Warmest Regards, Jeddah Mali. www.jeddahmali.com

Manitonquat (Medicine Story)

Assonet Wampanoag elder, philosopher, author of: *Return to Creation; Children of the Morning Light; Ending Violent Crime; the Circle Way; Wampanoag Morning, The Original Instructions, Changing the World*, and *Grandfather Speaks*.

Manitonquat (Medicine Story) is a storyteller, an elder and a keeper of the lore of the Assonet Band of the Wampanoag Nation of Massachusetts. Author of eight published books and a former columnist and poetry editor with the internationally acclaimed journal Akwesasne Notes, he has also edited Heritage, a journal of Native American liberation.

Manitonquat has spoken to peace conferences and groups on 3 continents, was the keynote speaker at the United Nations observance of the 50th anniversary of Gandhi's assassination, directs programs for native spirituality in 7 prisons, a nature school on his land, and, with his wife Ellika, annual international family camps in Austria, Germany, Denmark, Sweden and Finland.

An outgrowth of a course he taught at a Waldorf high school became a new book, *Changing the World*, which he has printed in a preliminary draft to get feedback from general readers that may later be incorporated into a final version for publication.

Manitonquat is now working on the final draft of a new book, *The Original Instructions*. His annual newsletter Talking Stick can be found with other articles and his schedule on the web at www.circleway.org

Contact:

Mettanokit, 167 Merriam Hill, Greenville, NH 03048

Tel. (603) 878-2310

Marris, Sheree

Victorian-based Aquatic Scientist Sheree Marris is one of Australia's youngest environment ambassadors who are committed to educating the community about their responsibilities towards water preservation, marine life and other environmental issues such as recycling.

The media-savvy 28 year old uses radio, television and newspapers effectively to channel her environmental messages. Through radio talk-back, television appearances, hosting documentaries and featuring in commercials, Sheree has gained a reputation and profile among the Australian community, national corporate organizations and all levels of government as an expert in her field.

A regular guest speaker at universities, school groups and youth organizations, Sheree has become a role-model for young environmentalists. Her down-to-earth approach in delivering education makes her sessions entertaining, informative and above all interesting to people from all disciplines.

In 2002 Sheree's profile was further heightened when she picked up three Young Australian of the Year awards: the National Unilever Environment Award, Young Australian of the Year (Victoria) and Victorian Unilever Environment Award. Among other numerous awards and accolades, Sheree was the year 2000 recipient of the Queen's Trust for Young Australians. This achievement gave Sheree the opportunity to present a paper on "Using the media as a powerful tool for environmental education" at an international marine education conference in Long Beach California, USA.

In January 2002 Sheree established her own environmental communications consulting business called Visions of Blue. In the short time the business has been in operation, Sheree has been commissioned by some of Australia's leading national organisations to provide advice and initiate environmental projects on their behalf. The Octopuses' Garden, Victoria's first snorkeling trail, was established at Rye Pier by Visions of Blue with sponsorship from Transfield Services. A further four underwater trails are planned for Victoria.

At the end of 2002 Channel 10 aired a two-part documentary series about marine life in Port Phillip Bay. This documentary was written, produced and presented by Sheree and future documentaries with the network are planned.

Sheree is also talented at putting her environmental messages on paper and has written and published many books. Her latest book, *KarmaSEAtra - Secrets of Sex in the Sea*, is a humorous read about the unique reproductive methods of sea creatures and the parallels they have with humans. www.visionsofblue.com.au

Martinez, James

James Martinez has a diverse history in the entertainment business. He's worked as a Casting Director, Manager, Actor and Radio personality. Throughout his years in the business he met a Director and collaborated to create meaningful programming that would create a better world. The subject of the programming was to be modern finance and its psychological effects on society.

Mr Martinez discovered that the ability to question the existing establishment on the nature of banking as well as challenging the credit card companies through consumer protection practices had to be done. Consequently after years of study, James managed to eliminate "alleged" credit card debts long before any documentaries were made exposing the credit card companies for who they really are. "Freedom to Fascism" Directed by Aaron Russo, "Maxed Out" Directed by James Scurlock and "In Debt We Trust" Directed by Danny Schechter became significant educational tools which provided an audience some of the tactics credit card companies used against their members. James has interviewed them all. However, none of them provided remedy for the millions of people affected by this national catastrophe. Long before these documentaries were made Mr Martinez successfully participated in eliminating over $700 million dollars of alleged credit card debt over a ten-year period. James managed to connect with people at The World Bank, International Monetary Fund and Bank of Warburg. This alliance with the help of the public has made this topic the number one concern of America today.

During this time Mr Martinez served as a member of the Board of Directors of the Freedom of Thought Foundation created by world re-known author and hypnotherapist Walter Bowart author of *Operation Mind Control*. It was during this time James discovered and studied all the behavior modalities associated with debt consciousness and began to uncover the necessary tools to inspire behavior modification in a generation of tragedy associated with credit card debt. In a time where suicide, broken families and bankruptcy are commonplace Mr Martinez managed to help thousands of families get their life back and see the world with a new perspective and life realization for a better tomorrow. In 2008 Mr Martinez was placed on the Board of Directors of the Marshal McLuhan Center on Global Communications.

Today Mr Martinez is currently working with Bob Neveritt in weekly State of the Union address and press conference to the world. The vital preparation and education of the public on new technologies aims to free the world from the inevitable failure of banking in an electrical environment. The implementation of free energy to the world via cold fusion and other suppressed technologies will obsolesce and even the playing field for the world. This operation began on 8-26-08 and will be one of the greatest achievements of the human race and one of the most important steps to the liberation of the human spirit. www.achieveradio.com

Maser, Chris

Chris Maser has spent over 25 years as a research scientist in natural history and ecology in forest, shrub steppe, subarctic, desert, coastal, and agricultural settings. Trained primarily as a vertebrate zoologist, he was a research mammalogist in Nubia, Egypt, (1963-1964) with the Yale University Peabody Museum Prehistoric Expedition and a research mammalogist in Nepal (1966-1967), where he participated in a study of tick-borne diseases for the U.S. Naval Medical Research Unit #3 based in Cairo, Egypt. He conducted a three-year (1970-1973) ecological survey of the Oregon Coast for the University of Puget Sound, Tacoma, Washington. He was a research ecologist with the U.S. Department of the Interior, Bureau of Land Management for thirteen years (1974-1987)—the last eight studying old-growth forests in western Oregon—and a landscape ecologist with the Environmental Protection Agency for one year (1990-1991). Today he is an independent author as well as an international lecturer, facilitator in resolving environmental conflicts, vision statements, and sustainable community development. He is also an international consultant in forest ecology and sustainable forestry practices. He has written over 270 publications, including his most recent book: *Earth in Our Care: Ecology, Economy, and Sustainability*. www.chrismaser.com

McKibben, Bill

Bill McKibben is the author of "a dozen or so" books on the environment, a scholar in residence at Middlebury College, and the co-founder of 350.org.

Miller, Dr Emmett

Often acknowledged as one of the fathers of mind/Body Medicine, Dr Miller is a physician, poet, musician, and master storyteller, whose multicultural heritage has given him a unique social, medical, and spiritual perspective. His commitment to helping us to reclaim our inborn personal wisdom, integrated with the scientific knowledge and techniques of modern medicine, has allowed him to unite seemingly disparate fields of knowledge and experience. For over 30 years, it has been his inspiration and his challenge to help people—individuals, families, and organizations—discover this truth for themselves. Millions have been touched by his message of hope, his vision of a brighter future, and his spirit of wellbeing. As a physician, health educator, and a pioneer in a field that is now on the cutting edge of modern medicine, Dr Miller brings us a deeper understanding of how the mind and body can work in harmony to produce healing, balance and wellness.

Dr Miller, a graduate of the Albert Einstein College of Medicine, has been a lecturer and preceptor at Stanford University and The University of California, as well as other universities and medical schools. In 1977, he gained international prominence as a founder and Medical Director of the Cancer Support and Education Center, (Now the Center for Healing and Wellness), and, in 1987, as a co-convener of the groundbreaking California State Task Force on Self-Esteem. A pioneer in the development of mind-body medicine, he has been widely acclaimed for his invention and development of the first deep relaxation/guided imagery intro audiocassettes. His tapes and CDs are widely used by such medical facilities as Kaiser Permanente, the Mayo Clinic, and by health professionals, business people, performers, and athletes, including members of the U.S. Olympic Track and Field Team.

Dr Miller is the author of numerous books, beginning with the seminal *Selective Awareness for Self-Healing*, in 1973, and including his latest contribution, *Deep Healing: The Essence of Mind/Body Medicine*. Deep Healing is a bold step forward in the theory, philosophy, and practice of self-healing and peak performance. In the book, Dr Miller shows clearly how beliefs and images become actual physical events in the body, and includes detailed instructions and training in how you can learn to use images and emotions to change your mind and change your life. His tapes and CDs do more than just talk about how it can be done; they take you by the hand and guide you through the experience of doing it, in a most enjoyable way.

The instruments Dr Miller offers here are not scalpels and drugs...but words and experiences—images, memories, and emotions. They do not substitute for or replace needed medical or psychological therapy—instead, they enable you to do your part in changing your diet, exercise patterns, thoughts and relationships. His techniques teach you to relax and his presentations inspire you to take charge of your life and realize your full potential. He has shared his insights into Deep Healing on hundreds of television and radio shows. He has appeared in the San Francisco Examiner, Los Angeles Times, Journal, as well as American Health, Prevention, Essence, Women's Day, Woman's World, Yoga Journal, and Shape magazines. His columns have appeared in more than 30 newspapers and magazines. www.drmiller.com

Mountrose, Drs Phillip & Jane
Pioneers in energy-healing and devoted to helping people live their life purpose, Drs Phillip and Jane Mountrose co-wrote *The Heart & Soul of EFT and Beyond*... The Mountroses offer high-quality holistic healing and spiritual counselor home-study certification courses, as well as their popular free e-newsletter "The Soul News." www.gettingthru.org

Murray, Jessica

Jessica Murray trained as a fine artist before graduating in 1973 from Brown University, where she studied traditional psychology and linguistics. After a stint in political theatre, Jessica began a study of metaphysics and has been practicing and teaching astrology in San Francisco for thirty years.

In addition to her monthly **Skywatch**, Jessica writes commentary for DayKeeperJournal.com, as well as articles for *The Mountain Astrologer, Psychic and Spirit Magazine* and other publications. Her new book *Soul-Sick Nation: An Astrologer's View of America* (MotherSky Press 2008) is an in-depth study of the global role of the United States, its recent past and near future.

Jessica Murray lives in the Castro District of San Francisco. She offers a full range of astrological readings, by appointment on weekdays, in a professional, comfortable setting complete with a pot of fine tea. **www.mothersky.com**

Nutt, Dr Samantha

Dr Samantha Nutt, MD, MSc, CCFP, FRCPC, is a medical doctor with more than thirteen years of experience working in war zones. Committed to peace, human rights and social justice, her ambition has always been to help war-affected women and children. She has worked in some of the world's most violent flashpoints with War Child, the United Nations and non-governmental organizations (NGOs) in Iraq, Afghanistan, The Democratic Republic of Congo, Liberia, Sierra Leone, Somalia, Iraq, Burundi, northern Uganda and the Thai-Burmese border.

Over the course of her professional career and as the Founder and Executive Director of War Child Canada (which is also responsible for War Child in the USA), Nutt has spearheaded efforts to provide direct humanitarian support and long term programming to war-affected children and their families, and to promote greater awareness across Canada and the United States concerning the rights of children everywhere.

Chosen by Maclean's Magazine for their annual Honour Roll as one of "12 Canadians making a difference", she is a role model to many Canadians and Americans, and has received numerous humanitarian awards for her work in support of war-affected children.

Nutt is a recipient of Canada's Top 40 Under 40 Award, has been profiled by Time Magazine as "one of Canada's five leading activists" and by CBC News Sunday as an "outstanding leader". Global Television has declared her a "Trailblazer". In 2006, she was also voted by Chatelaine readers as one of 12 women they would most like to see run for politics. Most recently, Homemaker's Magazine called her one of the "Ten Great Canadian Women to Know" and Chatelaine Magazine chose her as "Ms Chatelaine". Dr Nutt is the 2007 recipient of the Tiffany Mark Award for her humanitarian work in support of children affected by war and has also been recognized as an inspirational "Success Story" on CTV National News. She has been profiled in the USA by Marie Claire Magazine and her work has been featured in The Economist and on Good Morning America (2003).

Nutt has written for Maclean's Magazine covering war-related issues, is a published author and frequently appears on television and radio as an expert commentator on war and its impact on civilians. In 2007, she wrote and contributed a piece to CBC Radio One's *This I Believe* series. She is a highly sought after keynote speaker on the impact of war and on public engagement in global issues, inspiring others to make a difference.

A specialist in Maternal and Child Health in zones of armed conflict, Family Medicine, Public Health, and Women's Health, Nutt is also on staff at Women's College Hospital in Toronto, Canada and is an Assistant Professor at the University of Toronto in the Department of Family and Community Medicine. Nutt holds undergraduate degrees in Arts and Science, and in Medicine, from McMaster University in Hamilton, Canada and postgraduate degrees in Medicine and in Public Health from the University of Toronto as well as the London School of Hygiene and Tropical Medicine (London University).

Dr Nutt has received Honorary Doctorates from McMaster University, Brock University and Niagara University for her work promoting human rights and her role in delivering humanitarian assistance to some of the world's most vulnerable populations.

For information on War Child in Canada and the USA visit www.warchild.ca or www.warchild.us. War Child is a nationally registered American charity with 501c3 status.

O'Leary, Dr Brian

Dr O'Leary has published internationally ten trade books on the frontiers of science, space, energy and culture, with sales averaging over 10,000 copies per book. He was a NASA scientist-astronaut, assistant professor of astronomy at Cornell University alongside Carl Sagan, and has also taught Physics for Poets at Princeton University and technology assessment at the University of California Berkeley School of Law and Hampshire College. He has published over 100 technical papers in the peer-reviewed scientific literature and another 100 popular magazine and Op-Ed pieces worldwide. He has appeared frequently on American national television and radio, including the Today Show, Larry King Live, the Donahue Show and the Art Bell Show.

A passionate environmentalist open to innovative solutions, Dr O'Leary was special consultant to the U.S. House of Representatives Subcommittee on Energy and the Environment, wrote speeches and was senior advisor to environmental presidential candidate Morris Udall. He also helped presidential candidates George McGovern, Walter Mondale and Jesse Jackson on economic policies to convert from polluting and military activities to green initiatives.

He is currently on the faculty of the University of Philosophical Research in Los Angeles, teaching in the Masters program in Transformational Psychology. He is co-founder of the New Energy Movement (no longer President). He has recently completed the Sivananda Yoga Teachers Training Course and lectures widely at their ashrams and centers throughout the world. He is co-founder of the International Association of New Science and advisor to Dennis Weaver's Institute of Ecolonomics.

Over the past decade, Dr O'Leary has spoken or led workshops at the Esalen Insitute, the Findhorn Foundation, Oxford University, St. James Picadilly, State of the World Forum, the United Nations Youth Assembly, the International Conferences on Science and Consciouness, the International Forums on New Science, the Philosophical Research Society, the International Institute of Integral Human Sciences, Unity churches, Churches of Religious Science, the Yuba Seminars and dozens of other venues worldwide.

With his artist-wife Meredith, Brian has founded Montesueños, a retreat center and botanical garden in the Ecuadorian Andes dedicated to finding deep peaceful and sustainable solutions to humankind's war on nature and to implement these at local, regional and global levels of action, along with holding workshops and residences in the arts.

His latest book is *The Energy Solution Revolution.* www.brianoleary.info

Ortiz, Ernesto

Ernesto Ortiz, LMT, CST, KRM, is the founder and director of Journey to the Heart, a company dedicated to the upliftment of consciousness and the Well-Being of people. He is a noted artist, author, renowned and inspiring facilitator, teacher and therapist and is recognized for his innovative, explorative, and multi-dimensional training in massage therapy, Cranio Sacral therapy, Karmapa Reiki, Integrative/Shamanic techniques, Breathwork, Akashic Records, music therapy, and Trance Dance. His training started at an early age with Shamans and Curanderos in Mexico and South America and has continued with teachers from all over the world.

Ernesto has devoted his life to exploring and communicating the language of the heart, primal movement and deep inner spaces. Over the past 25 years, Ernesto has taken thousands of people on a journey from physical and emotional inertia to the freedom of ecstasy, from the chaos of the chattering ego-mind to the blessed emptiness of stillness and inner silence.

His Workshops and Retreats have an electric intensity that unifies the spiritual with the mundane, from the poetic discovery of the soul to the modern approach of ancient shamanic practices. He has facilitated numerous workshops and seminars in the US, Canada, Australia, the Caribbean, Indonesia, Egypt the UK and South America.

Ernesto is the author of *In the Presence of Love, Mastering the Art of Relationships* and others. His Akashic Records and Tian Di Bamboo workshop are also available on DVD. For more information visit www.journey2theheart.com

Pascoe, Ted

A graduate of Dartmouth College and the Daniels College of Business, Ted has spent a career in politics and nonprofits. He is currently the executive director of Senior Support Services, a non-profit providing resources and support to hungry and homeless seniors.

Perkins, Kelly

Kelly has expanded the possibilities of what a heart transplant recipient can do, climbing mountains that few thought possible, all the while using a visual approach to help promote the importance of participation and awareness for organ, tissue and blood donation.

Kelly has been featured in numerous TV and radio programs, as well as newspapers and magazines around the world. She has also become a sought-after speaker, inspiring audiences around the globe with her remarkable comeback story. Her memoir, *The Climb of My Life, Scaling Mountains with a Borrowed Heart,* (Rowman & Littlefield, 2007) details her inspiring journey back to good health. For more information, please visit www.theclimbofmylife.com.

Petersen, Carol

Carol Petersen had a private practice in holistic wellness which reached a critical mass when healing individuals jumped to a new level and her concerns became global. An eco-spiritual activist from the Maya of the ancient temples of the Central America, the Bolivian Aymara, and the native peoples of Argentina Amazonia, Carol Petersen became their voice. She is a council member Consejo de Saber Qulla, (Council of Knowledge) from Tiwanacu, El Alto La Paz, Bolivia, and a member of the Confederation of Consejos Ancianos Originarios de Abya Yala, (Confederation of Original Elder Councils of the Southern Hemisphere).

Founder of Rainbow Medicine Blanket, a council of native women advocates for human and ecological justice: to support Peace and Friendship, Cultural Awareness dedicated to earth keeping traditions.

Lectured on Sustainable Ecology at the Nevada Desert Experience, a watchdog group against atomic testing.

A candidate for Congress, California District 41, as an Independent.

Radio program host called Soul and Sage, http://www.therealpublicradio.net

("The Ecology of Soul" – copyright March 23, 2009)

Plotkin, Ph.D., Mark J.

Mark J. Plotkin, Ph.D. is president of the Amazon Conservation Team and research associate at the Smithsonian Institution's

Museum of Natural History. He served as Research Associate in Ethnobotanical Conservation at the Botanical Museum of Harvard University, Director of Plant Conservation at the World Wildlife Fund, Vice President of Conservation International, and Research Associate at the Department of Botany of the Smithsonian Institution. Author and co-author of several books including, *Tales of a Shaman's Apprentice*.

Powell M.D., Diane Hennacy

After an undergraduate education in neuroscience, Diane Powell received her medical degree from the Johns Hopkins University School of Medicine, where she also completed training in medicine, neurology, and psychiatry. She obtained additional training at Queen Square and The Institute of Psychiatry, both world-renowned medical institutes in London. She has been on the faculty at Harvard Medical School, was a member of a part-time think tank on consciousness at the Salk Institute in La Jolla, CA, and the Director of Research for the John E. Mack Institute. She currently is a member of the Board of Directors of the Jean Houston Foundation.

Her clinical practice has been diverse and international in scope. It has included being the Assistant Clinical Director of the Consultation-Liaison Service at Cambridge Hospital (a teaching hospital for Harvard); being the Chief Psychiatrist of the emergency room at Brockton Multi-Service Center; training and providing psychotherapy to Soviet psychologists; co-creating and serving as Clinical Director of the McCandliss Center for Women in Chula Vista, CA (which treated survivors of sexual assault, post-partum depression, and eating disorders); starting the psychiatric program for Survivors of Torture, International in San Diego, CA and providing treatment to its clients (refugees and asylum seekers from countries where genocide, torture, and terrorism have resulted in severe Post-Traumatic Stress Disorder). She currently has a solo practice in Medford, Oregon and incorporates psychotherapy, psychopharmacology, and pet therapy into her compassionate healing of people who want personalized care. She is frequently in Los Angeles, where she is available on a restricted basis for consultation.

She is the great niece of the famous peace activist, Ammon Hennacy, and has been a strong advocate for human rights. She participated in the United Nations Conference on Women and Children in Beijing in 1995 and is one of the panelists for the PBS documentary, *The Science of Peace*, which is still in production. www.dianehennacypowell.com

Ramirez, Magdala

Born a medicine woman she lived among the pyramids in Mexico in the ancient wisdom of the Maya and Aztec people. She was trained in her work from a very early age, spending many years studying and sharing information with the elders of knowledge near her home.

She has worked 35 years with the feminine ways, warrior woman and sacred dance. Magdala is a celebrated teacher and leader, she has traveled around the Continent speaking, creating ceremonies and seminars, she is a spiritual guide for Sacred Places, she is the author of six books, *Mayan Runes, Games People Play, Sacredness of the Union of Polarities, I am You, Sacred Sex*, and *Moon Codex*.

Roberts, Llyn

Llyn Roberts, MA is a prominent teacher of healing and shamanism. She has worked with original cultures spanning the globe. Her books include *The Good Remembering, Shapeshifting into Higher Consciousness* and (with Robert Levy) *Shamanic Reiki*. Roberts runs the non-profit organization, Dream Change www.dreamchange.org, dedicated to preserving indigenous wisdom and inspiring the transformation of human consciousness. She served as adjunct faculty for Union Graduate

School and teaches at the Omega and Esalen Institutes and at Rowe Conference Center with NY Times best-selling author, John Perkins—with whom she has worked since 1987. A modern day mystic and Buddhist-trained therapist, Roberts's work inspires a deep sense of belonging with the natural world.

Rosling, Hans

Hans Rosling, professor of International Health and Director of Gapminder.org. Gapminder is a non-profit venture promoting sustainable global development and achievement of the United Nations Millennium Development Goals by increased use and understanding of statistics and other information about social, economic and environmental development at local, national and global levels. Karolinska Institutet, Stockholm, Sweden.

Ross, Steven A.

Steven A. Ross has lectured to over 200 clubs, organizations, social groups, and private groups and has appeared in approximately 15 regional and national television programs. Steven is currently the CEO of the World Research Foundation, a 501(c)(3) nonprofit organization.

Since its inception in 1984, World Research Foundation has established a unique, international, health information network, so that people could be informed of all available treatments around the world, and so that they could have the freedom to choose based on complete and in-depth information.

The purpose of the Foundation is to locate, gather, codify, evaluate, classify, and disseminate information dealing with health and the environment. All countries are contacted to collect the best health information in an unbiased, neutral, and independent manner. The collected health information encompasses both ancient and current data from traditional and nontraditional medicine.

The World Research Foundation is one of the only organizations that provide comprehensive health information on both allopathic and *alternative medicine* techniques. In addition, WRF is the premier organization with established contacts with health practitioners and clinics in Europe. It has one of the foremost health information and philosophical libraries in the nation, and is considered a principal source regarding alternative medicine treatments and therapies. WRF has no bias, and strives to provide the most accurate health information to anyone in need. www.wrf.org

Russell, Peter

Peter Russell M.A., D.C.S., F.S.P., is a fellow of the Institute of Noetic Sciences, of The World Business Academy and of The Findhorn Foundation, and an Honorary Member of The Club of Budapest.

At Cambridge University (UK), he studied mathematics and theoretical physics. Then, as he became increasingly fascinated by the mysteries of the human mind he changed to experimental psychology. Pursuing this interest, he traveled to India to study meditation and eastern philosophy, and on his return took up the first research post ever offered in Britain on the psychology of meditation.

He also has a post-graduate degree in computer science, and conducted there some of the early work on 3-dimensional displays, presaging by some twenty years the advent of virtual reality.

In the mid-seventies Peter Russell joined forces with Tony Buzan and helped teach "Mind Maps" and learning methods to a variety of international organizations and educational institutions.

Since then his corporate programs have focused increasingly on self-development, creativity, stress management, and sustainable environmental practices. Clients have included IBM, Apple, Digital, American Express, Barclays Bank, Swedish

Telecom, ICI, Shell Oil and British Petroleum.

His principal interest is the deeper, spiritual significance of the times we are passing through. He has written several books in this area—*The TM Technique, The Upanishads, The Brain Book, The Global Brain Awakens, The Creative Manager, The Consciousness Revolution, Waking Up in Time,* and *From Science to God.*

As one of the more revolutionary futurists Peter Russell has been a keynote speaker at many international conferences, in Europe, Japan and the USA. His multi-image shows and videos, The Global Brain and The White Hole in Time have won praise and prizes from around the world. In 1993 the environmental magazine Buzzworm voted Peter Russell "Eco-Philosopher Extraordinaire" of the year. www.peterrussell.com

Salingaros, Dr Nikos

Nikos A. Salingaros is a mathematician and polymath known for his work on urban theory, architectural theory, complexity theory, and design philosophy. He has been a close collaborator of the architect and computer software pioneer Christopher Alexander, with whom Salingaros shares a harsh critical analysis of conventional modern architecture. Like Alexander, Salingaros has proposed an alternative theoretical approach to architecture and urbanism that is more adaptive to human needs and aspirations, and that combines rigorous scientific analysis with deep intuitive experience.

Prior to turning his attention to architecture and urbanism, Salingaros published substantive research on Algebras, Mathematical Physics, Electromagnetic Fields, and Thermonuclear Fusion before turning his attention to Architecture and Urbanism. Salingaros still teaches mathematics, and is Professor of Mathematics at the University of Texas at San Antonio. He is also on the Architecture faculties of universities in Italy, Mexico, and the Netherlands. (Wikipedia)

Schwartz, Robert

In a personal session with a medium in 2003, author Robert Schwartz was astonished to speak with nonphysical beings who knew everything about him—not just what he had done in life, but also what he had thought and felt. They told him that he had planned many of his most difficult experiences before he was born. Realizing that a knowledge of pre-birth planning would bring great healing to people and allow them to understand the deeper purpose of their life challenges, he devoted the next three years to studying the pre-birth plans of dozens of individuals. The extraordinary insights that emerged speak to our heartfelt, universal yearning to know…why.

Author—*Your Soul's Plan: Discovering the Real Meaning of the Life You Planned Before You Were Born*, www.YourSoulsPlan.com

Schwartz, Stephan A.

Research Associate of the Cognitive Sciences Laboratory of the Laboratories for Fundamental Research, and previously founder and Research Director of the Mobius laboratory, and Director of Research of the Rhine Research Center. Schwartz is part of the small group that founded modern Remote Viewing research, and the principal researcher studying the use of Remote Viewing in archaeology. In addition to numerous technical papers and reports he has written four books on the subject: *The Secret Vaults of Time, The Alexandria Project, Mind Rover*. His submarine experiment, Deep Quest, using Remote Viewing helped determine that nonlocal perception is not an electromagnetic phenomenon. He also conceived the original research that developed Associated/Associational Remote Viewing (ARV). Other areas of interest include research into creativity and Therapeutic Intent, including a continuation of the analysis of water exposed to therapeutic intent using spectroscopy that was begun by Grad and Dean. His latest book is *Opening To The Infinite*. He is the columnist for the journal *Explore*.

References for "Mind-Body and The Social Dimension"

1 Private communication. 23 March 1989.
2 Wolfgang Pauli, 1955.
3 Osis K and Dean D. The effect of experimenter differences and subject's belief level upon ESP scores. Journal of the American Society for Psychical Research 1964, 58,158-185.
4 Gertrude Schmeidler and Michaeleen Maher. Journal of the American Society for Psychical Research. July 1981.
5 Hazelrigg P, Cooper H, and Strathman A. Personality Moderators of the Experimenter Expectancy Effect: A Reexamination of Five Hypotheses. Personality and Social Psychology Bulletin, Vol. 17, No. 5, 569-579 (1991)DOI: 10.1177/0146167291175012.
6 Cooper H and Hazelrigg P. Personality moderators of interpersonal expectancy effects: An integrative research review. Journal of Personality and Social Psychology 55 (1988): 937-949.
7 Hazelrigg P, Cooper H, and Strathman A. Personality Moderators of the Experimenter Expectancy Effect: A Reexamination of Five Hypotheses. Personality and Social Psychology Bulletin, Vol. 17, No. 5, 569-579 (1991)DOI: 10.1177/0146167291175012.
8 Milgram. S. Obedience to Authority: An Experimental View Obedience to authority : an experimental view. New York : Perennial Classics, 2004.
9 Milgram S. The Perils of Obedience, Harper's Magazine 1974. E-version to be found at: http://home.swbell.net/revscat/perilsOfObedience.html. Accessed: 5 January 2009.
10 Burger JM. Replicating Milgram: Would People Still Obey Today? American Psychologist. Volume 64, Issue 1, January 2009, Pages 1-11. DOI: 10.1037/a0010932

11 Krieger L. Shocking Revelation: Santa Clara University Professor Mirrors Famous Torture Study. Mercury News. 21 December 2008. *SR Mind-Body and the Social Dimension* • *Schwartz* [9 \ http://www.mercurynews.com/breakingnews/ci_ 11285984?nclick_check=1. Accessed: 21 December 2008.

12 *Albert Speer: His battle with Truth.* By Gitta Sereny. (Vintage: New York, 1996). Pp. 136-137.

13 *Ibid.*

14 Carl Gustave Jung. *Memories, Dreams, Reflections.* Recorded and ed. by Aniela Jaffé. Trans. Richard and Clara Winston. (Pantheon Books: New York, 1963).

15 Unbroadcast BBC *Panorama* Interview. Roll 3; Rolls 4/1, 4/2.

16 Robert Gellately. *Backing Hitler: Consent and Coercion in Nazi Germany* (Oxford: Oxford, 2001)

17 Norton A. Happiness May be Good for Your Health. Reuters/Health 3 January 2008. http://www.reuters.com/article/scienceNews/id USPAR27336920080103?feedType=RSS&feedName=sc ienceNews&rpc=22&sp=true. Accessed: 3 January 2008.

18 Steptoe A, O'Donnell K, Badrick E, Kumari M, Marmot M. Neuroendocrine and inflammatory factors associated with positive affect in healthy men and women: the Whitehall II study. Am J Epidemiol. 2008 Jan 1;167(1):96-102. Epub 2007 Oct 4.

19 Stein R. Happiness Can Spread Among People Like a Contagion, Study Indicates. Washington Post 5 December 2008, pg. AO8. http://www.washingtonpost.com/wpdyn/conten t/article/2008/12/04/AR2008120403537.html?hpid=topne ws. Accessed: 5 December 2008.

20 Fowler JH and Christakis NA. Dynamic spread of happiness in a large social network: longitudinal analysis

over 20 years in the Framingham Heart Study. BMJ
2008;337:a2338, doi: 10.1136/bmj.a2338 4 December 2008.

Secours, Molly

As a writer/speaker/filmmaker/activist, Molly Secours has been
called an "uncompromising fighter for racial equity and social
justice".

Since 1995, Ms. Secours' writings have been published by over
50 mainstream and internet magazines and newspapers. She has
appeared on numerous radio and television talk shows to discuss
issues of racism, white privilege and reparations for slavery.

In 1998 Ms. Secours was invited to serve as an Advisory Board
Member at Fisk University's *Race Relations Institute* in Nashville,
Tennessee. In 2000, she presented an intervention to the United
Nations in Santiago, Chile, proposing that the U.S. "repudiate the
official histories and language(s) that maintain the hegemonic
and unearned privileges accorded to those who are identified as
'white'." During the Summer of 2001, Secours attended the
United Nations Prep-com in Geneva, Switzerland, and, as a
journalist, covered the *World Conference on Racism* in Durban,
South Africa (August 2001).

During 2000-2001, Ms. Secours wrote a bi-weekly column for
the daily *Nashville City Paper* until she was informed the paper
was "taking a hard right turn in order to attract financing" and
voices of the left were no longer needed. Since then, Secours has
become a contributing writer for *z-net magazine* and many other
progressive publications and has written and produced videos
for *Death Penalty Institute* and *Free Speech TV*.

Secours is a contributing writer in a book published by Harper
Collins (Jan. 2003) titled *Should America Pay?* Her chapter,
entitled "Riding the Reparations Bandwagon," addresses issues
of white privilege and reparations for the African Slave Trade.
She has also co-created a workshop entitled *"Straight Talk About
Race-a dialog in black in white"* which she co-facilitates with Dr.

Raymond Winbush, the Director of Urban Research at Morgan State University in Baltimore MD.

In Spring 2001, Secours testified before the *Tennessee Judiciary Committee* in support of a reparations study bill. In Fall 2001, *The Scene*, Nashville's alternative weekly, identified Secours as one of "Nashville's most influential public intellectuals". As a strong presence in the community, Secours has used her skills as a writer and orator to challenge state and local officials (as well as members of the community) to carefully consider the state's position on the death penalty and the racial disparities of the criminal justice system.

In a previous life, Secours worked in theater, film and television and recently founded a program called Youth Voice Through Video (Y.V.T.V.) wherein she teaches video-making to juvenile offenders and incarcerated youth in a Nashville prison. She has written, produced and edited documentary videos related to social justice issues and is working on several documentary film projects for her company, *One Woman Show Productions*. www.mollysecours.com

Silliphant, John

Co-founder of Seva Café, Friends Without Borders, DailyGood.org and numerous other projects designed to bring more love, inspiration, and magic to the world. Author and illustrator of *Here Come the Tickle Bugs!* a book designed to bring joy to kids. John is a work in progress...

Stamets, Paul

Paul Stamets has been a dedicated mycologist for over thirty years. Over this time, he has discovered and co-authored four new species of mushrooms, and pioneered countless techniques in the field of edible and medicinal mushroom cultivation. He received the 1998 "Bioneers Award" from The Collective Heritage Institute, and the 1999 "Founder of a New Northwest

Award" from the Pacific Rim Association of Resource Conservation and Development Councils. In 2008, Paul received the National Geographic Adventure Magazine's Green-Novator and the Argosy Foundation's E-chievement Awards. He was also named one of Utne Reader's "50 Visionaries Who Are Changing Your World" in their November–December 2008 issue.

He has written six books on mushroom cultivation, use and identification; his books *Growing Gourmet and Medicinal Mushrooms* and *The Mushroom Cultivator* (co-author) have long been hailed as the definitive texts of mushroom cultivation. Other works by Paul Stamets include *Psilocybe Mushrooms and Their Allies* (out of print), *Psilocybin Mushrooms of the World*, *MycoMedicinals®: an Informational Treatise on Mushrooms*, and many articles and scholarly papers. His newest book is *Mycelium Running: How Mushrooms Can Help Save The World*.

Paul sees the ancient Old Growth forests of the Pacific Northwest as a resource of incalculable value, especially in terms of its fungal genome. A dedicated hiker and explorer, his passion is to preserve, protect, and clone as many ancestral strains of mushrooms as possible from these pristine woodlands. Much of the financial resources generated from sales of goods from Fungi Perfecti are returned to sponsor such research. www.fungi.com

Steffen, Alex

Alex Steffen has been the Executive Editor of Worldchanging since he co-founded the organization in 2003, as the next phase in a lifetime of work exploring ways of building a better future.

Worldchanging is rated the 2nd largest sustainability-related publication on the Internet by Nielsen Online, and boasts an impressive archive of almost 9,000 articles by leading thinkers around the world.

Steffen was also the editor of Worldchanging's wildly successful first book, *Worldchanging: A User's Guide for the 21st Century* (Abrams, 2006), a 600-page compendium of writings from over sixty noted leaders around the world, with a foreword by Al Gore and introduction by Bruce Sterling.

Steffen's work has been subject of stories in the New York Times, the Wall Street Journal, The Guardian, and other leading publications. His essays have been translated into German, French, Japanese, Portuguese and Spanish, and widely reprinted and anthologized. Recently he was the subject of a CNN documentary, which envisions possibilities for the future, and was featured as one of six leading innovators in the New York Times Sunday Magazine's "Ecotecture" issue. He has also spoken and keynoted at many of the most renowned design and innovation conferences, including TED, Pop!Tech, and Design Indaba.

"We find ourselves facing two futures, one unthinkable and the other currently unimaginable," says Steffen, "My beat is looking for ways to create a future which is sustainable, dynamic, prosperous and fair—a future which is both bright and green. WorldChanging is based on the premise that such a future is not a distant possibility, but a growing reality. We seek to connect worldchanging people with the tools, models and ideas for building it." www.worldchanging.com

Tamminen, Terry

From his youth in Australia to career experiences in Europe, Africa and all parts of the United States, Terry has developed expertise in business, farming, education, non-profit, the environment, the arts, and government.

A United States Coast Guard-licensed ship captain, Terry has long been drawn to the undersea world, starting in the 1960s with a family-run tropical fish breeding business in Australia and continuing with studies on conch depletion in the Bahamas, manatee populations in Florida coastal waters, and mariculture in the Gulf States with Texas A&M University.

On land, Terry managed the largest sheep ranch east of the

Mississippi, assisting the University of Minnesota in developing new methods of livestock disease control. Terry also managed a multi-million dollar real estate company, owned/operated a successful recreational services business, and assisted the west African nation of Nigeria with the creation of their first solid waste recycling program.

An accomplished author, Terry's latest book, *Lives Per Gallon: The True Cost of Our Oil Addiction* (Island Press), is a timely examination of our dependence on oil and a strategy to evolve to more sustainable energy sources. He has also authored a series of best-selling "Ultimate Guides" to pools and spas (McGraw-Hill) and several theatrical works on the life of William Shakespeare. Terry is an avid airplane and helicopter pilot and speaks German, Dutch and Spanish.

In 1993, Terry founded the Santa Monica BayKeeper and served as its Executive Director for six years. He co-founded Waterkeeper programs in San Diego, Orange County, Ventura, and Santa Barbara. He also served for five years as Executive Director of the Environment Now Foundation in Santa Monica, CA and co-founded the Frank G. Wells Environmental Law Clinic at the School of Law, University of California Los Angeles.

In the summer of 2003, Terry helped Arnold Schwarzenegger win the historic recall election and become Governor of California. He was appointed as the Secretary of the California Environmental Protection Agency in November, 2003, and Cabinet Secretary, the Chief Policy Advisor to the Governor, in December, 2004. He continues to advise the Governor on energy and environmental policy. In April, 2007, he was named the Cullman Senior Fellow and Director of the Climate Policy Program of The New America Foundation, a non-profit, post-partisan, public policy institute. In September, 2007, he was appointed as an Operating Advisor to Pegasus Capital Advisors. Pegasus Capital Advisors, L.P., is a private equity fund manager that provides capital to middle market companies across a wide variety of industries.

Terry currently travels throughout the United States and the world, lecturing and providing private consulting services to a variety of clients, including several Governors and Canadian Premiers on climate and energy policy.

www.terrytamminen.com

Tennenbaum, Carla

Carla Tennenbaum is a young artist from São Paulo, Brazil. Working on the fertile intersection between Art and Design, Carla has not only created very original artwork and products from a wide range of materials, she has also developed innovative technologies for the creative and handcrafted *up-cycling* of industrial refuse and other discarded and undervalued resources. Her work with E.V.A. (ethyl-vinyl-acetate) waste has awarded her a first prize at the international contest *Design 21* 2005—"Love/Why?" (UNESCO/Felissimo Co.) and hOLAnDA 2003 (LADF—Latin-American Design Foundation), and in fostering project EVAMARIA Carla has won the support of Artemisia Brasil and the International Youth Foundation, who selected her as one of their 2008-2009 YouthActionNet global fellows.

Carla studied at the Armand Hammer United World College of the American West, in New Mexico/USA, from 1995-97, and graduated at the History Department of the Philosophy, Letters and Human Sciences College of the University of São Paulo (USP) in 2004. She has also completed a certified Gaia Education Ecovillage Design Curriculum at UMAPAZ, São Paulo, in 2008.

Project EVAMARIA was initiated by a sense of appal at the sheer volume of non-recyclable waste generated by commercial and industrial activities. Current estimates place the amount of E.V.A. refuse discarded in landfills in the State of São Paulo alone at 150 tons per month. Through EVAMARIA, Carla transforms this non-recyclable commercial waste into works of art, providing artistic development and opportunities of wage-generation for women excluded from the traditional job market. EVAMARIA's efforts focus largely on turning discarded industrial materials into functional and artistic objects. Through creating aesthetically stimulating products out of materials traditionally cast aside, EVAMARIA seeks to increase ecological awareness and conscious consumption.

Carla also provides creative services in the form of workshops, lectures and research projects, and offers consultancy for social organizations and artisans who need new productive strategies or innovative solutions for their products. www.caobaum.com www.evamaria.org

Tilsen, Nick

Nick Tilsen is a fourth generation organizer who has been active in many organizing efforts—from human rights to environmental justice and community economic development. Nick founded Lakota Action Network, a youth organization working to protect sacred sites while promoting sustainable alternatives in renewable energy. Nick served as the Executive Director for Lakota Action Network for four years. Tilsen has been a national correspondent for the Odyssey, an online non-profit producing original alternative content and interactive events on culture and politics aimed at educators and youth. The Odyssey serves over 75,000 k-12 students and 3,000 teachers worldwide. Tilsen has also served as the youth coordinator for the Teton Sioux Nation Treaty Council, working to get Lakota Treaty and human rights issues heard at the United Nations. He was also the director of LakotaMall.com for three years, working to create economic opportunities through the use of the internet. In 2002-2003, Tilsen served as the goodwill ambassador for the American Indian Higher Education Consortium promoting the Tribal college system. Nick is currently the Executive Director of the Thunder Valley Community Development Corporation, an organization that is dedicated to cultural education, sustainable community development and is currently engaging to create the Thunder Valley Community, the greenest community on an Indian reservation in North America. Both sides of Nick's family come from a tradition of resistance, dedication to the community and individual responsibility.

Tugwell, Frank

Frank Tugwell is President & CEO of Winrock International, a nonprofit organization that carries on the philanthropic work of the Rockefeller family around the world. He is responsible for leading the organization and advancing its mission to empower the disadvantaged, increase economic opportunity, and sustain natural resources.

Prior to joining Winrock, he served as Executive Director of the Heinz Endowments, a philanthropy that makes grants in the environment, human services, education, urban affairs, and the arts. Tugwell has also held positions as founder and President of the Environmental Enterprises Assistance Fund, a nonprofit venture capital firm investing in small and medium-sized environmental companies in developing countries; Deputy Assistant Administrator in the U.S. Agency for International Development in the Carter Administration; and Professor and Department Chair at Pomona College and Claremont Graduate School.

He holds a Ph.D. from Columbia University.

Vaughan-Lee, Emmanuel

Emmanuel Vaughan-Lee is the Founder and Director of the Global Oneness Project, a special project of the Kalliopeia Foundation. Prior to his work in the non-profit and foundation sector he was a critically acclaimed jazz bassist/composer and ran a successful entertainment company. In recent years he has worked with film and media based projects that focus on recognizing our common humanity and interconnectedness. www.globalonenessproject.org

Von Ward, Paul

Paul Von Ward with graduate degrees from Harvard and Florida State University, wrote *The Soul Genome: Science and Reincarnation* (2008) from the perspective of a psychologist and interdisciplinary cosmologist. Before becoming an independent scholar and creator of the Reincarnation Experiment, Paul's public career included roles as Protestant minister, U.S. naval officer, American diplomat, U.S. State Department official, and the founder/CEO of Delphi International. His other books include *Gods, Genes & Consciousness* (2004); *Our Solarian Legacy (2001)*; and *Dismantling the Pyramid: Government by the People (1981)*. His websites are: www.reincarnationexperiment.org and www.vonward.com.

Wagalla, Zablon

Founder of Trees for Clean Energy Network. Zablon Wagalla is an Agricultural Scientist and a social entrepreneur. He works to empower communities to develop clean and renewable energy to save the environment and alleviate poverty in Kenya.

Wann, David

David Wann is President of the Sustainable Futures Society; a board member of the Cohousing Association of the U.S.; a fellow of the Simplicity Forum; and recipient of various lifetime achievement awards for his work on sustainability. He's been a passionate gardener for 25 years and now coordinates a neighborhood garden in the cohousing community in which he's lived for 11 years—Harmony Village in Golden, Colorado.

Dave is author of many books, including *Affluenza* and the new *Simple Prosperity: Finding Real Wealth in a Sustainable Lifestyle.* www.davewann.com

Wise, Tim

Tim Wise is among the most prominent anti-racist writers and activists. Wise is the author of *White Like Me: Reflections on Race from a Privileged Son*, and *Affirmative Action: Racial Preference in Black and White*. A collection of his essays, *Speaking Treason Fluently: Anti-Racist Reflections From an Angry White Male*, was published in the Fall of 2008, and his fourth book, *Between Barack and a Hard Place: Race and Whiteness in the Age of Obama*, was released in Spring, 2009. He has contributed chapters or essays to 20 books, and is one of several persons featured in *White Men Challenging Racism: Thirty-Five Personal Stories*, from Duke University Press. He received the 2001 British Diversity Award for best essay on race issues, and his writings have appeared in dozens of popular, professional and scholarly journals. Wise has been a guest on hundreds of radio and television programs, worldwide. www.timwise.org

Wolf, Ph.D., Fred Alan

Fred Alan Wolf, Ph.D. works as a physicist, writer, and lecturer. His work in quantum physics and consciousness is well known through his popular and scientific writing. He is the author of thirteen books, numerous audio CDs, and video DVDs, and is best known for his contributions through technical papers, popular books, frequent demand as an international lecturer, keynote speaker, consultant to industry, and media personality including many international film, TV, and radio appearances.

Wright, Machaelle Small

Machaelle Small Wright is an author, researcher and co-creative scientist who has worked in partnership with nature intelligences since 1976. She lives in Virginia at Perelandra, her home and research center.

Ye, Quanzhi
Quanzhi Ye, undergraduate student and discoverer of Comet Lulin. He wishes to become a professional astronomer in the future.

Z., Mickey
Mickey Z. is a relentless purveyor of stand-up tragedy and can be found on the Web at http://www.mickeyz.net.

Zoriah
Zoriah is an award-winning photojournalist and war photographer whose work has been featured in some of the world's most prestigious galleries, museums and publications. Zoriah's clients include Newsweek, The New York Times, BBC News, The United Nations, CNN, NBC, CBS, ABC, PBS, NPR, The Wall Street Journal, Fortune and many others. With a background in Disaster Management and Humanitarian Aid, Zoriah specializes in documenting human crises in developing countries.

Charities

1 Sky - www.1sky.org

Alashanek ya Balady Association for Sustainable Development (AYB-SD) - www.ayb-sd.org

American Society for the Prevention of Cruelty to Animals - www.aspca.org

Argusfest - www.argusfest.org

Balarat - www.balarat.dpsk12.org

Bighart - www.bighart.org

California Heart Center Foundation - www.californiaheart-center.org

Chinese Red Cross - www.redcross.org.cn

Chuk Sar Cambodia (AIDS prevention and care)

The David Suzuki Foundation - www.davidsuzuki.org

Davis Research Foundation - www.help-kids-read.org

DIG - www.developmentingardening.org

Doctors Without Borders - www.doctorswithoutborders.org

Dream Change, Inc. - www.dreamchange.org

Environmental Justice Coalition for Water - www.ejcw.org

Erace Homelessness - www.eracehomelessness.org

EYES Project - www.eyesproject.com

Faithful Fools Street Ministry - www.faithfulfools.org

Girls for Gender Equity - www.ggenyc.org

The Glen Canyon Institute - www.glencanyon.org

Green Science Policy Institute - www.greensciencepolicy.org

Habitat For Humanity - www.habitat.org

Haller - www.thehallerfoundation.com

Heavenly Hats Foundation - www.heavenlyhats.com

The ICIS Foundation - www.iciscenter.org

Indigenous World Association

The Institute for Democratic Education and Culture (IDEC) - www.speakoutnow.org

Interface Environmental Foundation - www.interfaceglobal.com

The International Association of Metaphysics - www.internationalassociationofmetaphysics.com

Invisible Children - www.postcardsfromtheedge.ca

The James Redford Institute for Transplant Awareness - www.jrifilms.org

Kitezh - www.kitezh.org

Methuselah Foundation - www.methuselahfoundation.org

Mettanokit - www.circleway.org

MonNetA - www.monnety.org

The New World School of the Sacred Woman -www.thenewworldschoolofthesacredwoman.com

One Globe - www.1globe.ning.com

Our Sun Solar - www.solarenergyclasses.com

The Orion Project - www.theorionproject.org

Pachamama Alliance - www.pachamama.org

People for a Nuclear Free Australia - www.nuclearfree.com, pnfa.org.au

Pesticide Action Network - www.panna.org

PYE Global - www.pyeglobal.org

The Resonance Project Foundation - www.theresonanceproject.org

Royal Society For The Protection Of Birds - www.rspb.org.uk

The Ruckus Society - www.ruckus.org

Save The Peaks - www.savethepeaks.org

SEI (Solar Energy International) - www.solarenergy.org

Shelter - www.shelter.org.uk

Starting Artists, Inc. - www.startingartists.org

SUDC (Sudden Unexplained Death in Childhood) - www.sudc.org

Thunder Valley Community Development Corporation - www.ThunderValley.org

Transform - www.tdpf.org.uk

Treaty Total Immersion School - www.treatyschool.com

Trees for Clean Energy Network
Universal Oneness United Faith Canada - www.uoufc.org
War Child Canada - www.warchild.ca
Women Business Center - www.womenbizcenter.wordpress.com
World Research Foundation - www.wrf.org
World Wildlife Fund - www.worldwildlife.org

BOOKS

MySpiritRadio